BAD BOY
BALLMER

BAD BOY
] THE MAN WHO RULES MICROSOFT [
BALLMER

FREDRIC ALAN MAXWELL

wm

WILLIAM MORROW
An Imprint of HarperCollins*Publishers*

Grateful acknowledgment is made to reprint the following:

Excerpt from *Brave New World*. Copyright © 1932, 1960 by Aldous Huxley. Reprinted by permission of HarperCollins Publishers Inc.

Excerpt from *Startup: A Silicon Valley Adventure* by Jerry Kaplan. Copyright © 1994 by Jerry Kaplan. Reprinted by permission of Houghton Mifflin Company. All rights reserved.

FIRST EDITION

Designed by Kris Tobiassen

Printed on acid-free paper

Library of Congress Cataloging-in-Publication Data
Maxwell, Fredric Alan, 1954–
    Bad boy Ballmer : the man who rules Microsoft / Fredric Alan
    Maxwell.—1st ed.
        p.   cm.
    Includes index.
ISBN 0-06-621014-3 (hc.)
    1. Ballmer, Steven Anthony.   2. Businessmen—United States—
Biography.   3. Microsoft Corporation—History.   4. Computer
software industry—United States—History.   I. Title.
HD9696.63.U62 B355   2002
338.7'60053'092—dc21
    [B]   2002021918

02   03   04   05   06   WBC/RRD   10   9   8   7   6   5   4   3   2   1

To Howard Roarke, for living a life that nobody ever could.

To my kid sister Carla, for living the life that she did.

And to my librarian mom, Mignonne Marie Maxwell, who, when I was young and scared as only a kid can be, sat down on my bed, took my trembling hand in hers, held it, and, in a soothing voice, said, "Family. F-A-M-I-L-Y. It means 'Fredric Alan Maxwell I Love You.'"

The people who govern the Brave New World may not be sane (in what may be called the absolute sense of the word); but they are not madmen, and their aim is not anarchy but social stability. It is in order to achieve stability that they carry out, by scientific means, the ultimate, personal, really revolutionary revolution.

—A L D O U S   H U X L E Y

CONTENTS

PART THREE: POSTCARDS FROM THE BORG

GOOD BOY, BAD BOY, MONKEY BOY

Steve Ballmer can remind you of many people. The beefy, bald-headed, big-boned Ballmer bounces onto the stage, looking like a cross between Minnesota governor Jesse Ventura and *The Addams Family*'s Uncle Fester. He's acting like John Belushi on coke. He's totally in the moment in front of a bunch of computer folk. Singer Gloria Estefan's voice blares over the sound system, in the large auditorium packed with Microsoftians, eliciting the crowd to "Get on your feet." The boisterous, bellicose, sometimes belligerent Ballmer does just that. He runs and jumps and shouts, "Give it up for meeee!" He shoots across the floor like a banshee or Tasmanian devil. His arms are flailing. Turning at the wall, he jigs all the way back. Then he circles the stage again before running to its center. There he stands, behind a black podium bearing the word Microsoft, sucking air deeply, making Robin Williams seem laid back, an intense force of nature. Catching his breath, Ballmer screams, "I have four words for you! *I! Love! This! Company! Yesssss!*"

Look past the fact that he spoke five words. Steve Ballmer is on a roll, and he has been for over two decades. Since 1980, Ballmer has been the right-hand man of the famous company co-founder Bill Gates. And much more than that—Ballmer runs Microsoft when Gates doesn't. He has for a while. On January 13, 2000, Bill Gates officially stepped aside and gave the responsibilities and title of chief executive officer to his best friend, while he retained his chairmanship and gave himself the new position of chief software architect. *Time* magazine ran a cartoon of the event, showing Gates and Ballmer in running gear, with Gates handing Ballmer not a baton but a lighted stick of dynamite. Rarely does an American president comment on corporate personnel changes, but when President Bill Clinton was asked about the shift, he said, "Ballmer's obviously an able man." In many ways, he is more than able. Steve Ballmer often gets up and makes things happen. He truly loves his work, and the money's pretty good, too.

Twenty-two years ago Ballmer found the Maltese Falcon of jobs, the stuff financial dreams are made of. In his first eight thousand days working for Bill Gates, Steve Ballmer made around two million dollars a day. About eighty thousand dollars per hour. Twenty-four hours a day. Seven days a week. Fifty-two weeks a year. For twenty-two years. About fifteen billion, three hundred ninety-six million, twenty-three thousand nine hundred and fifty-six dollars, plus benefits. (An hourly tally can be found at www.cnet.com/investor under its CEO WealthMeter.) While many people railed about American CEOs' salaries averaging about 120 times that of their average worker, Ballmer was paid more than twenty thousand times what the average working American makes. The forty-six-year-old Ballmer has amassed one of the largest fortunes, if not the largest, ever made by somebody working for somebody else. Not bad for the son of a high-school-educated Swiss immigrant. Or so he says. Providing factual information isn't Steve Ballmer's strong suit. Nor is it Microsoft's.

When a streaming video of Ballmer's I-love-this-company antics suddenly appeared on the Web in August 2001 (www.globnix.org/ballmer/dancemonkeyboy.qui), people writing in on-line chat rooms wondered if it was Ballmer's screen test for the new movie *Planet of the Apes.* Another viewer compared Ballmer's footwork to the jig Hitler danced when his Nazis captured Paris in 1940. A third pointed out that a Microsoftian in the front row looks scared. An on-line editor wrote, "It's surreally disconnected from the impression that he's trying to create—one of simple, over-the-top enthusiasm. Is this a victory scream or a cry of fear—a sort of soul-searching wailing that occurs before a baited, trapped animal begins to chew off its own foot to escape the jaws of the trap. Is this a football rally or a Nuremberg rally?" A short while later, a second video appeared on the Web of Ballmer at another group meeting. He is wearing a solid blue shirt with huge sweat stains stretching from his armpits to his gut, which may have been computer-enhanced (www.ntk.net/ballmer/mirrors.html). On the tape, Ballmer shouts, "Developers! Developers! Developers!" over and over while maniacally clapping his hands together.

The Web site geekculture.com ran a cartoon parodying both videos. Picture two people looking at a Monkey Boy Ballmer Action Figure. A woman says to a man holding the toy "Hmmm . . . The sweat stains are a nice detail, but really . . . Don't you think a Ballmer action figure is just a little too scary for kids?" They also listed a poll of the favorite features of the Ballmer Action Figure: People liked the realistic sweat stains, the maniacal look on his face, his patented Flailing Limbs movements, and his vocabulary of four words. They also liked the fact that you can bend and manipulate him for a change.

The life of Steven Anthony Ballmer is the incredible story of tremendous ambition, genius, and charisma, of intense drive and merit, of insatiable greed and blatant arrogance. It's the up-by-the-bootstraps saga of how a young man born of modest means wrapped his need for great achievement in formal education, only to risk it all when he dropped out of Stanford Business School and threw his fate into the chaotic crap shoot called the computer industry with his Harvard dropout friend Bill Gates.

Ballmer adjectives abound. Steve's described as "richly experienced," "hyper-competitive," "hardworking," "relentless," "a bully," "Mr. Loud," "quick-witted," "impatient with fools," and "sharply critical." He's Microsoft's "chief coach, cheerleader, and hatchet man" who "focuses with laser intensity." Sun Microsystems co-founder and Java programming language co-inventor Bill Joy told me, "Gates is over the top but Ballmer's mad, he's insane." A former fellow executive says "his impact is felt in every molecule of Microsoft." *The Economist* pronounced him "maniacal . . . a rapid fire intervention force [with] relentless dynamism who's mean and brutal enough" to make, then implement, the tough decisions necessary to guide Microsoft through their antitrust litigation. This Ballmer does.

Out of all of Ballmer's truly extraordinary accomplishments, probably his greatest is putting up with Bill Gates for over two decades. Paul Allen couldn't, nor could any other Microsoftian. In fact, Ballmer is Microsoft's longest-serving employee. During the antitrust trial and appeals Paul Allen resigned from Microsoft's board of directors, for the second time, and quietly sold over 130 million shares of his company holdings, making Microsoft's second-in-command Ballmer its second-largest individual stockholder; he owns some 240 million shares.

When most people think of who made Microsoft, the names of co-founders Bill Gates and Paul Allen come to mind. Yet it was Gates and Ballmer who took Microsoft from fewer than thirty employees to some fifty thousand, annual revenues from twelve million dollars to more than twenty billion, and from relatively petty cash in the bank to over thirty-six billion dollars on hand.

Bill Gates and Steve Ballmer are the company's co-leaders, its intellectual equals, and its dynamic duo. They are the new economy's most powerful partnership, software's longest-running buddy act, twin sons of different mothers who donated the Maxwell Dworkin computer laboratory to their alma mater Harvard, named after their moms, Mary Maxwell and Beatrice Dworkin, respectively. Through luck, skill, and more than a little chicanery they set the standard for personal computer operating systems worldwide. Standards are needed, of course. Railroads became the first true American national corporations only after the gauges—the space between the rails and the rail's size— became uniform. American railroad lawyers successfully lobbied for a standard, based on the average wheelbase of a horse-drawn cart. (That standard gauge was set as the average width of two horse's asses.) Gates and Ballmer bought a personal computer operating system from a Seattle company, lifted part of another one from the industry leader at the time, cobbled these and other code parts together for the software that ran IBM's personal computer, were along for the ride as IBM established the PC hardware standard, then, at will, owning the de facto software standard, bent the rest of the industry to their will.

One analyst calls Microsoft "the Bill and Steve Show." A former company vice president talks about "the personality of Gates and Ballmer." Though much of the time Gates and Ballmer act as a single unit, when they divide it's along set lines. Gates is the techie, the strategist, the commander in chief. Ballmer's the business guy, the tactician, the field marshal. Gates ran the antitrust trial defense while Ballmer was running the company. Gates is Microsoft's ego, and Ballmer is the company's id. Gates is a "balance sheet" person. Ballmer is an "income statement" type. A former competitor, Novell's Ray Noorda, calls them "the Pearly

Gates and the Em-Ballmer: one promises you heaven, the other prepares you for the grave." A former co-worker says, "Gates likes really smart people, period. Steve likes guys who get shit done." Gates usually decides where Microsoft is going to go, but it's Ballmer who figures out how to get there. Captain Picard and Commander Ryker, only without the starship. Butch and Sundance, but without the charm.

Much has been made of Gates's admiration for Napoléon I, the math prodigy turned general who failed at Waterloo in his attempt at world domination. Microsoft antitrust trial judge Thomas Penfield Jackson told *The New Yorker*'s Ken Auletta that Gates "has a Napoleonic concept of himself and his company," and that he wished he could force Gates to write a book report on the emperor to see his own flaws in Napoléon's.

Part of Ballmer resembles not so much a Napoleonic general as a combination of the emperor's actual and fictional troops, brought together in the Nicholas Chauvin character in the 1831 French play *La Cocarde Tricolore*. Chauvin is a staunch loyalist, noted for his excessive patriotism and devotion and sometimes-comic blind faith in Napoleon. Throughout the play, about a French battle in Algiers, Chauvin shouts, *"I am Chauvin! I am French! I beat the Bedouin!"* Chauvin survives today as the father of the word *chauvinist,* often proceeded by the word male and followed by pig. Chauvinism actually means "an attitude of superiority toward members of the opposite sex" or "undue partiality or attachment to a group or place to which one belongs or has belonged." Both meanings describe sides of Ballmer and the Microsoft cult or culture, depending on how you see it. Make no mistake about it, Microsoft is Ballmer's country, and his actions pledge allegiance to its Windows flag logo.

And there are, at the least, two more Steve Ballmers.

The good boy Ballmer, his higher self, was the nearly perfect student and supportive classmate who won full-ride scholarships to prep school, Harvard, and then Stanford. He was the beloved but awkward valedictorian of his class at Detroit Country Day School, where the headmaster told me, "Every teacher is proud to get someone like Steve. He becomes your hero, really." He was the devoted son who made sure his father of relatively modest means received over a million dollars worth of stock in Microsoft's 1986 initial public offering (IPO). He spent twelve-hour bedside shifts as both of his parents succumbed to lung cancer. He's also the unpretentious, well-grounded corporate cheerleader who will do cartwheels on stage to prove a point, even if that means shouting out Microsoft's *"Win-doze! Win-doze! Win-doze!"* so loudly that he ripped his vocal cords. He is known for making his employees want to dig deeply into themselves and bring out their absolute best, if not for themselves then for him. In Douglas Coupland's novel *Microserfs*, he wrote about one employee's "Ballmer Shrine." There's the Ballmer who will only drive Ford cars, mainly because his father worked there. He never forgets where he came from or most of the people who've helped him along the way. There's the Ballmer who was instrumental in making over ten thousand Microsoft employees millionaires; the Ballmer who, if he was your friend, would be the best friend you ever had; the Ballmer who often didn't turn his back on his Jewish heritage even when doing so might have benefited him; the loyal Uncle Bill booster who'd take a bullet for Gates—and would fire one, too.

But, of course, there's also the bad boy Ballmer, the earthier level of his soul. It was this Ballmer who announced impending software release dates fully aware some couldn't happen until years later, a business practice he knew IBM had been forced to stop, a move coldly calculated to stifle Microsoft customers' interest in competing products. Ballmer proclaimed there was a "Chinese Wall" between Microsoft's operating system monopoly and applications division when no such thing existed. There's the

General Sherman war-is-hell Ballmer, who carried out the pilferage of competitor's products with a so-sue-us attitude, which many of the judges and juries forced to referee the conflicts would find Microsoft guilty of. Ballmer was the unabashed, unrepentant perpetrator of the serial date rape of businesses like Stac Electronics; the corporate hit man who led the military-style, scorched-earth, take-no-prisoners juggernaut against any threat to Microsoft's market share, effectively exterminating the WordPerfect Corporation and many other companies along the way. While the bad boy Ballmer was negotiating with another former partner, IBM, the hardware giant had the room swept and found bugs—listening devices. Ballmer continually proclaims what he privately acknowledges to be seriously flawed products as "great." He contends, in the face of overwhelming evidence to the contrary, that his company isn't a monopoly and has done "absolutely nothing wrong," then expects to be trusted. Then there's the large-lunged, blunt bully Ballmer who screamed at an employee, *"You fuckin' idiot! How could you make such a fuckin' stupid decision!? What the fuck were you thinking!?"* And there's the dark side of Ballmer, who ominously thundered at a client who'd signed up with rival Netscape, "YOU'RE EITHER WITH US OR AGAINST US, AND YOU'RE THE ENEMY NOW!"

Ballmer is vast. Ballmer contains multitudes.

It's easier to understand, if not feel for, all of the Ballmers when you realize that, not unlike Abraham Lincoln, and like Ted Turner and over two and a half million living Americans, he exhibits bipolar-like behavior. While he rarely appears depressive in public, he's a manic personality who rides his extreme mania to handle what to others would be a crushing workload, but whose doubts have taken him to the edge of quitting the company he runs, needs, loves.

Steve Ballmer's life is the story of how a victim became a perpetrator, how a virtue taken to excess becomes a vice, and how a product and proponent of the best America has to offer—the Ameritocracy—gradually became tainted. It shows how Ballmer's academic, geographic, temperamental, and religious backgrounds uniquely positioned him to exploit the phenomenal growth of personal computer use during the past twenty-five years. It chronicles how Ballmer, as he's acknowledged, learned about business from his father, from managing various school sports teams and publications, from his year and a half at America's premier marketing company, Procter & Gamble, from his ten months at Stanford Business School, and on the job at Microsoft.

Like most children, much of the buzzing, booming confusion of the world unfolded to Ballmer through the experiences of his parents. For Ballmer and the Microsoft molecules he affects, this has special significance. His Jewish mother, Bea, was born and raised in the center of American anti-Semitism. And, after dropping out of a Swiss university, Steve's Protestant father, Fritz (later Fred) Ballmer, learned about international business during his checkered eighteen months working under Americans in Germany after World War II. In fact, in January 2000, when tech columnist and curmudgeon John Dvorak mentioned that the Microsoft antitrust trial resembled the Nuremberg trials, Dvorak was more right than even he knew. Few people recall that the chief Nuremberg prosecutor, U.S. Supreme Court Justice Robert Jackson, had headed the Department of Justice's antitrust division for two years. Justice Jackson's great passion was convicting leading German industrialists and financiers for conspiring with Hitler to eliminate competition. Another odd connection comes through Ballmer, whose father, Fritz, punched his immigration ticket to America by working under Justice Jackson as a research analyst in the economic section of the first Nuremberg trial, studying Nazi methodology while he documented the underbelly of the Third Reich's economic miracle. He helped hang the bastards by wrapping their own word ropes around their necks.

The story of Steve Ballmer can be seen against a backdrop of two cities: Detroit and Seattle. Ballmer and I were both born in the Detroit area in the mid-1950s, both only sons of fathers who worked for Ford Motor Company. We graduated from high schools in the same small suburb a year apart, where we both managed our respective basketball teams. We both left Michigan in the early 1970s, and both now live in Seattle. Though I've lived here five years, it was only after I started researching this biography that I discovered just how protective Seattleites are of their winning hand in the Wall Street casino. *Wall Street Journal* reporter David Bank even received a death threat before a Seattle reading of his slightly critical text *Breaking Windows,* prompting police to join his audience.

This sometimes high-handed protectionism can seem almost understandable if you consider that the 2.2 billion shares of Microsoft stock owned by Rainy City residents once totaled over $260 billion. Factoring out the stock of Gates, Ballmer, and Allen, the average Seattleite's part of Microsoft—from homeless person to billionaire Jeff Bezos—is worth well over twenty-five thousand dollars even after the meet-the-new-boss economy contracted to the same-as-the-old-boss economy. It mattered far more that Microsoft had the money rather than how they'd gotten it—think in terms of local boys make good, and gift horses in the mouth. And, if they have the right connections, many Seattleites can get the retail-priced $579 Microsoft Office XP for about one hundred dollars at the company store, with similar discounts for Word and Windows.

Of course, Washington didn't join the twenty other states in the government's antitrust suit. Besides, in a certain Seattle state of mind, the whole thing was brought on by some whiny, La La Land Californians who complained about Microsoft's business practices, and who cares what they think. One local columnist ran a "Keep the Bums Out" campaign when Californians started to emigrate here in the 1990s. The columnist also blamed them for the huge rise in housing prices. (One relocated comedian noted that, when he lived in California, his skin was tan and his teeth were white. After moving to overcast Seattle and drinking lots of coffee, his teeth were now tan and his skin was now white.) Outsiders sometimes refer to Seattle as provincial, which it definitely can be, and have been known to call the local semi-laid-back style "Seattle lethargy." Seattle had long ago grown tired of being thought of as a stepchild to San Francisco, and almost since the city was founded it had been thinking of ways to get the best of Baghdad by the Bay. When Microsoft makes not-always-aboveboard profits from the discoveries of others around San Francisco, they're just carrying on a hundred-year-old Seattle tradition of roguishness.

In 1896, when gold was found in the Yukon some one thousand miles north, Seattle laid claim and scored a huge public relations coup. Seattle sold itself as the ideal prospector's staging area when a San Francisco–bound ship diverted to its port carrying two hundred thousand dollars' worth of gold, its arrival gleefully announced by city fathers, a story widely reported. Seattle then adapted San Francisco's gold rush business model, in spades and Levi Strauss–like, profiting from selling provisions to miners as they went rich rock hunting. When they came back from the fields, Seattle's nightlife included the world's largest whorehouse and many saloons and card rooms, near a street which birthed the term "skid row," all working hard to nudge the newly found nuggets out of the prospectors' pockets, if not outright robbing them blind. Into this history, both Microsoft and Steve Ballmer came of age.

Before I concentrated on Ballmer, he was part of a group portrait I was researching on seven now-famous people who were raised or educated in my surburban Detroit hometown around 1971. I wrote a letter to Ballmer, eliciting an e-mail from his longtime assistant, Debbie Hill. Ms. Hill wrote me that there wasn't a biography of "Steveb," but that "it would be a great book" and I should "let her know when I wanted to do the interviews." When I committed to writing this biography, I contacted Ms. Hill to set up the get-togethers. She got back to me, days after Judge Thomas Penfield Jackson handed down his ruling to break up Microsoft, and said that he'd decided to cancel the interviews. She said that Ballmer "doesn't care how accurate it is, he doesn't want the book written . . . he doesn't want attention drawn to himself." Much in Ballmer's background points to such reluctance—I didn't find a picture of him in any of the Harvard yearbooks when he attended, and he made his way in the professional world by putting Gates first (Mary *Maxwell* Gates and Beatrice *Dworkin* Ballmer). Also, Ballmer's cooperating with a biographer could be viewed as an act of disloyalty to his best friend.

Microsoft's veracity problems are sometimes exacerbated by its public relations word warriors, its propagandists. Reporters covering Microsoft call its PR people "obstructionist," "thought police," and "Orwellian." Other writers and journalists advised me that they'd "string me along" and "try to discredit me," and were "to be avoided whenever possible." One company propagandist actually told author John Heilemann, as they ate in the Microsoft cafeteria, that the employees hardly ever discussed the trial. As the flack spoke, Heilemann could hear employees talking about that very subject.

Unlike most corporations, Microsoft doesn't have a written code of conduct or ethics. In 1998 one executive, Mike Maples, failed in his attempt to draft such a code. He said, "I can't find the principles that would mean the world would like us more." Former vice president Cameron Mhyrvold told me he also proposed a code to Gates and Ballmer, who were strongly opposed to such a move, saying it was "too touchy-feely." After working there as a consultant, author James Fallows wrote that the corporation reminded him of the military. It's often said that the first casualty of war is truth. The truth, from what I found, is that the term "Microsoft business ethics" is an oxymoron. Microsoft's motto seems to be "all's fair in love and war and selling software," and if you get caught doing something wrong, deny, decry, and delay, and then deny some more.

Their lone corporate conduct directive lies on their Web site, www.microsoft.com, under "Living Our Values." It says, "Our managers and employees must always act with the utmost integrity, and be guided by what is ethical and right for our customers. We compete vigorously and fairly." Right.

Item: Ballmer told *Newsweek*, "People say a lot of things about us, but never has anyone said we're untrustworthy."

Item: Ballmer told a group of college students, "We operate with super integrity."

Item: About a dinner guest Emerson wrote, "The louder he talked of his honor, the faster we counted our spoons."

When I finally broke though Microsoft's gauntlet of propagandists and saw Ballmer in action, I was amazed. I've often thought that if muckraker Ida Tarbell had met John D. Rockefeller, it would have made her critical exposé of Rockefeller's Standard Oil show more of the human side of her predatory monopolist. My predatory monopolist was giving a speech at Overlake Hospital in Kirkland, a few miles from Microsoft's headquarters. His wife, Connie, a former Microsoftian, had raised a whole bunch of money for Overlake, and health care is an issue close to Ballmer's heart. Not only had both of his parents recently passed away from cancer, but more than a few of his aunts and uncles and grandparents, along with a famous cousin, Gilda Radner, had all lost their battles with various forms of the disease.

When I walked into the conference room at the Hyatt near Microsoft and saw Ballmer up onstage, what immediately grabbed my attention was that, like Hillary Clinton, he doesn't photograph well. While not a particularly handsome man, his strong features, especially his deep-set, almost ghoulish eyes, appear softer in person.

I was also struck by his hands—huge hands that would immediately go limp when not pointing, like Michael Jordan's tongue hanging out before a shot, as though every dram of energy was going into his brain. His hands looked as if the ones he was born with had been amputated and replaced with those of Andre the Giant, oversized hands on a man with an oversized drive and sense of loyalty. They are the hands of someone you want to watch over you, to protect that which you hold dear, hands which, when fisted, could easily instill fear.

Steve Ballmer is almost always in a sales mode. In character, he was up onstage touting the wonders of a Microsoft health care application still in the development stage, Dr. Goodwell, with which a physician supposedly could diagnose a patient from a distance. After he was finished, the six-foot-one-inch Ballmer moved through the friendly adopted-hometown audience, projecting a sense of pleasure and approval with a litheness one wouldn't expect from his girth, then posed for pictures with Connie. Seeing him brought to mind not John D. Rockefeller but something I'd read years ago, the observations of A. E. Hotchner when he saw Hemingway in the center of a crowd. Afterward, I found a copy of Hotchner's book *Papa Hemingway* and came across the passage I had in mind:

> He was massive. Not in height, for he was only an inch over six
> feet, nor in weight, but in impact. . . . Something played off
> him—he was intense, electrokinetic, but in control, a race horse
> reined in . . . something about him hit me—enjoyment: God, I

thought, he's enjoying himself! I had never seen anyone with such an aura of fun and well-being. He radiated it and everyone in the place responded.

That's the Ballmer many Microsoftians know and love, the man they'd damn as he led them on what they called "death marches," the coach they cheered when he said "to hell with Janet Reno," the knight they'd follow into such hell for a profitable cause. While in many ways Gates is the actual and intellectual head of Microsoft, Ballmer's is the heart above the belly of the so-named Beast from Redmond, and his soul is its soul.

PART ONE

GREAT EXPECTATIONS

"There was unanimous agreement about Hans Giebenrath's talents, however. Teachers, principal, neighbors, pastor, fellow students and everyone else readily admitted he was an exceptionally bright boy—something special. . . . This heightened activity and thirst for knowledge also coincided with a proud sense of self-esteem." At the school, the headmaster counsels Hans, *"That's the way, that's the way, my boy. Just don't let up or you'll get dragged beneath the wheel."*

—HERMANN HESSE

CHAPTER ONE

IN THE BEGINNING

Thirty years ago and twenty-three hundred miles apart, Detroit, where fifteen-year-old Steve Ballmer was being raised, and Seattle, where he'd end up, were vastly different places. Most people know of Thanksgiving in Seattle in 1971 by one name: D. B. Cooper. Though difficult to imagine after the World Trade Center and Pentagon airplane bombings, D. B. Cooper became a folk hero for his peaceful, soft-spoken skyjacking of a Northwest Airlines flight from Portland to Seattle that Thanksgiving eve. En route, Cooper demanded four parachutes and two hundred thousand dollars, showing a stewardess what appeared to be a bomb. Northwest officials radioed the pilot, saying, "We're giving him what he wants." The plane landed safely at the Seattle-Tacoma (Sea-Tac) airport. A few hours later, after he'd released the other passengers in return for the money and parachutes, and the plane was heading south, D. B. Cooper manually lowered the plane's rear stairs, jumped out, and parachuted into the Washington wilderness and American folklore, never to be seen again. As the news spread, many lauded the air pirate some called a modern-day Robin Hood, whom the *New York Times* would editorialize "didn't have the notoriety of John Dillinger, yet." D. B. Cooper T-shirts, books, and even songs would follow. As one professor observed, Cooper had "won public admiration through an awesome feat in the battle of man against machine— one individual overcoming, for the time being anyway, technology, the corporation, the establishment, the system." D. B. Cooper's name greeted Americans awaking to Thanksgiving Day in 1971, much to the chagrin of Henry Ford II.

The day before, "Hank the Duce" had announced his plans to build a two-hundred-million-dollar collection of offices and stores in downtown Detroit, which he optimistically called the Renaissance Center. Yet D. B. Cooper had stolen Ford's headlines in the *Detroit Free Press*. More than a few of his customers shared Ford's anger, but his products were their targets. The company's reputation for dependability had sunk to the point where the letters FORD were said to stand for "Fixed or Repaired Daily." Earlier in the year one customer, Eddie Campos, drove his Lincoln Continental onto the lawn of a Ford assembly plant, poured gasoline on it, and set it on fire. "I saved up for five years to buy that car new," Campos said, "and it turned out to be a lemon. I had it towed in for repairs ten thousand times and everybody just laughed at me—the dealers I took it to, the Ford people. I couldn't get no satisfaction." A deputy sheriff at the scene described Campos as "perfectly sober, perfectly rational, and completely disgusted." Thirty years later, more than a few of Microsoft's customers, competitors, and employees could relate.

Still, even though Ford was peddling generally mediocre cars that were supported by generally mediocre service, the company managed to sell over 2.4 million of them that year in North

America. Another highlight came when a Ford car, the Lunar Rover, was driven on the moon that July. And Ford attorneys were feeling upbeat about arguments they had made a week before, in front of the U.S. Supreme Court, to overturn their Sherman Antitrust Act conviction, for cutting competition in the spark plug market, a conviction the Supreme Court would uphold seven months later. All this was common knowledge in Detroit and at Ford.

Detroit was in a good mood for many reasons, a prime one being that it was surfing the crest of the great post–World War II economic tidal wave. Detroit's relative wealth and influence would never again be so vast. Record U.S. auto sales exceeded ten million units. (Meanwhile, Rolls-Royce went bankrupt.) These were the final days of Detroit's golden era. Having literally bombed out their German and Japanese competition a quarter century before, Detroit's automakers almost had to work at not making money. They would soon find a way.

In contrast, much of America was in a recession, and the Seattle area was reeling from Congress's elimination of funding for the airplane-of-the-future, the supersonic transport (SST). Though city leaders had backed Boeing's effort to produce the SST, to the point of naming their only major league sports franchise, their National Basketball Association team, the SuperSonics, the federal cutback, combined with low orders for its 747 aircraft, put Seattle's premier employer in a tailspin. Boeing laid off over sixty thousand workers to avoid the near-bankruptcy suffered by rival Lockheed earlier that year. This so-named "Boeing Bust" prompted such an exodus of residents that two Seattleites rented a billboard and printed this request: WOULD THE LAST PERSON TO LEAVE SEATTLE PLEASE TURN OFF THE LIGHTS? For some reason, however, this slowdown didn't deter three recent, grammatically challenged University of Washington grads from establishing a small coffee shop in the city's Pike Place Market. In tribute to Seattle's rich maritime history, they named the cafe after the chief mate in *Moby-Dick*. And that's how Starbucks got its start.

Back in Michigan, over five hundred thousand Detroiters braved the twenty-eight-degree cold and lined downtown streets to view the annual J. L. Hudson Thanksgiving Parade. Millions more watched on television as CBS broadcast the event nationwide. It could have been called "CBS Day in Detroit." Four hours later, the network showed the Detroit Lions' annual Thanksgiving game. Then, at 10:00 P.M., CBS Reports aired what the *New York Times* called a "superb, engaging, and totally rewarding documentary" on the parents, kids, and competitive nature in the Detroit suburb Birmingham.

Ten days before, far from CBS's cameras, a small California computer component manufacturer, Intel, had quietly announced that it had invented and was marketing what would become the most influential electronic device of the last half of the twentieth century: the computer chip. Intel's 4004 microprocessor included a central processing unit (CPU) measuring one-eighth of an inch wide by one-sixth of an inch long—about the size of Marilyn Monroe's black beauty mark—containing more computing ability than the moving-truck-size first electronic computer, the ENIAC, dedicated twenty-five years before.

On this day, one of the people who would profit the most from the invention of the chip—the chubby, excitable Steve Ballmer—was celebrating the holiday with his father, Fred, his mother, Bea, and his thirteen-year-old sister, Shelly, in their suburban Detroit home in Farmington Hills. Steve was taking a break from his classes at both a local college and the Birmingham prep school Detroit Country Day. Fred was taking a break from his accounting job at Ford, while Bea and Shelly cooked. Their world was as it should be. And how good their futures looked.

Frederic Henry Ballmer was born Fritz Hans Ballmer in the small northern Swiss village of Zuchwil in 1923, three and a half miles south of the Swiss village Balm, seventy-four miles south-west of the German village Balm, about fifty miles northwest of Zurich. When he wrote the U.S. Army twenty-three years later, saying, "I beg to apply for a position," then "offering my services for a federal employment [sic] in occupied Germany," he told them "I am a Swiss of German mother tongue who attended the grammar-school at Beinne (French-speaking part of Switzerland) for six and the high-school for five years. After leaving it I studied three years at the commercial school in Zurich (German speaking part), which I left with a degree for commercial purposes. . . . Spring 1944 I joined the University of Basel (Tropical Institute) for almost four semesters. I finished my studies of agriculture, economics and languages successfully (diploma)."

Fritz ended by saying that he was "looking forward to your answer with a keen interest [sic] I should be much obliged to you if you would favour me with particulars about the position I am applying for, the conditions of life, the possibility of becoming a U.S. citizen, the salary and when I could report for work." His intention was clear: he wanted to get to America. The why is a little more complicated.

On March 8, 1945, Fritz had married Dolores Koepf in Beale, Switzerland. Seven months later, on September 13, Dolores gave birth to a daughter, Kay Katharina Kutz. When Fritz expressed his desire to work for the army, then come to America, he was in the process of divorcing Dolores in a Swiss court. The divorce was granted on June 19, 1946, stipulating that Fritz would provide support.

Though the Second World War had ended the year before, there were numerous opportunities to help the victorious Allies, not only to assist implementing what would become known as the Marshall Plan, rebuilding the economies of various European countries, but dealing with the difficult question of punishing the conquered Germans. Fifty years later, many of the same arguments would be made for and against prosecuting and punishing Microsoft.

The question of punishment had come up in 1943, reportedly during a drinking match between Soviet dictator Joseph Stalin and British prime minister Winston Churchill. Stalin had killed hundreds of thousands of officers from the Soviet Army prior to the war, seeing them as a threat to his rule. It was in character that he proposed simply slaughtering the top fifty thousand Nazis. Churchill replied that a civilized society couldn't do such a thing. Stalin countered that they should first hold trials, then shoot the top fifty thousand Nazis. After the war, the International Military Tribunal (IMT) was established, with French, English, Soviet, and American components. President Harry Truman designated U.S. Supreme Court Justice Robert L. Jackson as the chief prosecutor.

Justice Jackson was fully aware of the problems the tribunal faced, not the least of which was trying Germans based on law which wasn't set when the alleged crimes were committed. Many thought that the tribunal would simply produce the show trial Stalin had proposed, convicting most of the defendants but acquitting a few to prove its legitimacy. Yet Jackson and his staff carefully used both international and German common law to establish the legal basis for prosecution.

Where to hold the trials was also carefully decided. Nuremberg had been one of the targets of the Allied carpet bombing of German cities, a policy implemented with the aid of physicists such as Freeman Dyson (computer guru Esther Dyson's father), the brutality fictionalized in novels like Kurt Vonnegut's *Slaughterhouse Five*. More to the point, Nuremberg had been the center of Nazi nationalism, where the famous Nuremberg rallies had been held, the town where the infamous Nuremberg Laws had been passed in 1935, putting Jews into a legal category similar to American slaves in 1835.

What we refer to today as the Nuremberg trials were actually a dozen war crimes trials, involving 190 defendants. The initial prosecution set both the stage and the legal basis for the rest. Whom to charge with what became the paramount issue. If an organization was found guilty through its leaders, than all members of the group could later be tried. Justice Jackson's two years as head of the Department of Justice's antitrust division, followed by two years as attorney general, prepared him for the intricacies of such trials. He wanted to ensure that those who helped Hitler paid the full, if not necessarily the ultimate, price for their profits and business practices.

After much study, an economic case against German businessmen and Nazis was formed. As Jackson's assistant Francis Lewis relayed to him in a memo,

> The chief industrialists and financiers, with knowledge of the conspiracy that Hitler planned, became his accomplices and were paid off handsomely. They gave Hitler funds to establish himself in power, worked together to limit imports, stockpiled raw material and products essential for war production, and lent their organizations abroad to the combined uses of propaganda, espionage, and limited other countries' production of materials essential to the war. Their payoff was that their Jewish and other minority competitors were knocked out of competition and the cheap labor of the concentration camps was made available for use in their factories. After the war broke out they were given the use of labor battalions conscripted from conquered countries and took consenting part in such atrocities as the starving of this labor and were given control of the industries in the conquered countries.

As Nuremberg prosecutor Telford Taylor noted, "Proof of criminality depended entirely on finding evidence that the economic defendants had sufficient knowledge of Hitler's plans, and shared sufficiently in his criminal purpose, that they might properly be convicted as co-conspirators with the Nazi leaders." A fellow prosecutor, New York lawyer Colonel John Amen, was outspoken against such a strategy. He declared that their job was to convict the major war criminals and then go home, not to "reform European economics." Amen thought that Shea's project would "overload things" and "turn the war crimes trial into an antitrust case." But Justice Jackson's mind was made up. Now they had to prove it.

Into the fray came the six-foot-three, 195-pound America-seeking Fritz Ballmer. He could speak English, French, German, Dutch, Italian, and Malay. He could take shorthand in German at seventy words per minute and type at fifty words per minute. After dropping out of college, he had worked in Zurich giving tours to American servicemen on leave. He became aware of the dire need for his verbal skills and in his introductory letter to the army command, he listed three lieutenant colonels and a major as references. Ballmer was hired on July 8, 1946, and assigned to Robert Jackson's office as a research analyst, working on the second floor of the Palace of Justice, next to the section prosecuting the feared SS Gestapo. (For some reason, he was one of the relatively few of the over eight thousand IMT workers who did not have a picture on his courthouse pass.) He not only translated captured German documents, but analyzed them to find the sections that could be used to convict the industrialists in their own words, bolstering Justice Jackson's case, and laying the groundwork for the future trials.

Though Germany was suffering severe food and housing shortages, IMT workers were well paid, bunking down in the best shelters, including Nuremberg's Grand Hotel, eating at banquets, and enjoying the pleasures of the captured and fully stocked wine cellars and liquor bars, fighting the good fight then partying with the numerous single female secretaries and clerks. It was, as

Telford Taylor wrote, "a festive time." Fifteen of the twenty-two defendants in the first trial were found guilty of at least one charge, four were found guilty of the antitrust conspiracy charge, and ten were hanged. The gallows were so poorly constructed that the men who were hanged didn't die for up to eighteen minutes. No one in the room, other than those suffocating, complained.

The first Nuremberg trial was the European media event of the war. Thousands of journalists from dozens of countries covered the trial, including United Press International's Walter Cronkite. Though Cronkite told me that he doesn't recall meeting Fritz Ballmer, a Colonel McConnell, the chief of Nuremberg's press section, certainly did.

Fritz Ballmer was "declared surplus" five months after being hired, and was transferred to work in Augsburg, Germany. Colonel McConnell called the commander of his new office and reported "that Mr. Ballmer had left Nuremberg with the key to his room, that he had broken the window from a taxi-cab, promised the pay for the broken window and failed to do so, that he had left Nuremberg without paying another taxi bill of $9.70, and that he was 'certainly glad to get rid of' Mr. Ballmer as he was a constant trouble-maker and guilty of misbehavior on several occasions." Ballmer had skipped town.

Already in Augsburg, Lieutenant Colonel Carroll Gray reported that Ballmer had a wild New Year's Eve. Specifically, he wrote, "On the evening of 31 December 46, Mr. Ballmer was observed at the Apollo Community Club, in a state of inebriation unbecoming a gentleman. His behavior and actions were such that he was requested to remove himself from the club. In view of [this], it is requested that the orders of Mr. Ballmer be revoked. His services are not desired by this branch." Given the need for Ballmer's language skills, Gray's commanding officer, Colonel Ellis, reported that he "talked to Ballmer and told him we would not tolerate any 'monkey business.'" So, even after provoking the press officer's ire, Ballmer stayed. He was needed. But others were looking for him, too.

Four months after his transfer came a request to the military attaché in the American embassy, from the Swiss General Welfare Administration in Basel, asking about Ballmer's whereabouts. The office was concerned about Fritz's "divorced wife (and whose) [sic] child must be supported by us." They wanted to talk to him "concerning payment of alimony, as stipulated in the divorce decree." There are no commendations in his personnel file, and his salary remained the same for his entire tenure until four months later, when he was arrested for trading on the black market.

According to the story Ballmer would later tell American immigration officials, he had been arrested under Article 96, behavior unbecoming a soldier (as a civilian in an occupied military area, he was covered by military law). His pay was suspended. It is unclear from his personnel file whether he was held in detention, but in February 1948 he was court-marshaled on the charge and found not guilty. He was immediately terminated. He left two days later, returning to Switzerland.

On October 18, 1948, Fritz Ballmer showed up in New York City, on a liberty ship, the SS *Ernie Pyle*, from Antwerp. (The public records of neither the Central Intelligence Agency [CIA] nor its predecessor, the Office of Strategic Services [OSS], show they employed a Fritz Hans Ballmer.) He immediately headed for Detroit. Ballmer went through three jobs within a year before finding employment with Ford Motor Company. A mutual friend introduced him to Beatrice Dworkin.

Imagine the impact the tall, handsome, glib, world-traveling Fritz must have had on the petite, Detroit-born-and-raised Bea. Not only had he lived in Switzerland and Germany, but he'd helped convict the head perpetrators of the mass murder of over six million of her fellow Jews. He was a hero. Even the Americanization of his name was romantic—Fritz Hans became Frederic Henry, Hemingway's protagonist in *A Farewell to Arms.*

Beatrice Dworkin was born in Detroit on September 7, 1920, one of three sisters and a brother, Irving, the children of the Russian-born Samuel Dworkin and the New York resident Rose Orning. As Irving tells the tale, "Sam was a cobbler with the czarist army in Russia. He built the best boots. The officers liked him. They treated him well. He didn't receive any of the harsh treatment the soldiers normally meted out to Jews. He came to America from Pinsk, Russia. [He] came through New York and met my mother." Ellis Island records show that a Samuel Dworkin did arrive there in 1898 from Russia with his family. He was three years old. Sometime later, Sam and Rose Dworkin moved to Detroit, where they found an infant auto industry.

Steve Ballmer was so close to his maternal grandfather that he'd name his firstborn Sam. Irving says, "Steve used to visit Sam every week. My dad loved the tumult of business. He liked the commotion of being a businessman. Steve probably admired him for that."

Irving's wife, who is Steve's aunt Olga Dworkin, is a kind, personable, compassionate woman who says that Steve was part of a small family and got used to being the center of attention. Someone close to the family says Bea favored her son, Steve, who consequently overshadowed his sister, Shelly, who only blossomed later on while studying speech at the University of Michigan and sociology at the University of Chicago.

Steve and Shelly Ballmer didn't socialize with their second cousins, the Radners, even though their grandfathers were brothers. One possible reason is that Herman Radner, who married Bea's sister Harrietta, had a shady side. His daughter, the late comedian and actress Gilda Radner, was raised in a well-funded lifestyle, graduating from an exclusive Grosse Point girls' school in 1964. Gilda adored her father. In her autobiography, she wrote, "By the 1920s he was able to buy the Walkerville Brewery in Windsor, Canada, just across the river from Detroit. It made whiskey and beer. No one in the family talks about it very much and they won't tell me for sure, but it's obvious to me that you were allowed to make and export beer in Canada during Prohibition. I know my father came out of the 1930s with a lot of money, and there's a story about how some people tried to kidnap him once in a dark alley and he was shot in the leg getting away. Now I don't know if we are talking about organized crime or what. He turned his brewery into a free lunchroom during the Depression and fed thousands of people." Many of Detroit's bootleggers were protected by the vicious Purple Gang, immortalized in the Elvis Presley song "Jailhouse Rock" as a group to be feared.

Bea helped her father at his Detroit Auto Parts shop. She eventually went to work for as a bookkeeper/office assistant for Hank Borgman at his small wheel-bearing shop. Borgman says, "Bea was very thorough, very competent. She worked in the office and the Negro girls—we called them Negroes back then—would be in the shop, greasing up wheel bearings. When Bea got ahead, she'd roll up her sleeves and go back and grease up the bearings. She didn't have to, she just wanted to help. That's something I can see Steve doing, getting his job done then helping others, doing whatever it takes to get the job done. Bea was the best employee I ever had."

Hank Borgman was a witness at Fred and Bea's wedding, and their families often vacationed together, camping at various sites in the park-rich Michigan. Borgman laughs when he talks about the wedding. "Fred was very old school and didn't know many American customs. He asked me if he had to pay the justice of the peace. I told him it was customary to tip him ten dollars, with another five dollars for his assistant. After the ceremony Fred gave the justice a twenty-dollar bill—and stood there waiting for his change."

Fred and Bea got married in 1951. The next year, he applied for citizenship, dutifully listing his arrest and court-martial, along with his first wife and child. Paul Schneider and his wife, Sharon, signed as references, saying they'd known Fred for two years. But, according to the hearing examiner's notes, Fred couldn't recall if his divorce decree required him to pay alimony or child support. Besides, said Fred, he didn't think the child was his. Not following the provisions of the divorce decree might have been grounds for denying Fred citizenship. But his second marriage was solid and valid, and that sealed the deal. His name was formally changed to Frederic Henry Ballmer.

One of Steve Ballmer's high school teachers describes Bea as a "very gentle, very kind" woman who was the family's religious force. Judaism is a maternal religion, passed on to a child by their mother. That her husband worked for Ford was bound to create certain tension for a native Detroit Jew. As Peabody Award–winning documentarian Aviva Kempner vividly detailed in her 2000 documentary *The Life and Times of Hank Greenberg,* about the Detroit Tigers' star first baseman, Detroit was the center of American anti-Semitism in the 1920s and 1930s, led by Henry Ford.

Not only had Ford authored a book, *The International Jew,* blaming Jews for everything ranging from World War I to high interest on bank loans, but his well-known views on Zionism made him the only American Hitler mentioned by name in *Mein Kampf.* Germany awarded Henry Ford the Order of the German Eagle, its highest civilian honor, in 1938, along with IBM's Thomas Watson and Charles Lindbergh. And when Lindbergh's admiration for the German military might and his anti-Semitic views turned him from America's first media hero into America's first former media hero, and he'd lost his secret clearance and become a pariah, Ford gave him a job at his Willow Run plant. Lindbergh lived with his family during the war in the northern Detroit suburb of Bloomfield Hills, just down the road from Father Coughlin.

As Howard M. Sacher writes in *A History of Jews in America,* Charles E. Coughlin was ordained a Catholic priest in 1926 and assigned to the lower-middle-class suburb of Royal Oak, adjoining Birmingham, which adjoins Bloomfield Hills, where he created the Shrine of the Little Flower. He bought time on a local radio station and broadcast the *Golden Hour of the Little Flower."* CBS picked up his show. He played into a distrust of both the Protestant ethic and communism. Then he started into the "shylocks" on Wall Street who were interested only in their returns on European investments. CBS canceled him. He bought time on other stations. By 1931, his *Golden Hour* reached twenty-six states, pulling in over sixty thousand dollars per month, attracting nearly 40 percent of the radio audience in his Sunday evening slot, ahead of the popular Burns and Allen, and Amos 'n' Andy. Franklin Roosevelt even welcomed him into the White House. Then Coughlin's dark side started to take control.

Coughlin had supported Roosevelt's decision to take America off the gold standard. When it was revealed that Coughlin's Radio League of the Little Flower had accumulated nearly five hundred thousand ounces of silver, Coughlin lashed out at the secretary of the treasury and "his Jewish cohorts," who acted "like Dillinger." He went on to blame "the Kuhn-Loebs, the Rothchilds," and the Jewish conspiracy behind communism and the New Deal. He praised Mussolini and supported Hitler's ambitions. In December of 1937 he flatly adopted the Nazi propaganda line of "world Jewish domination." He whipped his followers into rages, encouraging "the Franco way" of dealing with "traitors" (i.e., Jews). The Justice Department under future justice Robert L. Jackson went after

Coughlin for sedition, causing his Archbishop to order Coughlin to retire from politics. His hate-filled *Golden Hour* was finally silenced. But the feelings he flamed live on. Aviva Kempner speaks for many Detroit-area Jews when she says that she still shudders when she passes the Shrine of the Little Flower, on Woodward Avenue in Royal Oak, ten miles from the Ballmer house.

Bea Ballmer was an active reader who worked with Steve on his Hebrew school lessons. Ballmer recalls that he was "very shy" and would get sick to his stomach at the thought of going to Hebrew school. Bea calmed him down and drove him to studies. Steve said, "The importance of family to her was imparted to all. My mom always supported me in everything I wanted to do. She was a great partner and confidant." No one recalls him as ever being shy.

Steve's attachment to Bea, and his extreme sadness when she died in 1997, derives at least in part from of the concept of *naches* (knock-us), the Yiddish word for joy, especially joy from children. As Steve Silbiger details in *The Jewish Phenomenon*, a certain type of Jewish child becomes a "naches machine, and strives to satisfy their parents' own needs to be successful. The downside for these naches machines is that their self-worth is dependent on professional success. If they do not achieve material success and receive their appropriate kudos, they do not believe they are worthy of love and live unhappy lives. With their definition of success being a moving target, it is difficult for these naches machines ever to be satisfied."

By Thanksgiving 1971, Fred Ballmer had joined many former Detroiters and moved north. Fred and his family took an unusual route to the northern burbs—first they moved to Belgium. During the 1960s, politically savvy Ford employees learned that management's internal turf wars were best avoided if one wanted to advance. Ford International was the place to work. In 1963 Fred followed that route and accepted an assignment working on a U.S. Army compound near NATO headquarters in Brussels, Belgium, bringing his family along. (The European Union would locate its headquarters there years later.) They were there when President Kennedy was assassinated. At this point, young Steve was put ahead a grade, and learned to speak perfect French. The family didn't (and don't) talk much about the experience. When asked what Brussels was like, all Fred would say to Hank Borgman was, "Belgium was invaded by the French, the Germans, the Russians. They took all the good-looking girls. There aren't any pretty women left." Belgium had been invaded by the Nazis and by Napoléon. Waterloo is in Belgium. Brussels is headquarters for the European Union Competition Commission, which is also investigating Microsoft. The family made an impression when they returned.

Rather than come back to Oak Park, in August 1966, Fred and Bea scouted housing in the northern suburbs, deciding on a three-bedroom colonial on Lynford Road in the new subdivision of Lincolnshire Estates in Farmington Hills. The house is a block from the intersection of Middlebelt and Eleven Mile Roads. At the time, Farmington Hills was fairly rural (it still had farms), and Eleven Mile Road was unpaved.

It seemed the whole neighborhood turned out to marvel at the Ballmer's moving vans, including a flatbed truck with a crane, unloading the wood crates of their belongings, bearing exotic customs tags. Virtually all of their neighbors were, like the Ballmers, the first owners of their homes. The Ballmers' neighbors included Walt Whitman and James Mason, no relation to the like-named poet and actor. Walt Whitman was an engineer at Ford who lived a few houses down from the Ballmers for thirty years. Whitman says, "Fred and Bea were good neighbors, polite and friendly. They kept to themselves a lot. Bea did the gardening. Their lawn and house were well kept. They didn't socialize much with the rest of us. Steve was different, he played with our kids. But we rarely saw his sister Shelly.

"Something about Fred bothered me for a while. Every morning I'd pass the Ballmer house and see Fred's Thunderbird parked in the driveway. It was there in the evening when I came back. I wondered if he ever went to work. Then I found out he worked at the Wixom plant, located to the west. He drove against traffic and, in a few minutes, would be at work, while I spent an hour or so in rush-hour traffic. Smart guy."

Family lore has Fred Ballmer giving financial forecasts to high-level Ford execs, including president Lee Iacocca and CEO Philip Caldwell. (Philip Caldwell told me he doesn't recall Fred Ballmer.) For reasons Ford will not divulge, Fred didn't rise very high in the organization, only making it to the tenth rung of Ford's eighty-nine-step ladder, and after working there for thirty years his only extra retirement benefit was that he could still lease a car. Like Bea, Fred smoked, but unlike her, he smoked cigars. This was a point of contention between them, and Bea finally won and banished Fred to the garage to light up his stogies.

Though Fred wasn't athletic, he did compete with Steve in chess. They spent many hours facing each other over a chessboard. Fred was hard of hearing—he'd be almost completely deaf during the last ten years of his life—and so one would have to *raise their voice* for Fred to understand. According to a family friend, Fred occasionally talked about his Nuremberg experience, about his life in Switzerland, and about his current work. Steve recalled to *Newsweek*, "My dad like[d] to ask questions and think things through completely. I remember my dad, when I was a kid, explaining to me how domestic international sales corporations worked. It's a tax thing the U.S. government probably never should have done, but once they did it, Ford had to drive a truck through it. But it was so complicated. I never to this day could understand how my dad just went through all the details, saw all the opportunities. . . . Neither of my parents ever went to college but I can remember my dad just assuming I would." When Steve Ballmer reported his father's death to Washington state officials, though, he swore his father had "four plus" years of college, and Fred Ballmer provided certified college transcripts with his Nuremberg application.

Steve Ballmer quickly became known in the neighborhood. Actually, he became heard. Most area families had more than two children, and about every other house had a basketball hoop attached to their garage (the Ballmer house didn't have one). Steve joined in the pickup games whenever he could, playing half-court driveway ball with local kids. One of them, Rob Mason, observed, "You could see how Steve ended up where he did. He just kept driving toward the basket. He was hugely competitive. He'd organize these pickup games—we had them all the time. He'd be so loud, calling out to see if anyone wanted to play. His voice carries."

Mason's father, James, lived kitty-corner from the Ballmers for thirty years. He says he'd see Bea on her daily constitutional, her several-block walk to the grocery store for food and flowers. (She loved flowers.) She waved and said hello and kept walking. He clearly recalls one day hearing a disturbance on his front lawn. He came out to find Steve and Rob fighting. Steve was a few years older, and far bigger. Steve was wailing on his son, then pushed him aside, grabbed the basketball, and ran down the road to shoot baskets on another driveway court. A case of it's-my-ball-and-we'll-play-by-my-rules? "No," says James, "it was Rob's basketball."

Steve Ballmer was enrolled at East Junior High School, a few blocks from his house, a short walk every morning. At East a counselor, troubled by what her school could offer Steve's intellect, took him aside and said they weren't set up to handle someone like him, that they didn't have the advanced classes. The counselor told him that there was a private school close by, Detroit Country Day School, and every year they had a competition for a Headmaster's Scholarship. The counselor encouraged him to try. As Rob Mason recalls, "Steve aced the sucker. We all knew when he won the scholarship, he was off to better things. Not that it changed him as a person, he was still the same Steve to us, but we knew that he'd hit the big time, and we knew that he'd keep going. Once Steve gets it in his head he wants to do something, he's relentless." Steve Ballmer would spend most of his remaining Detroit-area days in the challenging environment of Birmingham.

CHAPTER TWO

BIRMINGHAM

Birmingham, Michigan, is a predominately upper-middle-class town of some twenty thousand well-to-do white people, a Wasp-dominated city containing streets named Puritan and Pilgrim. Located fifteen miles north of Detroit, and often linked with the neighboring community of Bloomfield Hills and referred to as Birmingham-Bloomfield, or simply Birmingham, the area boasts the second-highest per capita American income. Think in terms of Pacific Palisades or Mercer Island, of Scarsdale or Lake Forest. When Detroiters are asked what they think of their Birmingham residents, many respond with something akin to the Michael Dukakis statement, "Some people say I'm arrogant, but I know I'm better than that."

In 1971, Detroit was hot, cool, a muse. Both it and Birmingham were inspiring locations. After the huge commercial success of his movie script of a novel, *Airport*, Arthur Hailey received a then-record million dollars for his next book and came to the area to research *Wheels*. By Thanksgiving, *Wheels* was tenth on the *New York Times* bestseller list. Harold Robbins, never missing an opportunity to make a buck (or to describe a woman by her sex drive or body parts) saw his Detroit and Birmingham-based potboiler *The Betsy* a few notches below *Wheels* on the list (Robbins's book was made into a truly horrible movie, Hailey's into a truly horrible TV miniseries). Hailey and Robbins were following the lead of Joyce Carol Oates, who had set part of her 1968 novel *Expensive People* in Birmingham. The most recent Miss America emerita, Pamela Anne Eldred, lived in Birmingham. The town was a special place at a special time and CBS did a special on it.

In "But What If the [American] Dream Comes True?" correspondent Charles Kuralt began the well-written study with a voice-over while the camera showed a drive down the tree-lined Cranbrook Road: "Birmingham, Michigan, is to the north of *Huck Finn* and *Tom Sawyer*. It's to the east of *Babbitt* and to the west of *Leatherstocking Tales*, but echoes of all those American stories can be heard here. You know what's in those houses. A love affair with the obvious—good food, beautiful clothes, the best education. This is what America always said it wanted to become." A high school cheerleader appears on the screen shouting, "Hey, we're gonna beat you, you. Hey, we're gonna beat you, you."

The special concentrates on the family headed by bank vice president Sam Greenawalt, his troubled wife Jane, and his three kids—Sheri, fourteen years old; Tami, twelve; and son Sani, ten. Sam, a decorated marine combat veteran of the Korean War, describes how hard he has worked to get where he is. He is proud of this, but wonders why his children are rejecting him. Kuralt wonders, "If the women of Birmingham are away from home seeking their own identity and if the men of Birmingham are away from home seeking their fortune, what happens to the children of Birmingham?"

Around the time the special appeared, the town was raising or educating some kids whose influence would far exceed their numbers, extending to outer space, shaping cyberspace, touching television and film and most workplaces. The group includes a couple of Oscar winners, Robin Williams and Christine Lahti; an Emmy winner, Tim Allen; the Emmy-nominated Laura Innes from *ER*; and the editor cum talking head Michael Kinsley. Then there's the two constantly battling computer execs whose competition would overflow from the marketplace, through the halls of Congress, to the chambers of the Supreme Court: Steve Ballmer and Sun Microsystems co-founder and CEO Scott McNealy.

Why did such a small area produce more than its share of high achievers? One report suggests it could be because Michigan has the lowest natural concentration of the salt lithium and the highest incidence of manic depression in the nation. University of Michigan psychology professor Christopher Peterson shoots the it's-the-water theory down as urban legend, noting the regional statistics don't support that contention. I was born and raised in Birmingham, and would graduate from Birmingham's public Seaholm High School. I think my hometown petri dish spawned such stars because of its blend of intense and well-funded academic, athletic, and social competition, and a high level of parental expectation, involvement, and support. One should factor in the midwestern work ethic. And while in these northern suburbs of a city based on the internal combustion engine some kids would internally combust, those who didn't would be, if not prepared by the intense competition to prosper once they left, at least be familiar with it. It's also said that Hollywood is like high school, only with money. These kids, with the exception of Steve Ballmer, had money in high school. While none of the future high-profile kids are shown in the CBS special, Kuralt visits Birmingham's Youth Controlled Crisis Center, where some of the disaffected speak up. One states, "You're brought up to feel like everybody's, you know, like, if you're from Birmingham, you're better than the rest of the world."

Michael Kinsley, who went on to establish Microsoft's *Slate* magazine, told me, "If you had to pick a time and a place in history to grow up, just in terms of laying the groundwork for being successful, Birmingham would be it. It was a place obsessed with raising kids. Birmingham in the postwar era was probably the most advantageous place for a successful businessman to be raised in the history of humankind. That was a time after a lot of bad stuff—the Holocaust, the war—and before a lot of shit: Vietnam, drugs, and the reoccurring crisis of teenhood of sorts. It was a pristine place to go to high school and grow up. Because it was upper middle class, you had all the advantages, yet you weren't so rich that you would be spoiled and ruined. If you had a choice and were going to be hit by a bus and you had a kid you could leave behind, and you could leave behind an upper-middle-class kid or a poor kid struggling and he can build his way up from the log cabin, you'd pick the upper-middle-class kid."

In the special, of his fellow parents, Sam Greenawalt says, "They put a great deal of pressure on their children. I don't know whether it's too much or not, 'cause some children are going to crack, some people are gonna crack. But you have to have pressure to perform. You have got to have the pressure. I was trained to be competitive. To be better than someone else. To be better than someone else or to be better than what you ordinarily would be if you were lackadaisical. You have to push in order to get the best you can out of yourself and you have to hurt yourself to get it. This whole country was based on competition, and that doesn't mean that competition has to be bad. Competition can be clean and it can be forthright, and I think very good."

Sam Greenawalt decides to rejoin the suburban Bedouin and buys a house a mile and a half away in Bloomfield Hills. The special ends with Kuralt noting, "The American dream involves possessions and real estate and knows no limits. History may ask, 'Is this dream of acquisition the one you want to put your faith in?' We are all in a race, and there isn't any resting place, and there isn't any finishing line."

The next week the local paper, aptly named the *Birmingham Eccentric,* was filled with criticism of the critic. Given that a few of my friends were shown in the special, which took the parents many of us were rebelling against to task, we thought it was pretty good. And being the first generation raised with the electronic babysitter, it was fantastic to finally see ourselves coming out of the tube. For most people, it would be their fifteen minutes of fame. And for most, all they knew was that the rest of the world drove their fine cars, Bob Seger sang their sweet songs, their schools were the best, their girls were the prettiest, and didn't everyone go to Florida in the winter? They lived for the moment, and, like kids everywhere, most lived for the moment they could leave. Only about one out of every twenty of my classmates still lives there.

Detroit Country Day School was founded in 1914, mainly to educate the sons of the auto companies' growing professional class. Located six miles from the Ballmer house, on Thirteen Mile Road, it offered a very rigorous curriculum to a religious and racially diverse student body. What's more, Country Day virtually required parents to become involved in their kid's education. With Fred and Bea providing a great deal of support and encouragement, their son Steve took Country Day by storm.

A classmate recalls, "You'd hear Steve before he came around a corner. Not as much his voice, which was, of course, loud, but he wore the same black wing tips, I swear, the four years he was there. He must have had them resoled every year. And he had those metal cleats on the bottom. Click. Click. Click. They sounded like boots, shitkickers we called them. He had these shitkickers on, and he always wore the school uniform—a dark blazer, white shirt, dark tie, and gray slacks—every day. We only had to wear it once a week, but Steve wore it every day. He was hard core. He had a butch haircut, a crew cut. He told me it was easier to maintain. He looked a little like Sergeant Carter in the TV show *Gomer Pyle,* except he was about 250 pounds. He looked like the typical nerd, with everything but the pocket protector."

Todd Rich, a classmate who's currently a medical doctor and genetic researcher at Genentech in Silicon Valley, says, "Steve was the brightest of the bright. Everybody, after a few minutes, would know his amazing intelligence. Steve was always, I don't want to say overly animated, but certainly extremely animated. Both mentally and physically. He came here in the ninth grade, and he was probably a year or a year and a half behind us in math. By the end of tenth grade, he was a year and a half ahead of us. I'm not joking. We were in an accelerated class and in two years, he went from a year and a half behind us to a year and a half ahead of us, so he did five years when we did two. Amazing. He exhausted all of our math classes and started in college when he was only a junior.

"He would sit in the very front row. We'd be talking about something when the teacher would ask a question and you'd see him get really kind of agitated, because he couldn't figure it out. He's just voracious in his appetite for learning. He'd be almost despondent if he couldn't figure something out. He'd stay after class. He'd say, 'I don't care how long it takes.' He was really kinda driven that way. He'd even be excited explaining it to a classmate. He'd sit down and start drawing, you know, three quarters of the time you couldn't follow him anyway, because he was going so fast. It would just eat at him and eat at him." Rich laughs. "He'd be writing frantically, he'd be leaning over his desk, and he'd get so excited figuring out something for the first time.

And then, when he did, when he figured it out, he'd go 'OH! OH! OH!' We'd all say, 'Be quiet, Steve.'

"If you took the Steve we knew at Country Day, and flashed forward twenty years to where you'd think he'd be, I think he'd be designing [computer] chips. Or doing astrophysics. Or cosmology, or something with either equations and numbers and that kind of thing. Theoretical physics. He'd be more of a Freeman Dyson than an Esther Dyson. I think that when he went to P & G [Procter & Gamble], when he found a home in the marketing side of Microsoft, that just doesn't jive with my view of Steve in high school. P & G probably whetted his appetite and focused the same enthusiasm. Everything I read about Steve—whether he blew his vocal cords at some meeting, that he gets up and screams, sometimes screams things that are not always the most considerate—that's exactly what I would expect. [Those are all in] his personality traits. All that is totally consistent with exactly the same guy he was in tenth grade."

One of Ballmer's math teachers, Gerald Hansen, recalls, "Steve would get up in front of the class, at the blackboard, and explain a problem. Hands all over the place, chalk moving. He'd be writing with one hand and have an eraser in the other and be writing and erasing at the same time. He had this what I call intellectual energy. I don't know how he shuts down at night, to be honest with you. A very high level of intellectual energy. You couldn't stump him. Never. It's laughable, but he'd be a great candidate for *Who Wants to Be a Millionaire.*

"Bea and Fred would be at school a lot. They really supported him. Bea drove him to Lawrence Tech for his math classes there. Drove him all over the state for math competitions. He finished third in the state one year. Fred talked about his Nuremberg experience, how he got the job because of his language skills, how he was glad Steve had learned French. One of the things that teachers really live for is to see how their students turn out. Teachers sometimes are without an education in life—they're having a vicarious adventure through their students and everybody is always proud when you get someone who succeeds like Steve. He becomes your hero, really."

Hansen eventually became headmaster, and he sees Ballmer regularly. Ballmer is on Country Day's board of trustees, along with Sam Greenawalt. Hansen notes that Ballmer has been "very generous" to the school, donating over ten million dollars. One source claims that Ballmer provided the scholarship money for a promising basketball player, Chris Webber, to attend. (Webber's currently the star forward of the NBA's Sacramento Kings.) With great, and greatly unintended, irony, Country Day created a Diamond Member honor for donors, with Steve and Connie Ballmer its sole members. The irony is that, when the Ballmers were given Diamond Member status, Microsoft was in many courts for violating the Sherman Antitrust Act. As CBS's *60 Minutes* detailed, diamonds carry an artificial and very high price because the controlling distributor, DeBeers, is an illegal cartel whose executives can't enter the United States because they're under indictment for antitrust violations.

Another former classmate, Don Gregario, is a rehabilitation counselor with the Hazelden Foundation in Minnesota. He notes, "It's not abnormal to see people from the Birmingham-Bloomfield here at Hazelden. Their kids have a lot of substance abuse problems—they have the money and they're bored. But not Steve. Not at all. And not Country Day. Oh, maybe a few guys at Country Day smoked dope, but Cranbrook Academy had all the freaks, the drug users. We didn't have many."

Another classmate, K. C. Jensen, recalls, "Steve—I had a math class right after his, algebra for dummies or something like that, and the teacher walked in on him—he had stayed after class to work on a problem. The teacher, Don Hocevar, his eyes just kind of glazed over. He couldn't even deal with it. He just erased it. We begged him to explain what Steve was working on and Don Ho said, 'I don't have the time for that.'

"Steve was somewhat of an enigma. You never really knew what was going on inside. He came across as the quintessential nerd, physically, but he put you off guard because he was very personable, down to earth, easy to talk to, helpful. He really had a knack of fitting in whenever he wanted to. He wasn't Zelig-like, he never enmeshed himself completely. It's like he had a higher calling—and he knew it. He bridged all the cliques in the school. He didn't turn into the clique—he had a very good sense of himself, he was okay with himself. He could reach anybody. I could see his spirit then, what he's showing at Microsoft. He could reach anybody. That wasn't typical with your average brain at Country Day."

Steve was particularly close to a few teachers, among them John Campbell. Campbell is inevitably described as "a character," as "unorthodox." One of his former students, Robin Williams, has acknowledged that his portrayal of the character Mr. Keating in the 1989 film *Dead Poets Society* was based on John Campbell. The movie concerns a teacher who encourages students to carry on the tradition of a secret society, finding itself in poetry and prose, following Thoreau's credo to "suck deeply the marrow of life." It shows Mr. Keating telling his students to rip out the introduction of their poetry books.

Campbell says, "Rob—we knew him as Rob—was wrong. I told them to throw the whole book in the wastebasket." The film's credo, *carpe diem*—Latin for "seize the day"—quickly entered everyday use. Campbell says, "Rob was very quiet. I was also wrestling coach and Rob was on the wrestling team. One day I came into the locker room and overheard the wrestlers laughing. They went quiet when they saw me. I later found out that Rob had done a perfect imitation of my voice. Robin—when he became Robin—became famous, of course, playing Mork—an alien from the planet Ork—on [the late 1970s sitcom] *Mork and Mindy*." In the financially neurotic Birmingham, the middle class were considered poor, the upper middle class were considered middle class, and the rich were just that, with mansions and servants. Robin Williams, also a Ford kid, was the son of a senior Lincoln-Mercury vice president and one of the truly rich kids, raised in a forty-room mansion, on a twenty-acre estate, in Bloomfield Hills.

John Campbell continues, "Steve Ballmer. You don't forget Steve. He always sat in the front row and his hand was always waving, he always had the answer. Shy? No way. And it was funny to watch him. He'd sometimes get this puzzled look on his face and you could see he was trying to understand and then it would come to him and he'd almost jump out of his seat, saying, 'OH! OH! OH!' I'd say, 'That's fine, Steve, now shut up.'

"When I ran for the Michigan State House of Representatives, Steve's parents had a coffee klatch for me. It was hopeless. I was a liberal Democrat, for raising the minimum wage and the Equal Rights Amendment, and Farmington was, at best, moderately conservative, but Fred and Bea were Democrats. My students went door to door campaigning for me, including Steve. He handed out literature. He thought I'd helped him and he just was repaying the favor. Then every Saturday, for extra credit, I had a world United Nations–type political science competition. Groups of students would represent different countries and go into different rooms and plot strategy of how to use the resources they had—land, food, people, arms—to protect themselves or increase their dominions. Steve was pretty good at it, but then again, Steve was pretty good at anything he put his mind to. He loved learning. He loved competition. That came naturally to him."

After Robin Williams played him in *Dead Poets Society*, Campbell would suffer what's come to be known as "the Robin

Williams syndrome." Just like Dr. Oliver Sachs, who was canned after Williams portrayed him in *Awakenings*, Campbell lost his job. After twenty-eight years at Country Day he was, like Mr. Keating, fired, for "not adhering to the school's academic and professional standards." Campbell was the only teacher Ballmer had mentioned by name when he spoke at Country Day's commencement the year before Campbell was axed. Campbell notes, "I just didn't fit Country Day's corporate image." In retrospect, Campbell sees that "Steve developed the predatory monopoly personality after leaving Country Day. The Steve I see making speeches and all that, he wasn't like that at Country Day. He wasn't into theater. He was president of the political science and computer club."

Detroit's wealth flowed through places such as computer manufacturer Burroughs Corporation (now Unisys), which donated almost unlimited use of one of their mainframe computers via a remote TC-500 terminal. (In contrast, Seattle's Lakeside School, where Bill Gates and Paul Allen were programming away, had to hold rummage sales, in part to pay for the computer time of the future Microsoft co-founders.)

A Country Day exchange student from France recalls, "The school had probably one of the first high school computer rooms in the States, with machines that could now be shown in any antique museum. I remember that Steve spent a long time in that room. When the day at school was finished, we said, 'Steve, we are going out, would you join us?' He was glued at his keyboard and answered, 'No, sorry, I still have work to do.' He was a nice man, always giving me a hand as he spoke fluent French and my English was not very good when I first arrived in the USA."

One of Ballmer's English teachers, Beverly Hannett-Price, speaks of both him and his family in glowing terms. She notes that Ballmer read the prep school standards, almost regarded as a trilogy—*The Catcher in the Rye, A Separate Peace,* and *Death Be Not Proud*—but it was a Hermann Hesse work, *Beneath the Wheel,* that was his favorite. Ballmer's life at Country Day mirrors Hesse's novel. In the story, a headmaster counsels his star student, "That's the way, that's the way, my boy. Don't let up or you'll get dragged beneath the wheel." Hannett-Price says, "That's Steve, he was never going to let up, never going to be dragged beneath the wheel."

Like more than a few Detroiters, many Birmingham kids were obsessed with sports and cars. When the Detroit Tigers won the 1968 World Series, their march toward the crown was such a community bond that many credit it with preventing another downtown riot from breaking out, as had happened the year before, claiming forty-four lives. Yet that Thanksgiving it was amateur sports that captured the area's competition fanatics. Five days before, the University of Michigan football team had humiliated the Ohio State University diploma mill, winning the Big Ten championship, finishing their regular season undefeated and second in the nation. Ohio State's maniacal coach Woody Hayes threw one of his famous tantrums. Hayes picked up a sideline marker and broke it in two, took another sideline marker and hurled it on the field, and had to be restrained by his players from punching a referee. Michigan fans responded by pelting Hayes with snowballs as he was led off the field to chants of "Good-bye Woody, good-bye Woody, we're glad to see you go." The era's and area's Zeitgeist was reflecting the Green Bay Packer coach Vince Lombardi–attributed creed, "Winning isn't everything, it's the only thing." The saying was taped to a door in President Richard Nixon's campaign finance headquarters. (Lombardi would later say, "I wish I hadn't said the damn thing.")

Steve Ballmer got caught up in sports by playing on his junior varsity, then varsity football team in the fall, as basketball manager in the winter, and by putting the shot on the track team in the spring. Beverly Hannett-Price says, "I nominated Steve for athlete of the year the first year he came here. Oh, he didn't have much talent, but that wasn't what it was about. There was a tall, handsome, clear-skinned student, the quarterback of the football team, who had natural talent. I think he won, but I don't think that's what it should have been about. He was given the talent. Steve had acne and was overweight and simply worked harder and harder than everyone else. The terms of his scholarship required that he participate in three sports. And Steve worked."

Stephen Pollack, now a vice president with Fleet Boston, was an all-state center on the football team who would square off against Steve during scrimmages. Pollack remembers Ballmer enhancing his athletic ability with pure tenacity. "He used to keep coming at me," says Pollack. "He had great enthusiasm."

Steve also served under the basketball coach, John Hansen. He says, "Steve wanted to be part of the team and so he was manager. He was the best basketball manager I ever had. All the towels would be in place, the basketballs in order, and he kept perfect stats. He'd have water bottles waiting when they came off the court and a towel and, of course, he cheered. Everything was always in order. He was so disciplined."

Another classmate recalls, "I was on the hockey team. We didn't have our own rink, we played miles away. And we'd be in the middle of bumfuck, nowhere actually, playing some team or another, and they would have their home rink advantage and all their friends watching and cheering and then Steve would show up. And cheer. I mean, we'd have just Steve and they'd have dozens of people and, I swear, Steve would outshout them. Just having him there made you play better. He wasn't a hockey fan—basketball was his sport—but he came to almost every hockey game just to cheer. He's taking a crushing workload, he's taking math classes at the local college, he's got his own sports, and yet he'd show up just to cheer us on. You'd play better just knowing he was there. It was amazing."

Ballmer would be cheering for Country Day when they played their archrival, crosstown prep school Cranbrook, in hockey. As Todd Rich notes, "Country Day was the poor stepchild to Cranbrook. We only had one permanent building and three modular units while Cranbrook had an Ivy League–like campus." The forward on Cranbrook's hockey team was the tall, lanky sixteen-year-old senior Scott McNealy. In the three years McNealy and Ballmer were part of the Country Day–Cranbrook continuum, the better-funded, better-equipped, rink-owing Cranbrook won eight of its thirteen games with Country Day.

Scott McNealy's Harvard undergrad/Harvard Business School grad father, William Raymond McNealy, was a vice president at American Motors Corporation (AMC), working on, among other projects, its Pacer model. (He would later become AMC's vice chairman.) The office of one of his fellow auto execs boldly displayed a poster, popular among Detroit manufacturers at the time, proclaiming, YEA, THOUGH I WALK THROUGH THE SHADOW OF THE VALLEY OF DEATH I FEAR NO EVIL, FOR I AM THE MEANEST SON-OF-A-BITCH IN THE VALLEY. It was common knowledge in Detroit that AMC itself owed its continued existence to the Sherman Antitrust Act. If General Motors had flexed its marketplace muscle, it could have wiped both AMC and Chrysler off the map, and made Ford very nervous.

Just as Country Day and Cranbrook were on opposite sides of Birmingham-Bloomfield, Ballmer and McNealy were on opposite sides of the socioeconomic pecking order. McNealy lived close to Robin Williams, in a mansion where, he claims, he would talk business strategy with his father's friends Ford president Lee Iaccoca and GM chairman Roger Smith. McNealy shared Ballmer's involvement with sports but more as a participant: a self-described hockey and golf freak, he captained both teams.

Then there was the most famous Detroit passion: cars. While cars didn't turn Ballmer on—one friend recalled he drove an old, beat-up Buick—McNealy would drive to Woodward Avenue, which bordered the Cranbrook campus, and drag race. "Woodwarding," it was called. When Woodwarding, the best cars were by no means the prettiest or most expensive—just like, outside of certain Birmingham circles, people. Scott McNealy's car was an exception.

Given his father's position, he received fully insured company cars gratis—it's poor public relations for your car executives' cars to look shabby or break down. (One American Motors exec's son totaled three showroom-new cars in 1971 before his father took his company-car driving privileges away.) As it was heresy to drive a competitor's car, you could often tell who in Birmingham or Farmington Hills worked where simply by what make was parked in their driveway. Scott's father let him drive a Gremlin "X"—with a flashy, sporty accessory package that included Levi's denim bucket seats and an eight-track tape deck. But the secret of his success was unseen, at first.

Scott's father had gotten him a Gremlin especially made for the NASCAR production car series, powered by a 360-cubic-inch engine, a V-8 that took up every inch under the hood. Nobody in a muscle car would think twice when a cute little powder-puff Gremlin pulled alongside. McNealy's drag-racing opponents would take him seriously only after he'd shot off the light and accelerated like a missile, by which time they were too far behind to catch up.

His senior yearbook, the 1972 'Brook, mocked McNealy's jockish, bombastic ways and constant off-the-cuff talking: "Scott's quiet and unassuming manner won him a wealth of friends who have come to respect his always thoughtful advice. Although unconcerned about his athletic and scholastic endeavors, he excelled in both. Last, but not least, let it be known to all the world . . . that Scott's Gremlin X really was the fastest."

According to Ballmer's maternal uncle Irving Dworkin, and like the environment shown in *Dead Poets Society,* where actor Ethan Hawke's character is told that he must go to Harvard, Fred Ballmer told son Steve, when he was eight years old, that he was going to Harvard. Harvard has regional quotas and recruiters who look over and recommend students for admission. Says one accepted student, "The Harvard competition in Birmingham was so intense the advice I received was that if the regional recruiter, Don Hocevar, didn't recommend you, the only way you'd get in was to move to Montana and play the oboe. And Hocevar must have seen something in McNealy, something more than that he was a legacy [that his father had gone there], to recommend him." Of course, Don Hocevar taught math at Country Day. Don Hocevar taught math to Steve Ballmer, and he would stop by the Ballmer house on his way to school in the morning and give his student a ride. "Steve wasn't a brown-noser or anything like that," says a classmate. "You could just see how it was natural that they [Hocevar and Ballmer] would gravitate together." Ballmer and McNealy would meet with Don Ho for prospective Harvard student meetings. They weren't close, but Ballmer would bunk with McNealy in his Harvard freshman dorm room, A-31 in Mower Hall, when he toured the campus that spring.

Steve had taken the SATs and, like McNealy and Bill Gates and another Farmington Hills resident, Bill Joy, had received a perfect 800 on the math section. Though Steve was accepted at MIT and Cal Tech, and his goal was to be either a math or physics professor, his father's fiat had the good son Steve choose Harvard. And Harvard chose Steve. And no wonder.

In June of 1973 Ballmer graduated valedictorian of his class at Country Day. He also received the White Cup, given to the student with the highest grade point average over four years. His GPA was a perfect 4.0. His scores on the math, French, English, and History advanced placement tests were so high that Harvard actually accepted him as a sophomore. Bea and Fred would hear none of that. Like Tiger Woods's parents, they wanted their genius son Steve to progress as normally as possible.

Ballmer had worked odd jobs throughout high school, including caddying for two dollars an hour at the local Franklin Country Club. He continued doing the same the summer before he moved to Cambridge. No one recalls him ever even talking about setting up a business. Ballmer wasn't, said a friend, the entrepreneurial type. According to a friend, he had other things to concentrate on. He had another plan. And he was going to what many considered one of the better liberal arts college in the land.

CHAPTER THREE

HARVARD

In the summer of 1973, Steve Ballmer started his intellectual move to Boston by whipping through his summer reading list. Visiting the Harvard campus that spring had helped him quickly acclimate himself to that rarefied environment. Arriving in Cambridge in August, a declared mathematics major, he memorized all the faces and names in the freshman class book. Classmates were surprised to have this beefy stranger, looking like a bar bouncer, greet them by name and start up a conversation about where they were from and where they went to school.

Classmate Gordon Adler recalls, "I think Steve was like many of the rest of us, in celebration of deliverance, standing there in awe, thinking 'How is it possible I am here?' There wasn't one Steve Ballmer, there were thirty Steve Ballmers [valedictorian math majors]. It was as though we were being given the keys to the kingdom." Other classmates remember easing into the experience, learning more from their fellow students than their classes. Ballmer wasn't at Harvard due to family ties or money, he was there on merit. Like Country Day, he worked hard to belong, and succeeded, but it was an adjustment.

As one Harvard freshman at the time, a Birmingham public school graduate, relates, "Boston and Harvard were culture shocks. They hit you in two ways. First, we were from the midwestern suburbs and Harvard is the urban East Coast. Second, the rich in Birmingham-Bloomfield were the nuevo riche, the newly rich, but the rich at Harvard were the Cabots and the Lodges, the very definition of the old rich."

Another freshman that year, Jamie Coldre, says, "Harvard is so stratified. All the rich students seemed to know each other before they came. They hung together there. They'd look right through you. They'd act like you didn't exist." These rich were different from you and me in that they had their own secret societies, dining clubs, like the Porcelain Club, akin to Yale's Skull and Bones. Such clubs, says then freshman, now–*Baltimore Sun* editorial cartoonist Kevin Kallaugher (Kal), were peopled by "a bunch of eighteen-year-old kids sitting around smoking cigars and acting like forty-five-year-olds."

The Harvard that Steve Ballmer would absorb was, says Kal, "at an interregnum between the radicalism of the sixties and the 'greed is good' mentality of the eighties." Like all freshmen, Ballmer was required to live in a dorm at Harvard Yard—in his case Thayer Hall, with roommate Kenneth Argentieri, now a lawyer in Pittsburgh. Harvard had started to increase its puny number of coeds, and the Yard was undergoing one of the most radical changes in its three centuries: women could live there. As 1973 Yard resident Judith Kaplan says, "There were eleven hundred eighteen-year-old guys away from home for the first time and 280 of us women. They didn't allow us to live on the top or bottom floors, they felt they were protecting us. But many resented us being there." It seemed like a boys' club. Because it was.

During Ballmer's freshman year, the campus humor magazine, the *Harvard Lampoon,* gave its 1973 "Movie Worst" award to *Deep Throat* porno movie star Linda Lovelace. She won the uncoveted "Wilde Oscar," which was awarded annually to "the actor or actress most willing to flout convention and risk worldly damnation in the pursuit of artistic fulfillment." Lovelace arrived on campus in the Oscar Mayer Wienermobile—a twenty-five-foot-long plastic replica of a hot dog in a bun—her coming announced by the Harvard Orchestra, her path lined with jugglers, clowns, and a chorus of garland-bedecked maidens. This definitely wasn't Birmingham.

According to Beverly Hannett-Price, at the 2001 Father and Sons Dinner at Country Day, Ballmer revealed a freshman-year career epiphany. Entering Harvard, he fully expected himself to be a math or physics professor, but after struggling for seven straight hours with a physics problem, he said, "This isn't any fun. I wasn't having any fun. This isn't what I want to do with my life." Seven hundred miles away from Fred and Bea, freed from Birmingham's sometimes provincial and stifling conformity and conservatism, surrounded by some of the wealthiest, most privileged and gifted students in the world, Ballmer was unbound, wondering where he was headed. Slowly, the financially challenged idealist was changing. In August 1974, Ballmer moved almost a mile away from the Yard to Currier House.

Currier House is a complex of four five-story dorms, shaped like the letter E, with courtyards between each of its three arms and a two-story central commons building, connected by underground walkways. Audrey Bruce Currier, a 1956 Radcliffe grad, had died in a mysterious plane crash in 1967. Her mom, a granddaughter of former treasury secretary Andrew Mellon and wife of

Ambassador David Bruce, passed the hat among friends like David Rockefeller, Thomas Cabot, and Nelson Aldrich to erect a state-of-the-art living memorial to her daughter. Its dorms are named after four Radcliffe grads: historian Barbara Tuchman, newspaperwoman Mary Bingham, Radcliffe Board of Trustees head Helen Gilbert, and composer and musician Mabel Daniels. Steve Ballmer moved onto the fourth floor in Currier-Daniels, which, in honor of its namesake, had a one-hundred-seat auditorium and seven music practice rooms, along with a small computer lab. Microsoft's office park, also called a campus, would later resemble Currier House.

Currier House was an experiment. Project advisors, including the famed psychiatrist Erik Erikson, saw themselves as building more of a community than a dorm, one that would help residents "develop their intellectual interests, to venture into new fields and to enjoy and learn from each other." This was where Bill Gates met Steve Ballmer. When asked why he chose Currier House, Gates said it was an enclave of science types. In his more blunt manner Ballmer said, "Because there were more women there." He got that stat right. Currier House had 233 women and eighty-four men.

In the Harvard of Gates and Ballmer, the sexual revolution was going strong. With the Pill eliminating much of the fear of pregnancy, AIDS unheard of, free love was the call of the wild raging hormones. One student from Birmingham proudly announced that his goals at Harvard were "A's and lays." According to resident Jamie Coldre, "Currier was a cluster fuck. My friends and I thought that, sooner or later, everyone in the dorm would sleep with everyone else. Except Bill Gates. Nobody wanted to be with Gates. He was weird." Water, water everywhere but not a drop . . . Known for not washing himself or his clothes regularly, known as a twerpy math guy, the girlfriend-challenged Gates spent time collecting *Playboy* and *Penthouse,* and ventured out to Boston's red-light district, the notorious Combat Zone. Gates told biographers Stephen Manes and Paul Andrews, "I used to hang out at the Zone for a little while, just watching what was going on. Mostly I just sat at this pizza place and read books." Dr. Judith Kaplan, who lived on the same hall with Gates and Ballmer and is now a practicing psychiatrist in Seattle, says, "Ballmer was definitely manic. I never saw the depressive side, it could have been there or developed later."

If a vote had been taken for the nicest guy in Currier House at the time, it almost certainly would have gone not to Ballmer or Gates but to music prodigy Yo Yo Ma. Ma, who began studying at Julliard when he was eight years old, practiced in the dorm's auditorium or outside on the roof, where he'd heft his cello and serenade his fellow students. And how proud the loyal Democrats Fred and Bea Ballmer must have been when Steve told them about his new dorm mate, a princess in the closest America comes to a royal family, Caroline Kennedy. Says Jamie Coldre, "Caroline was very self-possessed, a woman who could almost never go anywhere without being stared at. Her mom was very lovely, gracious, and would show up without any fanfare and be just like most other moms."

While one report has a dorm mate introducing Gates and Ballmer, with Mr. Loud in room 403 and Gates just down the hall in room 417, the two math whizzes seemed destined to meet. Gates told PBS, "I had my friends and Steve had his friends and they were different circles. Steve was this middle-class guy who wanted to experience all of Harvard. I'd spent most of my time with the computers." Ballmer is Gates's only remaining friend from his Harvard days.

Ballmer said, "In the sophomore year we lived down the hall from each other and I kept hearing about this kind of crazy guy who was always out late at night and he came from Seattle, which was far away, at least from Boston, and most of us had not been out to the Great Pacific and he didn't sleep a lot and he had these sort of weird patterns, but people told me, you know, he's a real smart guy, he's a math-science guy. I was a math-science guy, and I met him probably two months later and we quickly got to be pretty good friends because we both liked sort of talking about sort of science and math stuff and it was fun."

Neither Ballmer's lust for knowledge nor his general mania allowed for much sleep. The introverted Gates, with underdeveloped social skills, found a sense of belonging at the dorm's regular poker games. Gates just couldn't get enough of the regular seven-card stud games. In a move to rid itself of its roguish past, Seattle had outlawed legal gambling. But now, a short walk away from his room, Gates, with a million-dollar trust fund, could indulge himself at will. His poker buddies would rub their hands together when he entered the room, saying, "Here comes the Gates gravy train." It was not unheard of for Gates to lose hundreds of dollars in a night (a month's worth of Ballmer's caddying), and win almost as much on other nights. He once gave his checkbook to Paul Allen, another time to Ballmer, telling them to keep it from him. Despite reports to the contrary, Ballmer never gambled. Never. (In fact, gambling is illegal in his father's native Switzerland.)

After a long night of poker, Gates usually stopped by Ballmer's room, where they'd do a brainiac version of rock around the clock. Picture the dweebish Gates sitting down and starting into his usual, autistic-like pattern of rocking back and forth when talking. Picture the highly animated Ballmer, rubbing his thighs, rocking back and forth as he had at Country Day. Though part of their neuroses matched, their personalities didn't. Says Gates's suitemate Andy Braiterman, "Bill and Steve were polar opposites. Bill was really not a social guy. He was not the sort of person who hung out with a lot of people." Says Jamie Coldre, "We called Steve 'Old Man Ballmer' because he was losing his hair. He was very nice, none of us had an inkling of what he would become." Gates, along with Paul Allen, had started a computer programming business while they were at Lakeside School in Seattle, and continued it while he was Harvard. Ballmer didn't have an entrepreneurial bone in his big body. Gates had a heightened sense of entitlement, Ballmer worked to feel entitled. The cold, calculating Gates. The passionate, glad-handing Ballmer. Gates got away with things—stealing time on both Lakeside and Harvard computers, throwing temper tantrums, gambling—that Ballmer wouldn't even consider doing. Ballmer was tactful, Gates was tact-challenged. Gates was deep-pocketed, Ballmer was deeply ingratiating. Gates's parents gave him a wide berth. Ballmer's parents propelled him down the straight and narrow. Gates had a high opinion of himself (which few of his classmates shared, nor did the head of Harvard's computer lab, who called him "the most obnoxious human being" he ever knew.) Then again, neither had a girlfriend. Neither had a brother. Both were very close to their mothers. Gates contemplated. Ballmer elated. And both their brains and their rocking were syncopated.

Ballmer told author John Heilemann that one of his first serious conversations with Gates involved the Wonder Bread antitrust case Gates's lawyer father had worked on. Formally called *Utah Pie Company v. Continental Baking*, the suit was prompted when Continental (Wonder Bread) cut prices in Salt Lake City on loaves that were sold side by side with bread from local bakeries, represented by Utah Pie. Being local, Utah Pie had less transportation costs than Wonder Bread, a natural competitive edge. So Wonder Bread simply sold at a loss, which they were able to sustain until they put local bakeries out of business. They then raised their prices. It was a strategy straight out of Rockefeller's 'You, too, can be a monopolist' handbook. The Supreme Court ruled that such price discrimination, intended to have "immediate destructive impact," was a no-no under Section 2(a) of the Sherman Antitrust Act.

One of Gates and Ballmer's first social outings was viewing a double feature of the musical *Singing in the Rain* followed by Stanley Kubrick's *A Clockwork Orange*. While singing in the rain would be de rigueur for a Seattle vocalist, the so-named song was key to Kubrick's plot; *A Clockwork Orange* involves an out-of-control gang of punks in England who brutally beat, rob, and rape while singing that tune. When the gang leader is finally imprisoned, he is chosen for a government study to see if aversion therapy can be used to reprogram his antisocial behavior. Yet by removing the thug's natural tendencies, the therapy leaves him unable to protect himself after his release, causing his demise. It's a move Kubrick posits as a metaphor for excess government intervention, similar to Microsoft's anti-antitrust frame of mind. According to authors Stephen Manes and Paul Andrews, Ballmer and Gates reveled in the film, Ballmer singing the title song so loud that he was almost punched by a dorm mate.

At Harvard, Ballmer had a wide group of friends, ranging from fellow Country Day student Stephen Pollack through his cronies in the Fox Club, a dining club which, in part because of his prep school background, he'd been accepted into. Using his ability to bridge diverse groups, Ballmer pulled Gates out of himself and brought him into the Fox Club fold. Gates was initiated in a ritual involving many drinks, a blindfolded tour around parts of the campus, a forced discourse on some arcane computer topic, and memorizing secret songs and a secret handshake. (All they lacked was a secret decoder ring.) Still, Gates was an outsider, and recalls it as a depressing time; he was having problems living in a world where he wasn't the alpha intellect.

Gates and Ballmer buddied up to study and compete. Unlike Country Day or Lakeside, going to class wasn't required. Having attended only the first session of a macroeconomics class, when the midterm arrived, Gates said, "We're just fucked in this course." He pulled all-nighters with Ballmer, whose prep school exclamation "Oh! Oh! Oh!" became "We're golden!" when he solved a problem; his despondency became "We're screwed!" They both aced the test. Then they attacked the prestigious Putnam math exam. Ballmer finished in the top one hundred. Gates was an also-ran.

When he gave the graduation speech at Country Day in 1990, Ballmer told the captive audience, "I found out that the person who was manager of the football team at Harvard every year was almost assured a chance to go to Harvard Business School, and I said, 'Business, that's the new thing for me. I'm going to get interested in business.'" (He also recalled that, upon graduation from high school seventeen years before, "I weighed about 160 pounds, I was very, very shy, and I hated computers," none of which is true.) Ballmer became equipment manager of the varsity football team, which was headed by a former Canadian Football League head coach, Joe Restic. Called "The Razor," Restic was famous for his philosophy "Ya gotta pay the price." Tackle Dan Jiggitts captained the Harvard team, and would go on to play pro football with the Chicago Bears before becoming a sportscaster in Chicago.

Jiggitts, a garrulous man who chooses his words carefully and quickly, says that when he got to the NFL, he saw how advanced Joe Restic's style of play was; because of that he had a leg up on the other rookies in training camp. Jiggitts recalls that Ballmer was "extraordinarily organized and quiet and nice. When he talked to me you could tell that he was afraid of saying something that I might not like. He was very buttoned-down, almost reverential. Ten years ago, one of my daughters wrote him and Steve responded with a sweet letter and some free software. When Steve came to Chicago and the head of our public schools was talking to him about how to give a group of underprivileged kids computer training, he opened the Microsoft training facility to the kids, telling me that 'we might need to hire them someday.' "

Knowing both Ballmer and Michael Jordan, Jiggitts thinks they're alike. He offers, "Steve loves the team aspect of business, the camaraderie, like Michael loves the team aspect of basketball; nothing else—not family or church—is like it. Once Steve, like Jordan, got it in his blood to compete and realized success, he also realized that he needed the success and the need to work for it. They're both competition addicts, they need the rush. Jordan left the NBA with a picture-perfect shot, with so many MVP trophies that you think he'd done it all. But he can't get enough. Both are family men who protect their families from the limelight. But once they switch on the competition gene, the competition switch, they can't turn it off. The switch is broken." Surprisingly, Ballmer would be toned down on the sidelines as Harvard played. Not surprisingly, he was a part of a group at the center of Harvard's social life, and in a supporting role.

Strangely, Harvard football had influenced Hitler as well. According to Hitler's former foreign minister, Ernst "Putzi" Hanfstaengl, Harvard '09, Hitler got the idea for having crowds at his rallies shout "Seig!" with the response "Heil!" from Putzi's stories of how the in-unison response "Harvard!" to the chant "Harvard!" got the football fans excited. The influence can be most notably seen in the films of Hitler's Nuremberg rallies.

In character, Ballmer would take coach Restic's "Ya gotta pay the price" credo so much to heart, and repeat it so loudly and often, that, as Judith Kaplan recalls, Ballmer's suitemate Paul Valenstein, composed a song about Old Man Ballmer, which ended with the line "you've got to pay the goddamned price."

While Ballmer didn't take any official role in Harvard's freshman or varsity basketball teams, he did join in pickup games. Classmate Kal, who played on the freshman squad, says, "Given his size, Steve couldn't jump, but he set great picks," which would block an opponent so his teammate would have a clear shot. Ballmer would later set great picks for Bill Gates, too.

Gates's best friend while he was at Harvard was his schoolmate from Lakeside, Paul Allen, who not only had a girlfriend but had moved to Boston to be around Gates and to work at a job at Honeywell. Unlike 99 percent of the rest of the world, Ballmer could understand a good amount of Gates's geek speak; Allen could follow even more of it. (Allen shares some of Ballmer's basketball fanaticism and would later purchase the Portland Trailblazers.)

After Allen saw a cover story in *Popular Electronics* about the Altair personal computer, he gleefully raced to Currier House to tell Gates, who shared his enthusiasm. Gates conned a shy classmate, Monte Davidow, to help him steal time on Harvard's Defense Department–provided computer and write a crude program for the Altair in BASIC, prompting Harvard to issue Gates a stern reprimand and change its computer use policy. Davidow wouldn't receive any ownership interest in what he helped create, and though he did some work with Microsoft later, Gates would forget Davidow's contribution to the building of his company.

One day in spring 1975, future cartoonist Kal and his roommate were walking across campus when they came across the odd couple Ballmer and Gates. Gates was full of many things, mainly himself, and said, "I've learned all I can from Harvard. I'm dropping out." Kallaugher, initially put off by Gates's brashness, found himself thinking that this was an impressive guy. For various reasons, one of which is to keep face, one does not drop out of Harvard, one goes "on leave." Though he dropped out of Harvard at the end of his sophomore year, twenty-seven years later Bill Gates is still listed as being on leave. (Twenty-five years later, Judge Thomas Penfield Jackson called Gates "sophomoric.") That summer the on-leave Gates moved to Albuquerque, New Mexico, and set up Microsoft with Paul Allen, a company that wrote programming languages for the Altair computer. Ballmer stayed at Harvard and matured.

Ballmer told tech columnist Dan Gillmor that he had taken a course at the Harvard Business School called Management and Leadership in the Arts. According to Beth Potier at the Harvard News Service, undergraduates are not normally allowed to cross-register for classes at the B-school, and the school itself has no record of Ballmer enrolling for the class. The B-school, physically distant from Harvard College, located across the Charles River, was politically and intellectually isolated from undergraduates as well. But, taking Ballmer at his word, if he took a class at the B-school in his first year, a classmate might have been the verbicidal son of financially and socially gifted parents, George W. Bush, who was in his final year at the B-school, a member of a class so instrumental in establishing the next business world order that Professor John Kotter would track their progress in his 1998 text *The New Rules*. The future president wasn't mentioned.

While his class work was average, Ballmer rightly named himself "Mr. Extracurricular" at Harvard; he increased his appeal to business school admissions officers and gained management experience by getting involved with both the campus newspaper, the *Crimson*, and the literary magazine, the *Harvard Advocate*. *New Yorker* Washington correspondent and author Nicholas Lemann was the *Crimson*'s editor in chief in 1975. Lemann told me, "Ballmer was selling ads. He was obviously the best ad salesman the paper had. This was much appreciated by me because the paper had to be profitable. It was very important that the *Crimson* maintain its financial independence from the school. Ever since 1969, when students went on strike, the *Crimson* had lost a lot of revenue and advertisements and was operating in the red. It had been in crisis. Our board was upset. We were in a modified receivership of sorts. The worst-case scenario was that the school would take us over.

"The *Crimson* has a very elaborate process for choosing editors. Editors pick their successors. All of the juniors go in and give a pitch for themselves. Steve went in and applied for the top job [business manager]. He didn't get it. And the reason he didn't get it was because they thought he was too abrasive. 'Too abrasive,' I thought. I didn't care, he was exactly what the *Crimson* needed. He exudes confidence."

It was in the paper's offices, visiting his good friend Lemann, that Michael Kinsley first met Ballmer. Kinsley had finished his Rhodes scholarship at Oxford and was studying law at Harvard, along with being a tutor in the Kirkland House. Kinsley says, "The stories that Steve was a loud, maniacal adrenaline junkie at Harvard are all true. But out of all the people I knew there another student, Scott McNealy, would be low on my list of those who would become successful businessmen. I was at the dining room when I saw this guy wearing a Cranbrook Hockey sweatshirt, not something you see every day, so I introduced myself."

McNealy never made the varsity hockey team at Harvard—it was among the top teams in the country—and, by his own admission, majored in beer, coming across as the typical frat boy, save for the fact that Harvard doesn't have fraternities. McNealy formally majored in economics, and would graduate with honors in 1976, having authored a thesis, involving antitrust, entitled *Competition and Performance in the United States Transit Bus Manufacturing Industry.*

Ballmer spent the summer of 1976 in Boston, in part because of the Bicentennial, when an estimated seven hundred thousand people took over the Boston Commons to celebrate. He lived off-campus with a roommate who remembers that Ballmer had bought some sheets for his bed which turned out to be too small. He used them anyway, exhibiting a trait that he would become known for—some would call Ballmer thrifty, others would say he was simply cheap.

Ballmer also became publisher of the nation's oldest college publication, the *Harvard Advocate*. It was the first enterprise Ballmer led, and it was profitable. The *Advocate*'s previous heads included future president (and Standard Oil trust-buster) Teddy Roosevelt, and had published some of the first work by T. S. Eliot and a short, Jewish guy from Brooklyn, Norman Mailer, who was serving on the paper's advisory board. Ballmer oversaw the *Advocate*'s "rejuvenation and reorganization" process. Says *Advocate* writer Peter Alter, "Ballmer had no literary airs whatsoever. He was there to handle the business side." While Harvard is often thought of as a bastion of liberalism, populated by the "pinko commie fags" of the sixties, and while its faculty is generally liberal, Harvard students make up all wings of political and philosophical thought. Ballmer would publish liberal authors such as Maura Moynihan, daughter of future U.S. Senator Daniel Patrick Moynihan, and poet Mary Jo Salter; he also worked closely with noted arch-conservative Grover Norquist, who would become a lobbyist for Microsoft and who's currently leading a crusade to have a Ronald Reagan memorial built in each county of the fifty states. Ballmer's literary endeavors were less out of a love for literature than pumping up his résumé. Not one line of his own prose ever appeared in the *Advocate*.

During the spring of his senior year, Ballmer met Gates in New York, where Gates was selling a BASIC program. They went to a Fox Club dinner, then talked (or bought) their way into the swinging hot spot du jour, Studio 54. It was there Ballmer ran into his second cousin, Gilda Radner, who was out on the town with her *Saturday Night Live* co-star John Belushi. (Belushi's body language resembled Ballmer's.) There are no reports of Ballmer mimicking Belushi's drug consumption.

It has been reported that Ballmer graduated in 1977 with magna cum laude honors, and Harvard's News Service wrote me that he was magna, though Harvard's registrar doesn't support this claim, and there is no record of his authoring an honors thesis, as such a designation would require. (The 1994 feature film *With Honors,* staring Brendan Fraser and Joe Pesci, details the Harvard honors process.) Microsoft's Press Pass Web page (microsoft.com) says Ballmer received a degree in mathematics and economics. Harvard's registrar lists him not as a double major but as getting a B.A., not a B.S., in applied math, his coursework dominated by humanities, not science, classes. None of the Harvard yearbooks published while Ballmer attended have his picture. What lay ahead?

Harvard Business School doesn't have a record of Ballmer applying, but he had applied, and was accepted, to Stanford Business School. Both schools encourage students to spend a few years in the "real world," getting practical experience, before attending. He took a two-year deferment of entering Stanford. An Occam's razor explanation is that Ballmer needed to work to earn some cash.

Where were the best and brightest wanna-be businessmen going after graduation? Ballmer didn't have to look far to see that Ford's president, Lee Iacocca, had mastered that private bureaucracy through the marketing side. True to his midwestern roots and his lust for sales, Ballmer decided to join consumer products giant Procter & Gamble in Cincinnati, Ohio, a three-hour drive from Farmington Hills and Fred and Bea, Ballmer's first journey into the way of the commercial world.

PART TWO

THE WAY OF THE WORLD

Make yourself necessary to someone.

—RALPH WALDO EMERSON

CHAPTER FOUR

PROCTER & GAMBLE AND STANFORD

I n the 150 years before Steve Ballmer went to work there, Procter & Gamble had gone from making soap and candles for Cincinnati residents to producing a wide variety of products worldwide. The company expanded to shampoo and laundry detergent and many other product lines, including disposable diapers (Pampers), cold remedies (Vicks), and food: it added to the Crisco line it developed by acquiring Folger's coffee, creating Pringles potato chips, and marketing cake mixes, most notably Duncan Hines. By the time Ballmer started there, P & G was recognized as the world's leading consumer-products marketing company in the world's largest consumer-oriented economy. According to one informed source, something like 80 percent of the cost of Crest toothpaste is its marketing, not ingredients. P & G took great pains to train its sales force, and gave them both ammunition and entrée with the largest advertising budget in the nation, if not the world.

Steve Ballmer says that he didn't have a grand plan when he joined Procter & Gamble's Food Products Group as a brand assistant. P & G had virtually created and pioneered brand management over the previous fifty years. Branding is the proprietary visual, emotional, rational, textual, and cultural image that one associates with a company or a product. Branding is the main reason that many Americans think of soap when they hear the word *ivory*, not piano keys or elephant tusks but soap, and not just any soap, Procter & Gamble's. Branding was eventually listed in corporate financial reports as an asset, under company goodwill (there isn't a listing per se for bad will, though it tends to show up under litigation. Think in terms of the ship *Exxon Valdez*). Today, branding is a separately listed asset. In its 2001 world survey, the consulting company Interbrand found that the brand Microsoft was second only to Coca-Cola in value, worth over sixty-one billion dollars to the soft drink's sixty-eight billion; P & G's collection, called a brand portfolio, is also second in the world, listed at $45.5 billion, albeit almost twenty-five billion dollars below Johnson & Johnson's.

Brand management is the concept that, by putting one product brand in the hands of a capable manager, they can focus all their managerial and marketing skills on just that. In fact, it wasn't unusual for P & G's brand managers to compete against one another in the marketplace. Ballmer was immediately put into the field as a sales trainee, working in Dallas and Denver with the field sales force on their Duncan Hines brownie and muffin mixes, the Moist & Easy line.

Ballmer managed his own sales section, and this was his first meeting with the consumer marketplace. He had to wear a suit. He helped make presentations to new clients, and he analyzed competitors' businesses, along with his own. He learned how to plan an idea that had been initiated by his brand manager, and he learned how it was implemented by the sales force. Ballmer found out what made a good display piece. He went to supermarkets, saw how and where the product was displayed, how it competed for shelf space. Then he got a simple idea, which he carried back to Cincinnati and, getting approval from his boss, Nes Cockburn, he put into action.

Ballmer realized that if the brownie mix box was turned on its side, and its label printed horizontally rather than the traditional vertical, it would take up more shelf space. If the supermarket simply kept the status quo and ordered the same amount of Moist & Easy, then some of the competing mixes would be pushed off the shelves. Smart.

Ballmer also took on the task of introducing Coldsnap Freezer Dessert Mix, which was a dismal failure. (Ballmer keeps a framed label from the mix on his office wall at Microsoft, a reminder how even the best-laid plans of marketing men can go awry.) One night in 1978, Ballmer joined other co-workers for a bachelor party. As *PC Week* reported, "In a downtown Cincinnati pub, after several rounds of beers, the patrons started up an all-hands trivia contest. 'Steve blew the place away,' recounts co-worker Gordon Tucker. 'He remembered what Beaver Cleaver said in episode 43, that kind of thing.' Later, they got kicked out of a pizza parlor for making too much noise. They then trekked across the bridge to wild and woolly Kentucky. Something noteworthy happened there, but Tucker swore to Ballmer he won't tell."

Ballmer not-so-eventually grew bored at P & G. Invited later to speak at Country Day, he told students that, when working at P & G, "I would sit back in my cubicle and play Nerf basketball with my cubicle mate, a guy named Jeff Immelt." Immelt is currently CEO of General Electric. (Of working with Ballmer, all Immelt says is "We were incorrigible.")

As he was with all of his major adult endeavors, Ballmer was surrounded by exceptionally bright and talented people. At P & G, Ballmer was among a group of hard-driving young executives who would charge out into the marketplace in other areas: Scott Cook was working just down the hall on the Crisco and Fluffo accounts. He would become a co-founder of the software company Intuit, best known for its Quicken financial software. (Cook would get tired of competing with Microsoft, and accept Bill Gates's billion-dollar-plus acquisition offer, only to have it nixed by the Department of Justice, who thought it would unlawfully give Microsoft dominance in the financial software market.) Cook now sits on P & G's board of directors. Drinking buddy Gordon Tucker, who worked on the Pringles account when he and Ballmer knew each other, would go on to set up E-Greetings. Just after Ballmer left, a guy named Steve Case joined P & G, working as an assistant brand manager on a wipe-on hair conditioner called Abound! and the Lilt home permanent kit. Case would go on to become CEO of America Online, and then chairman when the company became AOL/Time Warner. *Business Week* noted that, with brand values quickly becoming the company jewels, those trained in brand management naturally became more influential. So there was Ballmer, in the right place, at the right time.

When Ballmer joined P & G it was well known to be involved in an antitrust suit, as even a cursory survey of its annual report would have revealed. In 1957, acting on a complaint by Purex Corporation, the Federal Trade Commission ruled that P & G's purchase of the Clorox Corporation had restrained trade under the brother of the Sherman Antitrust Act, the Clayton Act. The case worked its way through various appeals with the FTC and federal courts before the Supreme Court upheld the decision requiring P & G to divest itself of Clorox. P & G immediately complied. The antitrust case continued when Purex then filed a new suit, claiming the treble damages allowed under the Clayton Act for the loss it suffered at Clorox's hands. That case spent twelve years in litigation before Purex finally accepted the fact that it was its own poor judgment, not anything Clorox did, that caused its market share and profits to drop. All of this showed the complexity and near-glacial pace antitrust litigation takes. More good experience for what lay ahead for Ballmer.

Ballmer told *Rolling Stone* in 2000 that he never saw people at P & G get passionate about selling Tide laundry detergent or any of its product line. He credits such lack of emotional involvement as being one of the reasons he left. Whatever the reason, in early 1979 he loaded up his Mustang and headed west, to Hollywood. Of course, he had deferred his acceptance to Stanford Business School, and was scheduled to start there that fall, so his Hollywood fling seems to have been just that. His fellow Country Day alum Robin Williams had just achieved fame with the sitcom *Mork and Mindy*, and Mindy was played by the Farmington Hills–raised Pam Dawber. Maybe Ballmer was caught up in the hype and wanted the attention they were receiving. He met with another Harvard grad, then–CBS executive Jeff Sagansky, now head of PAX television, who recalls that he recommended Ballmer become a studio script reader. So Ballmer read scripts for NBC and parked cars at celebrity functions. It is within the realms of both possibility and his personality that he auditioned for roles, yet Sagansky doesn't remember him doing so.

That July, Ballmer found time to drive up to Seattle and hang out with his buddy Bill Gates. Seven months before, Gates and Paul Allen had moved their fledgling software company there, in part to avoid the animus Gates had created with his main contract, Micro Instrumental and Telemetry Systems, or MITS. Ed Roberts, who headed MITS, says Gates "was impossible to deal with. He literally was a spoiled kid, that's what the problem was." Roberts sold MITS to Pertec Corporation, which would end up in court-ordered arbitration with Gates and Allen over their Microsoft contract. The mediator was the first in a long line of arbiters who were forced to rule on the Microsoft frame of mind. Microsoft won. Ballmer drove back to California and entered the Stanford

Business School class of 1981 with high hopes and high confidence. According to Ballmer's aunt Olga Dworkin, at the time he had nary a thought of moving to Seattle or working for Microsoft.

Stanford Business School was established in 1925 at the suggestion of Stanford alum and future president Herbert Hoover. Just before Ballmer enrolled, the dean, former Ford president Arjay Miller, resigned and Rene McPherson was to take over the next year. McPherson, retired chairman of Dana Corporation, one of the ten companies profiled in Tom Peters's bestselling text *In Search of Excellence,* was in tune with the winds of change, and saw that Stanford was rivaling Harvard because of, among other things, its encouragement and support for creating new businesses. Besides, McPherson's mantra at Dana had been "Question authority." This fit well on a campus where, in 1975, the students had voted to change the school's nickname from Indians to Robber Barons, the late-nineteenth-century group of ruthless thieves to which school founder Leland Stanford had belonged. (The administration immediately nixed the change, and the color cardinal, not the bird, was chosen.)

Formally called the Stanford Graduate School of Business (GSB), its advisory board members included Thomas Murphy, chairman of General Motors; Frank Cary, chairman of IBM; John Young, president of Hewlett Packard; and Warren Buffett, the head of the private investment firm Berkshire Hathaway. GSB was challenging Harvard as the number one place for postgraduate business study. In a few years GSB students would start to say to their counterparts at Harvard, "You went to the B-school, too bad you couldn't have gone to the A-school."

Ballmer joined a class of 260, whose members recall him in the same terms as his Harvard classmates: "loud," "maniacal," "driven." But unlike his Harvard classmates, not one of the people in Ballmer's class of 1981 contacted would talk on the record. His classmates included Frank Quattrone, future head of Credit

Suisse First Boston Technology Group; venture capitalist Vinod Khosla; and the future head of Great Plains software, Doug Burgum, which was bought by Microsoft in 2001—the company retaining Burgum as a senior Microsoft VP. Ballmer's required classes included Management Use of Computer Models and Systems. This class mandated that students would get hands-on experience using both time-share computers (DEC 2040 and HP 2000) and "small computer models." Ballmer was required to learn the BASIC programming language and develop a case project focused on a managerial problem.

As for his electives, classmates don't recall Ballmer taking either Business and the Law or Management and Ethics. The class Regulatory Aspects of Law wasn't offered that year, but if it had been, it might have been taught by Stanford law school's noted Ronald Reagan devotee William Baxter. Following Reagan's election in 1980, Baxter would be confirmed as head of the Department of Justice's antitrust division. At Stanford at the time it was said that "it's better to know the judge than know the law."

During his first year Ballmer entered two ten-thousand-dollar competitions and won both: one from the Boston Consulting Group, the other from Bain & Company. He also picked up a new characteristic: fellow students recall hearing him brag about the summer internships he'd been offered, and a few were turned off by this trait. And for the second time in as many schools, a year ahead of Ballmer was Scott McNealy. (Unlike Ballmer, McNealy had twice been rejected by the school, even though, according to McNealy, he had recommendations from people like Donald Peterson, the president of Ford.)

Ballmer recalled to the *Detroit Jewish News* that, as his first year at Stanford came to an end, "I had interviewed at Ford and I was talking to all of these investment banks. My dad was really excited about me being in business school. He said, 'You'll come home, you'll work in the auto industry—it'll be great.' " It wouldn't have been great because, by 1980, the American auto industry was severely depressed. As David Halberstam noted, in his 1985 study *The Reckoning,* a combination of some poor management decisions, high labor costs, and both German and Japanese auto companies responding better to customers' needs saw hundreds of thousands of auto workers laid off. This implosion of the shared American auto-making monopoly found many workers and executives blaming "the government" and the cost of mandated safety and emissions regulations for their fate, denying that foreign auto makers faced the same laws and simply built a better mousetrap—so much better that in 1980 the bestselling car in Detroit was the Volkswagen Rabbit.

Detroit wasn't the place to be, and Bill Gates was desperate to get someone to handle the business side of his partnership with Paul Allen. Ballmer was looking for a summer job before his final year at Stanford. Gates called him, but Ballmer said he was available only for the break. Gates needed a full-timer and convinced Ballmer to visit Seattle, where his well-placed parents became involved. Though William and Mary Gates had met Ballmer before, this time they had him over for dinner and gave him a tour of the big town. At his mother's funeral in 1994, Gates spoke of how his mom had influenced Ballmer to come aboard Microsoft. According to Ballmer's aunt Olga, William Gates was so impressed with Ballmer that, after dinner was over, he took son Bill aside and said, "You *have* to get Steve. He's just what you need." As Ballmer said in his 1990 Country Day commencement speech, "So I finally thought, There's one thing about this Bill Gates, he's absolutely the smartest guy I ever knew, and he had more enthusiasm, more focus; he had relentless focus. He had more of an ability to really concentrate and know what he was doing, to think about it completely, and just love it. Well, I thought, at least I'll be working for a guy I really think is great. He is a friend of mine and that will be a lot of fun."

Ballmer's aunt Olga says, "It was very interesting because Steve couldn't make the decision to leave [Stanford]. His father would say, 'Now, you stay in school' because, naturally, education is the thing. And he talked to his mother and she said, 'Well, maybe you ought to try it.' Bea even called [my husband] Irv, who said, 'I think he should try it. He could always go back to school. With his intelligence, he doesn't have to worry. He could always walk into any university and they'd take him.'" Still, it was a gutsy decision, one that Ballmer feared his father wouldn't accept. Bea and Irv convinced Fred otherwise. After some negotiation, conducted in part over ship-to-shore radio while Gates was vacationing, Ballmer was hired as assistant to the president. And so, the son of a college dropout dropped out to join the Gates & Allen chapter of Dropouts "R" Us.

CHAPTER FIVE

BILL AND STEVE'S EXCELLENT ADVENTURE

Americans had explosions on their minds on Tuesday, June 10, 1980. The *New York Times* reported the then-radical, now-accepted theory that an asteroid hit Earth about sixty-five million years ago, leading to the extinction of dinosaurs. In New Jersey, the president of United Airlines was injured when a package bomb blew up as he opened it, a victim of an anti-technology zealot who would be come known as the Unabomber. In Los Angeles, comedian Richard Pryor was given a fifty-fifty chance of surviving burns over half of his body, the result of distilling cocaine (freebasing). In Washington State, as President Jimmy Carter spoke to the mayor's conference in Seattle, there was still ash in the air from Mount Saint Helens, 130 miles to the south, which had erupted three weeks before (and would do so again the next day). Bob Dylan was singing "Gotta Serve Somebody." And Steve Ballmer went to work for Bill Gates at Microsoft. He, too, would explode, many times. But, within the next three months,

Ballmer, Gates, and Paul Allen would negotiate what are arguably the two best business deals of the twentieth century, from which a volcanic hundreds of billions of dollars—and much acrimony—would flow.

Ballmer became Microsoft employee 28, though he would later tell The *Washington Post* that he started as employee 24. (In Microsoft's official history, *Microsoft: Inside and Out,* Ballmer says he was employee 15. He later told Country Day students that he considers himself a founder of the company.) For the first time in his life, Ballmer got a job based on whom he knew, not what. When Ballmer was hired, Microsoft had $12.5 million in annual sales, which were kept track of by hand on a paper ledger.

Ballmer was not, as *Vanity Fair* reported, the first nonprogrammer hired. The other twenty-seven employees included a few secretaries and support staff, whom Bill Gates so underpaid that they were forced to file a complaint with the State Board of Labor and Industries. The employees won. As he normally did when he didn't get his way, Gates went wild. Bookkeeper Marla Wood recalls, "Bill came into my office saying he had a phone call from [Labor and Industries, and he was] just livid. This was the first time I was really on the receiving end of one of his rages—I mean, screaming about this and how it was going to ruin his reputation." Marla Wood and her husband, general manager Steve Wood, would soon leave the company.

Microsoft was essentially a company of programmers—"code monkeys," they'd come to be called. Ballmer's hiring did not sit well with the code monkeys. When a programmer saw a copy of Gates's agreement confirming his offer to Ballmer—that Ballmer was to be paid fifty thousand dollars a year (more than they) and get somewhere between a 5 and 10 percent ownership interest while they received none—he tacked the letter to the office bulletin board. Sure, Ballmer was a Harvard guy, but they weren't exactly dull tools themselves; they wondered what Ballmer really knew about business. He'd spent a year and a half marketing cake mix and ten months in business school. Besides, it's reported that they thought he wasn't technical—a tech weenie—and Microsoft was a tech company.

Ballmer is more technical than he allows outsiders to think. As we've seen, not only did he head the computer club at Country Day but he used computers at Harvard studying applied math and learned BASIC programming at Stanford. One of the boundaries between Gates and Ballmer, however, is that Gates is the technical guy. Ballmer doesn't encroach on that territory, though he's very familiar with it.

(Writing code—programming—is akin to writing, say, a book. A line of code is the same length as one line of this book. The main difference is that computer code uses the numerals one and zero to communicate. It's binary. Just as a line of prose can be verbose, code can be clunky, inexact, indirect. A code monkey can sit back after reading someone else's program and, like a Hemingway or Raymond Carver work, be amazed at the elegance of its simplicity or, like a Dickens novel, wonder why the writer took so long to tell the story [Dickens was paid by the word]. If code tries to be all things to all people, it tends to be like a poor political speech. Windows ME contains over twenty-nine million lines of code, which, if printed out, would fill over 970 volumes of five-hundred-page books.)

Upon accepting Gates's offer, Ballmer drove up from Palo Alto in his Mustang and stayed with his friend. His office consisted of a space on the couch in Gates's office. His title was assistant to the president. His role was to take care of operations—recruiting, accounting, legal, and related functions. Yet within a few weeks Ballmer had moved out of Gates's house and was on the verge of quitting. Gates and Ballmer had a fight. Ballmer quickly realized that the company needed at least fifty more people to handle the contracts already on hand. Ballmer's assertiveness caused Gates to throw one of his tantrums. As he would become known for doing, Ballmer stood up to him, not becoming subsumed as Gates fumed. Gates, not used to this, shouted, "You're trying to bankrupt me! You're trying to bankrupt me!" Ballmer left. Gates's father became involved, and eventually Gates relented. When Ballmer came back, he set out to make himself indispensable.

First, Ballmer was determined to control the skyrocketing payroll cost. He devised a new compensation plan for programmers, which became about as popular as herpes. Before Ballmer, the code monkeys were being paid overtime, which, given the huge amount of hours they were required to work, was becoming astronomical. The new plan called for straight salary without overtime but a 15 percent year-end bonus. Tech weenies tend to have a working knowledge of arithmetic and they figured out that the annual bonus would amount to just over five hours' pay per week, when many of them were putting in twelve-hour days. Code monkeys complained. The plan stayed.

Long hours. Crummy climate. Mediocre pay. Why would a programmer want to work at Microsoft? "It was fun," says an early programmer. "We were on the leading edge, technology-wise. And we'd dress however we wanted [to], barefoot if that's what you liked. Bill Gates was like a god to us. He was one of us. He talked tech. We knew it was important to work for him."

In his seminal 1984 study of programmers and their culture, *Hackers,* Steven Levy writes about "the peak hour" when a code monkey "attained a state of pure concentration. When you programmed a computer, you had to be aware of where all the thousand bits of information were going from one instruction to the next. . . . When you had all that information glued to your cerebral being, it was almost as if your mind had merged into the environment of the computer. Sometimes it took hours to build up to the point where your thoughts could contain that total picture, and when you got to that point, it was such a shame to waste it that you tried to sustain it by marathon bursts, alternatively working on the computer or poring over the code you wrote." Microsoft was a place where you lived for peak hours. Yet now that Ballmer was taking care of business, code monkeys started having less influence in the company they'd created.

Ballmer quickly became head recruiter, a job he was good at, a duty he's never really given up. He looked for people with "enormous intelligence, energy, and drive," saying his recruiting philosophy was "Whenever you meet a kick-ass guy, get him. Do we have a head-count budget? No way. There are some guys you meet only once in a lifetime. So why screw around?" Ballmer told tech author and PBS host Robert X. Cringely, "Recruiting is a constant challenge. I interviewed absolutely everybody for my first three years. You couldn't get hired [without going through me] because I was the personnel department. We thought it was important to sort of set a culture about making sure we get super-bright, super-motivated people."

Among the new tech weenies he thought kicked ass was the "Mad Hungarian," Charles Simonyi. (For complex reasons, many who left Hungary, including nuclear bomb developer Edward Teller and Intel's Andy Grove, are called the "Mad Hungarian." See John McPhee's *The Curve of Binding Energy* for details.) Unwittingly, Ballmer tapped into a golden source for quality code monkeys that future headhunters would come to know: former communists. As one Microsoftian relates, "Since the computers that these commies used didn't have much memory, their code had to be tightly written, nearly perfect, to get the machine to work. It's like the Indians and the buffalo—they used every buffalo part they could, from hide through the hoofs and dung, while the white man tended to use only the hide. They had to, they didn't know when they were going to come upon another herd. The commies also worked well in teams."

Simonyi was born in Budapest, Hungary, in 1948, the son of a professor of electrical engineering, which gave him access to the school's moving-truck-size Russian Ural II computer, which had about the same amount of memory as the Altair machine Gates, Davidow, and Allen had programmed at Harvard, then for MITS in Albuquerque. In 1955, the year Bill Gates was born, the sixteen-year-old Simonyi defected to Denmark, before emigrating to the States and enrolling at the Left Coast bastion of computer geekdom, the University of Michigan of the West, also known as the University of California at Berkeley.

Simonyi recommended that Ballmer hire a programmer friend, Richard Brodie. Brodie recalls, "Steve Ballmer knew as much about computer programming as I know about yacht racing. Still, he knew people pretty well. He had a trick—he would always ask programmers about hash tables. Hash tables are a computer science trick for looking things up in a table. They are a highly efficient mathematical tool that stores and processes index numbers in the computer. I told Steve about hash tables. He didn't know much about them, but he knew when an answer was good or not." A post-1986 IPO hire remembers, "Ballmer's interviews were this psychoanalytical bullshit." Ballmer would ask questions like "Why are manhole covers round?" or "How many gas stations are there in the United States?" just to see how one would arrive at an answer. The new hire continues, "And you were paid less by Microsoft, but they supplemented your income with these pieces of candy called stock options."

Six weeks after Ballmer signed on, a call from IBM in Boca Raton, Florida, to Bill Gates in Seattle would change computerdom as we know it. The largest computer company in the world, IBM, was so dominant that not only had the Department of Justice's antitrust division filed suit against it in 1969, but the lawyers fighting in the action had set up their own law firm. Suing IBM had become an industry in itself. Undaunted, by 1980, "I've Been Moved," as IBM came to be called, had seen the minicomputer blip on its radar screen, led by Radio Shack and Apple, and was ready to respond. As was the case with Data General, which was well chronicled in Tracy Kidder's Pulitzer Prize–winning book *The Soul of a New Machine,* IBM took a small group of renegade employees and empowered them to produce a minicomputer in what they termed Project Chess (PC). At the time, it didn't take much for employees in the straitlaced, regimented, lockstep IBM to be thought of as rebellious: a standard joke had an IBM employee showing up for work one day wearing a blue, not the mandated white, button-down oxford shirt; his boss quipped, "Are you on vacation?"

Led by twenty-year IBM veteran Jack Sams, this group was given one year to produce the small machine. To meet that deadline, they decided to use as many off-the-shelf components as possible, those that were already in production. In August 1980, they contacted Bill Gates about creating an operating system for their hush-hush microcomputer. Gates referred them to Digital Research, run by Gary Kildall, whose CP/M operating system was far and away the leader for small computers. In his 1999 study of contemporary computer culture, *The Silicon Boys and Their Valley of Dreams,* David A. Kaplan relays what happened next. Kildall's partner, Tom Rolander, told Kaplan, "Gary and I had already scheduled a morning appointment at Oakland Airport with a CP/M distributor." So they flew up in Kildall's plane and the reps from IBM met with Kildall's wife, Dorothy. IBM presented Kildall with its standard nondisclosure agreement, which was so overreaching and one-sided that Dorothy called the company attorney. Gary Kildall arrived in the afternoon and balked at IBM's instance that they license his operating system for a flat fee of several hundred thousand dollars rather than a ten-dollar-per-copy royalty. Kildall was already earning millions of dollars from royalties and wouldn't budge. IBM left, then met with Bill Gates. Why Gates? Mary Gates had served on the national board of United Way with an IBM bigwig who, when he heard of Microsoft, reportedly said, "That's run by Mary Gates's son, isn't it?" IBM asked Gates to come to Boca Raton, Florida, to discuss a consulting contract. Many Microsoftians would later say that DRI didn't get the contract because "Gary went flying."

Gates, Ballmer, and programmer/mathematician Bob O'Rear flew on a red-eye from Seattle to Miami to meet with IBM. Microsoft had no problem signing the nondisclosure agreement. As Ballmer would tell Paul Andrews, "I was a good suit-type guy. . . . We're big boys, and we can decide what we're going to tell [IBM] and we can decide what we are going to tell them. And there was nothing in particular we didn't want to tell them." Over two days they hammered out an agreement whereby Microsoft would supply four high-level languages—BASIC, FORTRAN, COBOL, and Pascal—for IBM's personal computer, along with a disk operating system. It is through the operating system that the application programs tell the computer's bells when to ring, its whistles when to blow. Think of an operating system as a wall socket into which you plug a program. Microsoft convinced IBM that Microsoft should retain copyright on the operating system and would license it to IBM. At least that's the tale they tell. IBM's Jack Sams remembers it differently: "We had a terrible problem being sued by people claiming we had stolen their stuff. It could be horribly expensive for us to have our programmers look at code that belonged to someone else because they would come back and say we stole it and made all this money. We lost a series of suits on this. We went to Microsoft on the premise that we would license his product."

Given the breakneck deadline that IBM was under, and that it seemed to them Microsoft could do the job, on November 6,

1980, IBM signed them up, with Ballmer wearing a suit while Gates sported "a sweatshirt, with the emphasis on sweat." Gates then said to Ballmer, "Well, Steve, now we can get to work." One problem for Gates and Ballmer: Microsoft didn't have a PC operating system. Paul Allen had begun to take care of that a few weeks before.

Allen was well liked among programmers and knew that a small local company, Seattle Computer Products, had developed an operating system that worked with the same computer chip IBM was using. A programming whiz at Seattle Computer Products, Tim Patterson, had developed what he called QDOS—Quick and Dirty Operating System. Allen contacted Rod Brock, Patterson's boss, and put him in touch with Ballmer and Gates. Ballmer put the deal on paper. For seventy-five thousand dollars, the dynamic duo quickly licensed the product, not revealing, of course, that it was for IBM's PC. They also allowed Seattle Computer Products to sell QDOS to other original equipment manufacturers (OEMs), a move that would come back to haunt them. Now they had to adapt QDOS, which they renamed MS-DOS. They had three months. As often happens, especially with Microsoft, they would find their deadline impossible to meet.

IBM brought nine boxes of their computer-in-progress to Seattle, along with a mandate that, at all cost, the system needed to be kept secret. Ballmer took the boxes to a ten-foot-by-six-foot supply room, which would become the first Microsoft version of hell. There, the programmers would work in this windowless, unventilated room, where temperatures often exceeded one hundred degrees Fahrenheit. IBM was so paranoid that they supplied the Microkids with safes for all documentation, and demanded that the door be kept shut at all times. On one visit, IBM found—egad—the supply room door cracked to get some air. Another day, Ballmer got a call from one of the IBM people. As he schmoozed the IBMer, he asked about the weather in Boca. The executive said he didn't know, he was in Seattle and would be over soon. Ballmer ran down the hallway, shouting, "Close the door! Lock the safe! They're here!"

Up to this time, Microsoft was still a partnership between Gates and Allen. Reflective of his view of himself and the rest of the world, Gates owned 64 percent, Allen, 36 percent. Ballmer started pushing for a corporate structure, but that wouldn't happen until the following July.

Gary Kildall, who died as a result of a freak accident in 1994, left behind an unpublished memoir—unpublished, says his son, for fear of a lawsuit by Gates. In the text, he calls Gates "manipulative," a man who "has taken much from me and the industry," and "divisive." No wonder. He told Robert Cringely, "Ask Bill why function code 6 [in MS-DOS] ends in a dollar sign. No one in the world knows that but me." After IBM got wind that Kildall thought Gates's operating system was "suspiciously similar" to his, IBM came calling again, agreeing to license Kildall's CP/M for royalties and offer it as an alternative to QDOS, which Microsoft had renamed MS-DOS. The problem was that, though IBM allowed the customer to choose between CP/M and MS-DOS, CP/M would cost them six times what MS-DOS would, effectively killing the system.

Kildall suspected Gates had a hand in the pricing structure. Both Gates and Ballmer had studied what's called game theory in their math classes at Harvard. At the core of game theory lies the simple fact that it is easier to win if there are fewer players; it's like winning a yacht race by sinking the other boats. Game theory is the nub of Microsoft's business strategy, the fountainhead of its wealth.

After working for NASA on spy satellites, Bob O'Rear had joined Microsoft in Albuquerque and moved with the company to Belleview. He became the head program adapter on Project Chess. After receiving the Project Chess parts, O'Rear's daily regimen became what would be normal Microsoft working hours for many programmers: wake up, go work for eighteen hours, come home, sleep. Thanksgiving and Christmas and New Year's became abstracts. He concentrated instead on how the IBM hardware interacted with the QDOS software. He told Cheryl Tsang, author of *Microsoft First Generation,* "I was trying to make software work on the prototype PC and it wouldn't work as advertised. I'd try to write on the disk but the printer wouldn't respond or funny things like that. I was just desperate to get things to work and it just drove me nuts! I'd be banging my head against the wall [in the hot, windowless room] for days on what should have been simple easy problems." Alas, Microsoft missed its January 12 deadline, and wouldn't get the system up and running for another month.

While many Microsoftians had a hand in MS-DOS, the suit-wearing Ballmer would handle the business side as the system came together. It was Gates, Allen, and O'Rear who carried the reprogramming load, shuffling between Seattle and Boca Raton as needed. June 1981 found MS-DOS almost finished and the company getting good press, even though its biggest project was still under wraps. That month, *Fortune* magazine did an article on leading computer industry people, including Gates and Allen, which prompted Ballmer to send a memo to all employees saying, "As slow as progress may seem, some times [sic] we are having an impact."

MS-DOS trudged along. Rod Brock, the head of Seattle Computer Products, had received a $250,000 offer to purchase a QDOS update called 86-DOS. Brock informed Gates of the offer. Brock says, "Microsoft must have been getting antsy, because they sent Steve Ballmer over. He tried to get us to hurry up and agree to the thing and sign [an agreement giving Microsoft exclusive license to 86-DOS]. I met with him personally. He basically told me how it was a good deal, how it would not change anything whether or not they owned it or we owned it, since we would have unlimited right to use it. I guess he convinced me, because Paul called a few days later and said come on over to Belleview and sign the papers." Brock did.

After the IBM deal was signed, Ballmer became closer and closer to one of Gates's business acquaintances, the engineer/venture capitalist David Marquart. Both Gates and Ballmer became impressed with his business smarts, Ballmer working closely with him to reorganize or, more accurately, organize the partnership into a corporation. With Marquart's help, Microsoft filed corporate papers the first of July listing, of course, William H. Gates III as chairman of the board and Paul Allen as a director. Stock was shuffled out in percentages: Gates 53, Allen 31, Ballmer 8, Simonyi 1.5, other programmers splitting the remaining 6.5 percent. Still, by now Microsoft had over a hundred employees, most of them shut out of stock ownership, including O'Rear. The Microsoft natives quickly became restless. Ballmer thought he'd figure out a way that, if the employees worked hard, they might be able to earn a down payment on a house. Of course, raising salaries was not an uncommon way to get more money to employees, and loaning employees money was another (one Ballmer himself would use, to the tune of over five hundred thousand dollars, to pay an unexpected tax bill on his shares). Instead, Ballmer devised and implemented the "pieces of candy," a stock option plan, allowing Microsoftians to purchase at least two thousand five hundred shares, at ninety-five cents each, which, after a year-long wait, would be handed out every six months for the next four years. This was brilliant.

Unlike the bonus plan, which was still in effect, stock options cost Microsoft virtually nothing out of pocket and gave employees a feeling that they had an ownership interest in what they produced, albeit small. (James Fallows would later observe that this put everyone on the same team: the Microsoft Stock Option Team. Many employees refer to their company as MSFT, their NASDAQ symbol.) It was another carrot to offer new recruits. What's more, it tied employees to the company for five years, until they became fully vested, a situation termed golden handcuffs. Further adding to the magnificence of the program is that the stock options are taxed at, at least, a one-third lower rate than earned income.

As usual, Microsoft didn't invent the program; its much larger rival, Apple Computer, had offered stock to its workers before its successful initial public offering the previous December, though Apple co-founder Steve Jobs was so anal in sharing Apple's financial pie with his workers that his partner, Steve Wozniak, sliced his piece, dividing it among those who deserved it.

On August 12, 1981, IBM released its personal computer to the world. It was named Personal Computer. At the time, the PC market was dominated by Commodore, Apple, and Radio Shack, which together held 75 percent of the market. IBM ran a mass of successful television ads featuring a Charlie Chaplin look-alike doing Chaplin's famous Little Tramp routine—the message being that even a good-natured fumbling idiot could use the machine. Within two years, IBM sold over five hundred thousand PCs. More importantly, especially for Microsoft, IBM would set the hardware standard, ergo MS-DOS became the de facto standard operating system.

On November 13, 1981, Gates and Ballmer staged the second installment of what would become their annual company-wide meeting. Over a hundred employees crammed into a conference room at the Ramada Inn of Belleview to hear, generally, Gates and Ballmer talk about how well the company had done the year before and what the future held. Ballmer reached back to his experiences at Country Day and Harvard and showed why they call him the company cheerleader. This year Microsoft would report sales of fifteen million dollars. But this year it was the Mad Hungarian, not Mad Dog Ballmer, who would take center stage.

Charles Simonyi was in charge of developing Microsoft's application programs. He had spent four years at Xerox's Palo Alto Research Center, commonly referred to as PARC. Xerox had recruited some of computerdom's best and brightest, including an MIT Ph.D. and Stanford professor named Bob Metcalfe, to basically sit around and think about what interested them the most: how to improve computers. PARC had an uncanny ability to create things—the computer mouse, the graphical user interface, some say the first personal computer—and an equally uncanny inability to bring these inventions to market. It was Metcalfe who suggested Simonyi see "this crazy guy in Seattle" about a plan he had. Since Gates was busy, Simonyi met with Ballmer, detailing a project for a word processor and other applications he had in mind. Ballmer shouted, "Bill has to see this!" which Bill did, and immediately bonded with Simonyi. Gates would later visit PARC, his eyes wide open, absorbing all he saw, with the Mad Hungarian as his tour guide.

At the 1981 company meeting Simonyi proposed that Microsoft "adopt" applications for spreadsheets, word processing, something new called electronic mail, and computer-assisted design (CAD). Simonyi brought along a chart showing what would happen if Microsoft applications ran on every possible platform. His graphic looked like a ski slope, viewed from the lodge at the bottom. He told the crowd that if Microsoft successfully developed these applications, it would experience a "revenue bomb," some of the most prophetic words ever spoken. Simonyi hugged capitalism like an Ayn Rand character, bonded with Gates like a brother, and worked well with Rah Rah Ballmer.

At the time the best-selling application was VisiCalc—visual calculator—which provided an electronic spreadsheet. Small businesses loved the simplicity of entering data once and having it simultaneously update numerous accounts. What's more, you could immediately project the effect of a change in cost or price.

VisiCalc, owned by the top provider of personal computer software, VisiCorp, was wildly popular, yet it ran only on the Apple II. A nascent programming company, Lotus Corporation, was on the verge of releasing its spreadsheet, called Lotus 1-2-3, which ran exclusively on the IBM PC and its clones. Gates and Ballmer realized that Simonyi was on target and a revenue bomb would explode if one had the right applications. So Microsoft played catch-up by developing its VisiCalc/Lotus 1-2-3 knock-off, called Excel.

At the same time, the company was improving MS-DOS. How to get people to use Excel rather than Lotus 1-2-3? One way was to make a superior product—not Microsoft's forte. Another way was to make it appear that Microsoft had a better mousetrap. According to published reports, Microsoft programmers were parroting Gates when they said, "DOS isn't done until Lotus won't run." By monkeying around with the operating system code, the code monkeys could make an application run slower, if at all. By executing game theory in updating MS-DOS, Microsoft gave a virtual reality to Robert Frost's observation, "Work is play with mortal stakes."

At the same time James Fallows wrote in *The Atlantic Monthly* that "the war of standardization for personal computers is just about over. The crucial, bitterly contested territory [of operating systems was won by] a DOS called CP/M, which has become the industry standard and is earning millions for a formerly small company known as Digital Research. Almost any kind of computer you buy these days will have CP/M . . . an important exception [being] IBM."

Given its high price—about four thousand dollars when fully loaded—IBM left itself wide open for other personal computer makers to enter the field, which they did in what came to be called IBM clones. One of the clones was made by Compaq. Compaq had developed a chip similar, but not identical, to IBM's, making it compatible with IBM's personal computer. Due to various efficiencies, however, mainly less overhead, Compaq sold at a markedly lower price. Gates wove a deal with Compaq that it would receive a version of MS-DOS, which Compaq would then have Microsoft adapt to its machines. Then, when Ballmer got wind that Hewlett-Packard was considering going with Gary Kildall's CP/M-86 as the operating system on its latest computer, he convinced HP that, since IBM was dominant and ran on MS-DOS, it would be far less risky to go with Microsoft.

Gates and Ballmer continued selling MS-DOS using a pricing system that was ingenious. They basically gave the systems away to original equipment manufacturers (OEMs)—a flat-rate licensing fee of fifty thousand dollars no matter how many computers the manufacturers sent out the door. If one sold one hundred thousand units, the price would be fifty dollars per. If one sold two hundred thousand units, the price would be twenty-five dollars per. Given a retail price of between one thousand five hundred and two thousand dollars, the operating software could be less than 5 percent of the total cost of a personal computer. By 2002 one could buy a Dell computer with 20 gigabytes—20 billion bytes—of memory for less than eight hundred dollars. Given that IBM's 1981 Personal Computer had between zero and forty-eight thousand bytes of memory, a single, low-end 2002 Dell computer contains more than the memory of all of the two hundred thousand IBM PCs sold in their first year combined.

CHAPTER SIX

GET OUT OF JAIL FREE

I n 2000, Steve Ballmer told *USA Today* that he isn't a student of history, although John Campbell recalls him as being an excellent history student at Detroit Country Day. Ballmer's view is reminiscent of Henry Ford's famous credo that "history is bunk," an early voicing of the contemporary "What have you done for me lately?"—the mantra of sales managers worldwide. If Ballmer had studied the history of the Wild West, he would have discovered that January 8, 1882, was a sad day in San Francisco. This was the date that Emperor Norton had died. Several years before, Joshua Norton had been one of the more successful businessmen in town, but he had gone broke trying to corner the Bay Area rice market and simply disappeared. A few months later, Norton showed up at a local newspaper office, dressed in full military regalia, with a story for the paper's editors: He, Joshua Norton, had declared himself Emperor of the United States and Protectorate of Mexico. The story was published, and Norton became the city's reigning eccentric: he issued his own money in script, which was accepted by local merchants, restaurants, and taverns. The upper crust pandered to his whims. Newspapers quoted him on events of the day. When his uniform became ragged, the city council voted to buy him a new one. When one of his dogs, Bummer, died it was front-page news. Emperor Norton's funeral attracted over ten thousand mourners. Exactly one hundred years later to the day, in Washington, D.C., came another passing, one which would eventually create many times more San Franciscan mourners than Emperor Norton's death, in part because of Steve Ballmer's actions. It would take the better part of a decade to fully realize the implications of that January day.

On January 8, 1982, President Ronald Reagan's Justice Department announced that it was dropping its thirteen-year-old antitrust suit against IBM, and that AT&T had agreed to divest itself of its regional Bell operating companies. IBM was said to have won, AT&T was labeled a loser: the future would show just the opposite was true. At the time of the announcement the stock of both companies was selling at about sixty dollars per share. Over the next eleven years one hundred shares of IBM would return nine thousand five hundred dollars, one hundred shares of AT&T returned $25,901. The *New York Times* called the Justice Department's announcement "the end of an era in antitrust law."

As many regulatory attorneys in Washington were aware, the head of the DOJ antitrust division, William Baxter, who had been a professor at Stanford when Steve Ballmer was there, believed that the marketplace, not the government, should decide what was best for consumers. Says one well-placed Washington attorney, at the time "you'd have to be an idiot not to know [the Justice Department] wasn't going to bring a Section 2 [monopolization] case anytime soon." Given Microsoft's savvy legal department, plus its daily contact with IBM—with Ballmer as the point man— it is virtually impossible that Ballmer wasn't aware of the no-holds-barred regulatory climate. For the twelve years that President Reagan and then the first President George Bush were in office, the Department of Justice wouldn't file a single monopolization case. In essence, these two administrations let it be known that the monopoly police would be on holiday, and that the Microsoft mouse was free to play. Yet in January 1982 IBM was only beginning to set the personal computer hardware standard, few outside the industry had even heard of Microsoft, and the company was just one of many producing PC software.

At issue in the antitrust suit was how IBM used its dominance in mainframe computers to prevent others from competing with them. IBM had signed a consent decree in 1968 agreeing not to announce products until they were certain they could be delivered. Key in the Justice Department's decision to drop the case is that most observers believed IBM was on the verge of losing: all the evidence had been heard. A ruling was imminent.

AT&T's settling was another matter. Like Microsoft seventeen years later, it was obvious that the company was going to lose. In Washington, D.C., a brilliant man, the presiding federal judge, Harold Greene, had said in open court that the government's evidence demonstrated "the Bell system has violated the antitrust laws in a number of ways over a lengthy period of time." As Thomas Penfield Jackson would do in the same courthouse concerning Microsoft, Greene telegraphed what his ruling would be in the hope the parties would settle. AT&T and DOJ attorneys struggled with the immensely complex consent decree. AT&T agreed to break up into seven regional companies: NYNEX, Bell Atlantic, Bell South, Ameritech, US West, Southwestern Bell, and Pacific Telesis. In return, they received permission to enter the information services market, with their well-funded Bell Labs eventually split into the well-funded Lucent Technologies.

Almost immediately, long distance companies like MCI and

Sprint started eating into AT&T's market share. The external source which forced AT&T to be competitive did it a favor: it had grown so large and immobile that it had forgotten what the true marketplace was like. Indeed, the IBM trial judge David Edelstein later said, "It appears, in the entire history, going back to the earliest times, that when enforcement proceeds and a monopolist is broken up the parts grow stronger than the whole. They are able to survive and flourish, instead of being part of an albatross." One need look no further than the 1911 Standard Oil case to see that the thirty-four companies it was broken up into became far more profitable than it had been as a whole, though this may have been due more to the fact that rocketing auto sales greatly increased demand for gasoline.

Back in Seattle, Steve Ballmer, the master networker, kept in touch with his Harvard classmates, as evinced in the five-year anniversary report each class publishes, in essence a letter to the whole group. For the 1982 report, Ballmer wrote,

> After Harvard, I spent two years marketing at Procter and Gamble then a short stint in Hollywood learning about the movie business. I returned to Stanford in fall, 1979 [actually the first term he attended Stanford], and did the first year of my M.B.A. I left school prematurely to come work in Seattle, working for a friend and classmate from Currier House, Bill Gates. Bill co-founded a computer software company, Microsoft, during our sophomore years. That company is now the leading supplier of systems software for microcomputers. We sell our products through a network of more than 2,000 computer stores as well as hardware manufacturers like Apple, IBM, and Radio Shack. Growth has been phenomenal—the company has at least doubled

in size every year since Bill started it. This year we will do over $15 million in sales and have over 110 employees. I enjoy my job, which includes professional recruiting as well as overseeing the finance, marketing, communication, and technical writing areas.

Gates responded to the alumni query by simply listing his address.

After two years on the job Ballmer realized his limitations and recognized that Microsoft needed more experienced management. Gates even suggested that Ballmer go back to Stanford. Ballmer instead recommended that they hire a president. A recruiter came up with the forty-year-old James Towne. Towne was a product of Stanford Business School, and most recently had headed up a nearly three-quarters-of-a-billion-dollar, seven-thousand-employee division of Tektronix, the Portland, Oregon–based engineering equipment producer. Again, getting top-notch programmers and executives to come to computerdom's boondocks of Seattle wasn't easy, especially when the center of the American computer solar system was split between Boston in the east and Silicon Valley in the west. Yet Ballmer and Gates convinced Towne that software, not hardware, was where the industry future lay and that Microsoft's relationship with IBM gave it a leg up on the competition. Towne signed up. He would last less than a year.

One Microsoft executive said, "Frankly, Gates needed a big brother more than he needed a president." Author James Wallace claims that Towne was more of a baby-sitter for the maturity-challenged Gates than an executive. And a big problem was that Towne didn't fit into the Gates-Ballmer on-the-wing management style—they would make decisions in the middle of the night, for instance, without bothering to tell Towne.

At the same time, Paul Allen and Bill Gates were fighting, even more than normally. This wasn't unusual, as that's what one does with Gates; it's how he connects with many people. Gates lore gains richness looking at his often-uttered pejorative, "That's the stupidest fucking thing I've ever heard." Microsoft's propagandists want you to believe that his brusqueness is Gates's way of forcing one to defend their position, which it does. A more objective source, the head of Harvard's computer center, observed that Gates would put people down as a matter of course, many times unnecessarily. At Henry David Thoreau's funeral, Ralph Waldo Emerson eulogized, "He had no friends. He only felt himself in opposition." Like Thoreau, Gates seems to bounce off of those surrounding him, energizing robust verbal intercourse, providing intellectual structure at an emotional price. Ballmer isn't intimidated by Gates, and he had passed Gates's "Are you worthy of my attention" test long before.

After a decade of working with Gates, Paul Allen was becoming weary of the Gates grind, which was taking its toll on his physical health. Just after Towne became president, Allen was on a European sales trip when he became ill. He flew back to Seattle and checked into a local hospital, where it was discovered that he had a form of cancer called Hodgkin's disease. Allen underwent a rigorous X-ray therapy that left him drained, yet he managed to work half-time for a few months until he resigned. After he left, his Hodgkin's went into remission. Allen, a very private man, publicly speaks only in positive terms about Gates, Ballmer, and Microsoft. And many Seattleites express far more admiration for Allen's philanthropy and civic-mindedness than Gates's, which includes building the Experience Music Project museum, though some wonder why a decabillionaire charges a twenty-dollar admission to the general public.

The branding of Microsoft didn't just happen but came about as the result of an intense, and sometimes high-handed, marketing campaign championed by Steve Ballmer, beginning at New York's Plaza Hotel in November 1983. The company realized that the graphical user interface (GUI) on their much larger rival Apple's soon-to-be-announced Macintosh was, in their words, cool. With a GUI, called a gooey, rather than type in commands such as LOGIN (for trivia fans, the first word sent over the Internet), a user could tell his or her computer what to do by simply pointing on a command and clicking, using a device called a mouse. But neither Apple nor Microsoft invented such a system, nor were they first to use a windows GUI on a personal computer.

As the cover story of the September 1977 issue of *Scientific American* relayed, both windows and a mouse were created at PARC. The article, written by Dr. Alan Kay, the head of PARC's Learning Research Group, detailed both a mouse and a GUI so easy to use that high school students were pictured interacting with a self-contained "windows" machine. The students used overlapping graphical files to simultaneously show a clock, a graph, a chart, an index of files, and text notes. Bill Gates, who regularly reads *Scientific American*, and was given a tour of PARC by Charles Simonyi, knew that inventing technology was one thing, yet bringing it to market was something else. So Microsoft took it upon itself to bring the GUI operating system to market.

Gates and Ballmer's main concern about Apple's Macintosh was that its users would be tied to Apple, and not Microsoft. In November 1983 in New York, to much fanfare, Microsoft announced that it was bringing something called Windows to market. What the announcement didn't say was exactly when this would happen. Later that month, at the fall Comdex computer convention in Las Vegas, to even greater fanfare, the term *Windows* was everywhere—from ads on taxicabs to key chains handed out by rental car companies to discount coupons at city restaurants. As one Microsoft executive recalls, "You couldn't take a leak in Vegas that year without seeing a Windows sticker." Another ex-Microsoft exec said, "I think Steve Ballmer saw himself as carrying the water bottle, making sure the towels were there, making sure [Microsoftians] had the proper equipment, just like he'd done with the Harvard football team." While it isn't certain whether Ballmer helped supply the head of team Microsoft with bedmates, there's no doubt that he was at the core of the Windows marketing and branding strategy.

Working with Gates, Ballmer helped recruit a marketer named Rowland Hanson, who had worked for many years selling food products (Betty Crocker and Contadina) in retail markets. And in 1983, Microsoft hired its second president in as many years, Jon Shirley. Shirley's experience at Tandy Corporation (Radio Shack) had also been in retail sales. At the time, most people referred to MS-DOS as simply DOS, and had little idea what the MS stood for. Windows became Microsoft Windows. Their word-processing program became Microsoft Word. Again, it was brilliant. Twofold. Microsoft was using retail techniques to market their product to businesses and getting immediate cash while building a branding cachet.

So Microsoft announced that it was developing Windows, a GUI version of MS-DOS. And, just as it had licensed MS-DOS to IBM even before it had such a product, Microsoft told the world it could expect Windows. When IBM settled its antitrust suit with the Department of Justice, one of the minor restrictions it consented to was that it wouldn't announce products in advance that might chill their competitor's sales. But Microsoft had never consented to any such thing, Gary Kildall's CP/M was still the dominant operating system, and the monopoly police were on vacation. In the Microsoft frame of mind, it was just fine to announce something nowhere near completion. Little did those at the 1983 Comdex know, it would take two long years—nearly an eternity in computer technology time—before Windows would be shipped, and it would be a crummy Windows at that.

Put yourself in the position of an independent software developer in late 1983. IBM and Microsoft are in bed together, clearly on their way to setting the PC hardware and software standards. Microsoft announces it is bringing a GUI operating system to market. The success of the IBM PC and its clones has given Microsoft a huge boost in the operating systems market (it would soon surpass CP/M), and only Microsoft knows its lead time for getting Windows shipped. Could be out within the next few months. If you're a developer, why go up against this by writing your applications only for CP/M and Apple when there appear to be great gobs of gold in applications written for the IBM PC and its clones?

For two years Windows would be in the ether. Where? Nobody knew (including many working on it). The delay provided a Microsoft-inspired addition to the American lexicon: vaporware. Windows was all talk, no product; it seemed to vaporize. The term also created a new twist on an old story. According to the latest version, a woman in her forties goes to a doctor for a physical. During the examination the doctor becomes puzzled and says, "Mary, it says on your medical history that you've been married three times, yet I see that you're still chaste, still a virgin, how could that be?" Mary sighs and says, "My first husband, Tim, was the nicest, kindest, guy you'd ever meet—friendly, helpful, a great confidant—but it turned out he was gay and so he wouldn't. My second husband, Jim, was rough, tough, macho, but he was a wounded Vietnam combat vet and, well, he couldn't. My third husband, Bill, he was a Microsoft programmer. He just sat on the end of the bed and told me how good it was gonna be." Tech magazine *InfoWorld* would give the first version of Windows, Windows 1.0, a 4.5 rating on a ten-point scale.

As if he didn't have enough recruiting, marketing, and putting-up-with-Gates responsibilities, Ballmer was also in charge of getting Windows shipped, formally assuming the new title vice president of systems software. Ballmer recalled to Robert X. Cringely how his new duties began. "I went into one of my cheerleading routines and the programmers just looked at me and rolled their eyes. One laughed. That programmer left [Microsoft]. It was good for Microsoft and good for him." In Microsoft's first decade, the programmer was always a him.

A little-known fact: the first American computer programmers were women, working on the ENIAC while the boys were off fighting the Good War. In fact, it was one of the women—future navy admiral Grace Hopper, the inventor of the COBOL programming language—who found the first known computer bug. Literally. On September 9, 1945, at 3:45 P.M. Boston time, Hopper found a moth lodged in panel F of relay #70 of a Mark I computer at Harvard. Hopper duly recorded not only the date, time, and place in her log, but taped in the electrocuted culprit as well. (Thomas Edison had called any electrical systems flaw a "bug," and the term dates back to fourteenth-century Welsh, meaning a hobgoblin.) While in the 1990s female Microsoftians would set up a loosely connected women's club of sorts and call themselves Hoppers, nine years after the company's founding Microsoft was still a boys' club, reflecting the Harvard environment Gates and Ballmer were schooled in, with relatively few female employees, virtually all in clerical roles. This became a problem while Ballmer was heading up Windows.

In 1984, Microsoft coveted a twenty-five-million-dollar programming contract with the U.S. Air Force. The civil rights legislation passed in the sixties included a mandate that a federal government contractor would have to take affirmative action in recruiting female and minority employees. As Pulitzer Prize–winning *Chicago Tribune* columnist Clarence Page pointed out in his 1996 collection of race relations essays, *Showing My Color,* the biggest beneficiaries of affirmative action are white women. Simply put, Microsoft needed at least a few women in higher-profile positions. At the suggestion of Ballmer, Gates hired the head of Apple's applications division, Ida Cole, as Microsoft's vice president of applications. Microsoft got the Air Force contract. Ida Cole stayed five years, until her stock options were fully vested, and left a multimillionaire.

Given the dinky memory of personal computers at the time, code monkeys were forced to program PCs on larger machines. Microsoft purchased some of the computers for their programmers to work on from a small Silicon Valley manufacturer named Sun Microsystems. Two years before, Sun had been founded by four men, including Ballmer's Stanford classmate Vinod Khosla, Ballmer's fellow Farmington Hills–raised Bill Joy, and Ballmer's Cranbrook rival and Harvard and Stanford schoolmate Scott McNealy. Joy was studying programming at Berkeley, grew tired of academic office politics, dropped out, and became head code monkey at Sun (the name is an acronym standing for the Stanford University Network). Unlike Ballmer, McNealy had graduated from Stanford Business School, where he concentrated on manufacturing, and for a year had helped build tanks for FMC Corporation in Chicago before becoming director of manufacturing for a small San Jose minicomputer maker, Onyx Systems. McNealy headed up manufacturing Sun's workstations before taking over as president and chief executive officer in 1984.

As vice president of systems software, Ballmer pushed and pushed to get, as he put it, Windows! Windows! Windows! out the door. Gates said, "Developers accepted him early on because he was smart. He would sit and listen to them, understand the things that they really liked to do." Ballmer told *InfoWorld,* "I learned that you have to get the right guys and you've got to look them in the eyes and listen, and find the guys you can trust. Then ride them." And ride them he did, implementing what the employees called a death march. In fact, one programmer posted a political cartoon on an office bulletin board showing a Middle Eastern terrorist executing people, with the name BALLMER handwritten on his body.

During the Windows Death March, it wasn't unusual to have programmers sleeping in their cubicles. As novelist Douglas Coupland showed in *Microserfs,* some programmers simply closed their doors, wrote code, and slept. Concerned about a friend who had locked himself in his office, some co-workers went out and bought flat food—Kraft cheese singles, Premium Plus crackers, Pop-Tarts, Freezie-Pops—and slid them under his door. One report has Gates actually threatening to fire Ballmer in the summer of 1985 if Windows wasn't finished "by the time the first snow falls in Seattle." Ballmer succeeded, mainly because it doesn't snow much in the Rainy City. Though, according to one report, he was watching a Denver Broncos–Seattle Seahawks football game being played in Seattle while he was on the road. When it started to snow at the game, Ballmer became "quite nervous" and had to be settled down. It wasn't until November 1985 that Windows 1.0 was shipped. It had taken so long to get out the door that PC journalist John Dvorak quipped, "When they announced Windows, Steve Ballmer still had hair."

Along with being head Windows slave driver, Ballmer was still Microsoft's point man with IBM, which was becoming increasingly concerned about MS-DOS becoming the software standard. One of the main reasons IBM had become so dominant was that it pushed a concept called "systems compatibility." While its high-end System 360 computer was more than one thousand times as powerful as the low-end model, any of these machines would be able to run the same application software—

except their PC. It was IBM's dominance in compatible software that led to the increasing dominance of IBM hardware in what economist Stephen Siwek calls "a kind of perpetual feedback loop." But with their PC, they'd allowed Microsoft to set the standard. IBM initially ignored the fact that an installed base of software, not hardware, locked in computer users. Realizing its mistake, IBM sought to actively limit Microsoft's influence by developing its own proprietary operating system, which came to be called OS/2. Gates convinced IBM that it should partner with Microsoft in creating the new system. In the summer of 1985, IBM and Microsoft signed a joint development agreement for OS/2, giving Ballmer two masters. Guess which operating system would receive most of Ballmer's attention? IBM's would. In fact, in spite of his public statements, Ballmer wasn't a fan of Windows, and didn't want to upset another animal in the software zoo.

Ballmer said his strategy at the time was what he called "riding the bear." IBM was the bear and "you just had to try and stay on the bear's back and the bear would twist and turn and try to buck you and throw you but, darn, we were going to ride the bear because the bear was the biggest, the most important—you just had to be with the bear, otherwise you would be under the bear in the computer industry, and IBM was the bear, and we were going the ride the back of the bear. So we said okay, this isn't our delight, but who are we? We're just these little punk kids in Seattle, Washington. We're not going to thumb our nose at the bear, we're going to hang on and do our best." Internally, Ballmer was blunter. He said, "The strategy with IBM was BOGU—'bend over, grease up.'" Some of his subordinates would give him a jar of petroleum jelly with BOGUS written on the front: "Bend Over, Grease Up, Steve." Bogus Ballmer.

Given their radically different cultures, it isn't surprising that the Microsoftians working on Windows clashed constantly with the IBMers. So much so, in fact, that an IBM executive would be quoted as saying that he wanted to "put an ice pick into Bill Gates's head." And some Microsoftians came to call IBM "an Incredible Bunch of Morons." The Incredible Bunch of Morons might have been just that, simply because they trusted Microsoft. It would take a few years before IBM became convinced that Gates and Ballmer had been fooling them into thinking they were devoted to OS/2. One IBM executive, Jim Cannavino, would later come to believe that "Gates has a small team of people tied up making OS/2 shit. I've gone through the plans and added up the number of people they have working on our stuff and the number they had at the same operating systems group doing something else. They must be doing something else."

Cannavino did some research and discovered that Microsoft's Developer Relations Group was getting independent companies to develop software not for OS/2 but for Windows, Windows, Windows. As he relates, at the same time and with a straight face, "Gates is coming and telling us at IBM that DOS and Windows are dead. Microsoft is saying to [customers like] General Electric and Boeing that IBM is fucked up." Combined with the fact that OS/2 would challenge Windows for market share was the realization that, unlike OS/2, with Windows, Microsoft wouldn't have to pay any royalties to IBM. The acrimony between a PC father and spoiled child, the once and future computer chieftains, started to seep into the media.

At the 1989 Comdex convention, after much squabbling, IBM and Microsoft announced they were still working together, with OS/2 being developed for more powerful machines, and Microsoft would make applications for it before offering a more refined Windows. Just after the announcement, an IBM executive was talking to Ballmer, telling him that it was going to be a challenge to write a tighter OS/2 that didn't use more than two megabytes of memory. "Oh," Ballmer told him, "we're never going to do that." Incredulous, the IBM exec replied, "What do you mean? That's what we just announced!" Ballmer just grinned. According to author Wendy Goldman Rohm, the same day Jim Cannavino had a security man scan his Las Vegas hotel room. The investigator found three listening devices—bugs. Cannavino would never trust Microsoft again.

Whether Ballmer's troops outright sabotaged OS/2, as IBM and many technophiles thought, or simply put more effort into their proprietary system Windows, is a question still fiercely debated in computerdom. However, to the Federal Trade Commission it looked less like competition between two operating systems than collusion between IBM and Microsoft. By 1990, the FTC started to investigate.

Steve Ballmer's "thrifty" ways, combined with Bill Gates's similar inclinations, kept Microsoft salaries below market, sometimes well below. Unlike California or Massachusetts, where Microsoft's main competitors lay, Washington State didn't (and still doesn't) have a state income tax, so a lower salary wouldn't necessarily mean less take-home pay. But it was the golden handcuffs, the stock option promise, that kept many Microsoft code monkeys in the fold. By late 1985, Microsoft had offered so many employees options that they were quickly approaching the five hundred mark, at which point, due to Securities and Exchange Commission regulations, Microsoft would be required to register the stock. Besides, an increasing number of Microsoftians owned stock but had nowhere to trade it. On October 28, 1985, Gates recommended to his board that the company go public. Board member and president Jon Shirley said, "We decided to do it when we wanted to, not when the SEC said we had to."

After auditioning a dozen or so underwriters, Chief Financial Officer Frank Gaudette decided on both Goldman Sachs and Alex Brown. Never one to miss a chance at free publicity, in early 1986 Gates gave *Fortune* magazine the exclusive on the inside story of taking a company public. As Microsoft and their underwriters prepared the prospectus, they underwent due diligence, the fiduciary responsibility which basically says that, to the best of our knowledge, this is our company. If, say, the company officers were aware that they were liable for damages anytime Windows crashed and failed to report that, a stockholder could bring suit. Adding to the problem was *Fortune* shadowing Microsoft's efforts, so if they revealed something to the reporter that wasn't shown in the prospectus, they were open to other suits, including fraud. A security analyst for one of the underwriters recalls, "Steve Ballmer was pretty wild during the due diligence. He was his normal, ebullient self. Once, he was right behind one of the minions from Goldman Sachs and he clapped his hands together to make a point and the guy jumped about five feet out of his chair." According to James Wallace and Jim Erickson, "Ballmer, even more so than the other Microsoft executives, came up with so many potential developments that could result in Microsoft's demise during due diligence that one of the investment bankers quipped, 'I'd hate to hear you on a bad day.'" This was Ballmer at his best and worst, the "we're golden! we're screwed!" persona that would attract some and repel others, the locker room Ballmer lambasting his team then picking them up.

The impending IPO created more stir in Seattle than when Asa Mercer returned from Boston in the nineteenth century with a boatload of bachelorettes, the basis for the television series *Here Come the Brides.* It seemed everybody wanted in on it. For weeks, Gates fielded calls from people he hadn't seen in years: teachers at Lakeside, boyhood friends, old neighbors, even his doctor. He refused most. He did allow his grandmother, his two sisters, and a former maid to purchase shares. Ballmer made sure that his father, Fred, had shares but, for some reason, he didn't reserve any IPO stock for his sister, Shelly.

Once the prospectus was ready, some thirty-eight-thousand

copies were sent out, giving a window into the inner workings of the Windows producer and its top executives. Microsoft now had 998 employees (840 domestic), with 326 in product development, 402 in sales, marketing and support, 113 in manufacturing and distribution, and 157 in finance and administration. For the first time, the public became aware of the extent of Microsoftian holdings. Gates owned 11,222,000 shares, just less than 50 percent, his family another 134,000 shares. Paul Allen owned 6,390,000 shares, 28 percent. Ballmer owned 1,710,001 shares (7.5 percent), and his father 33,666. Programmer Charles Simonyi held 305,000 shares; fellow code monkey Gordon Letwin had 293,850.

Gates, and to a lesser extent Ballmer, spent a few months traveling around the country extolling the virtues of Microsoft to analysts and brokers. Though he was of the mind that Microsoft shouldn't pay its underwriters more than 6.5 percent of his stock's selling price, when Gates discovered that Sun Microsystems had negotiated a 6.13 percent fee on its sixty-four-million-dollar offering, Gates wanted the same and demanded Gaudette get it. The IPO was nearly withdrawn until Goldman Sachs agreed.

The week of March 10, 1986, was the most empowering, energizing, and yet emasculating seven days in American information history. Taking advantage of an IPO-friendly market, within several days, and with much fanfare and phenomenal success, Wall Street voiced its opinion of the information revolution when Sun Microsystems, Oracle, and Microsoft all went public with their stocks. The same week, citing budget cuts, our national Library of Congress, which was first housed on Wall Street when New York briefly served as the nation's capital, and which protects Microsoft's copyrights, eliminated most evening hours (though, after loud protests, the cuts were later rescinded). In early March of 1986, the path of the information revolution started to move, albeit slightly, from the printed page to electrons and protons, and Microsoft would get the most attention.

Feigning disinterest in the IPO, Gates was on vacation, sailing off the Great Barrier Reef in Australia, when the stock hit the floor and the opening bell sounded. It was as though he was saying, "A great programmer like me can't be bothered with this crass financial stuff." On March 13, 1986, at 9:35 A.M. eastern standard time, the first shares of Microsoft, offered at twenty-one dollars, were publicly traded at $25.75 per share. The NASDAQ action made Ballmer seem laid back. *Fortune* reported that Gaudette called Shirley from the floor, shouting, "It's wild! I've never seen anything like it—every last person here is trading Microsoft and nothing else." Over three and a half million shares traded hands. The stock closed at $27.75. Within six hours, Bill Gates was worth $311,410,500.00, Paul Allen $177,322,500.00, Steve Ballmer $47,452,527.75, Fred Ballmer $1,017,481.00. Fred Ballmer made more money in those six hours than he had in at least twenty years working for Ford. Thirteen days before his thirtieth birthday, Steve Ballmer was a millionaire forty-seven times over.

Yet things weren't totally sunny in Seattle. Just prior to the IPO, Seattle Computer Products had filed a twenty-million-dollar suit based on the agreement Ballmer had Rod Brock sign, granting Microsoft the right to use Q-DOS but allowing Brock some use as well. Brock found out—the hard way—that Ballmer wasn't exactly right when he had told him "it would not change anything whether or nor [Microsoft] owned it or we owned it." According to Paul Andrews and Stephen Manes, during the subsequent trial the jury had a chance to see Gates testify in person. When he was asked about "your company," Gates reportedly responded, "You mean Microsoft?" Seattle Computer Products attorney, Kelly Corr, then asked if Gates owned about half of the company stock. Gates said he owned about 40 percent.

"You own about eleven million shares, don't you?"

"Yes."

"The last time I looked, it was about fifty dollars a share, right?"

"I don't look," Gates responded.

While the jury was deliberating, Microsoft and Brock settled for $925,000. It was a good move for the bigger company. A poll of the jury found that they were leaning eight to four against Gates & Ballmer. For a total of one million dollars, Microsoft finally and fully owned MS-DOS.

PART THREE

POSTCARDS FROM THE BORG

Monopoly is business at the end of its journey.

—HENRY DEMAREST LLOYD

CHAPTER SEVEN

THE BORG

I n 1925 a businessman, Bruce Barton, published a book, *The Man Nobody Knows*, about how Jesus was the best salesman ever. It sold extremely well, as did the 1995 book *Jesus, CEO*. Combining religion and sales took a new form in 1984 when Apple decided to set up what it called its evangelists—a group that would try to convince independent software developers to write applications for their Macintosh machine. Three years later, Steve Ballmer decided that Microsoft needed its own evangelists, so he created the Developer Relations Group (DRG), headed by Cameron Mhyrvold. Says one former DRG member, "Cameron told us, 'Your job is to fuck up a competitor. A competitor will never adopt your technology. It's like cocaine. They're not going to willingly get addicted. You have to push the cocaine on them.'" This former employee also says, "We were the storm troopers, the SS. In my office, we had a picture of the Borg. We were the Borg."

The Borg is a race of part-human, part-mechanical characters from the television show *Star Trek: The Next Generation*. The Borg have no single brain but operate as a collective, each member interconnected with the other. The Borg are infamous for announcing at the beginning of a battle, "Resistance is futile. Prepare to be assimilated."

Ballmer would go on account calls with Cameron Mhyrvold, who recalls, "We would be driving to an account and Steve would turn the radio to a Top 40 station, turn the volume all the way up, and bang on the dashboard like a drum. It was an outlet for his energy. He's an amazing barrel of energy, even when he was sick, except when he was sick he was a little subdued. He would stimulate you to be at the top of your game. He was very appreciative of what you did. Steve was always willing to come along. He would really think the account calls through. [The DRG] was in the trenches. What I got from Ballmer was the best strategic feedback of anybody in the company. And Steve is a guy that it's easy to be loyal to because you always had a sense that he's loyal back.

"In the eighties there wasn't any training at the company. You learned by following the footsteps of others. The place didn't have much institutional memory. When I'd been at the company for a few weeks, Ballmer asked me a question, and I said I didn't know. Ballmer said, 'That's unacceptable. It's your job to understand. You have to understand. You are going to be the company expert on the issue.' There are two types of meetings with Steve. One is where he does all the talking, the other is when I did all the talking—new issues, I was educating Steve. I'd take him through the thought process. And Steve listened, he always listened. Then he would very much give you his point of view. He'd go, 'Oh! Oh! Oh!' when he saw my internal logic. He wanted to know what the opportunity map looked like. He'd ask, what is the map of the market? Where is the low-hanging fruit for us? Steve is always logical and consistent and he demands you be the same.

"When I was running the DRG, I decided that we needed to staff it with techies, not marketing people. Techie talk [what Ballmer calls 'geek sex']. Techies understood the functions. Alex St. John is a prime example of a DRG evangelist." St. John was home-schooled in Alaska, scored a perfect 1600 on his SAT, and got his job, in part, by telling the recruiter, "Bill [Gates] kicks ass. I like kicking ass. I enjoy the feeling of killing competitors and dominating markets." Mhyrvold continues, "One day Alex wrote a three-page memo to Bill saying that we needed better technical support, that Microsoft didn't have great technical people to be deep enough in technical space. St. John was the best evangelist we ever had." Reading the memo, Gates was angry at first, but then came around to St. John's point of view. St. John would do things like give tours of the campus in his Humvee, not bothering to be constrained by the streets. He told Michael Drummond, author of *Renegades of the Empire,* "You'd insert your hand into [developers'] brains and adjust them. You'd put the world in terms of Microsoft for them. To make [Microsoft] a thought for them on a daily basis. If they loved you or hated you, that didn't matter, so long as they were thinking about you." St. John currently heads the 3-D game developer Wild Tangent.

Ballmer used the Chinese Wall fiction to put developers at greater ease, giving them a sense that they could show Microsoft how their applications were programmed without worrying that the code would be incorporated into DOS or Windows. Invoking yet another comparison to religion, Ballmer told *Business Week,* "There is a very clear separation between our operating systems and our applications software. It's like the separation of church and state." The problem was that such a wall didn't exist. Ballmer was head of systems software, and his best friend, Gates, was head of applications. In fact, Microsoftians working under Ballmer on the operating system worked with the applications people under Gates to ensure that, surprise, Microsoft applications worked best on Windows. This was due in part to Microsoft using an under-handed method called "hidden APIs" in their operating system. APIs are programming codes integrated into an operating system such as Windows to allow it to respond to commands from an application program. If you didn't know where all the APIs were, your programs would run slower, more clumsily, if at all. (Recall that Gates allegedly said, "DOS isn't done till Lotus won't run.") True to its corporate ethic of denial, Microsoft refused to admit that such hidden codes existed until a programmer, Andrew Schul-man, published his book *Undocumented Windows* in 1992, prov-ing that the operating system programmers slaving under Ballmer had, in fact, coded in hidden APIs, something they would later do with Sun Microsystems' Java. Microsoft later admitted that two of its applications bundled into Windows, Excel and Word, used "at least" sixteen APIs that had been hidden in their operating sys-tem. Developers were leery of working with Microsoft, but by now, MS-DOS and Windows had become the dominant personal computer operating systems, so they had little choice. Resistance was futile.

By 1989, Fred Ballmer had retired after thirty years at Ford, and his son, Steve, managed to amend his well-earned tightwad reputation and sprang for a class-act retirement gift: he bought his parents' Farmington Hills house for them. His father's pension from Ford (including the previously mentioned car leasing dis-count), combined with his IPO stock, provided Fred and Bea Ballmer with a comfortable living. According to a family friend, Fred's hearing was getting worse. Steve Ballmer's demeanor was getting worse as well. According to 3Com founder Bob Metcalfe, formerly of Xerox's PARC team, working with Steve Ballmer and the troops he famously motivated was "like mating with a black widow spider."

By now, personal computer networking—one PC being able to talk with another—was becoming the rage. While the Utah-based Novell Corporation held about 70 percent of the networking market, San Francisco's 3Com Corporation, with over four hundred million dollars in revenues, was a major player. Ballmer contacted Metcalfe to work out a joint development agreement. Ballmer flew to California and proposed that the two companies finish developing Microsoft's OS/2 Local Area Networking (LAN) Manager and then sell it through 3Com's network of dealers. After some tough negotiations, 3Com and Microsoft became partners. They started to fight almost immediately.

Metcalfe told James Wallace and Jim Erickson, "Our engineers were treated like shit by Microsoft people. They ended up testing all the buggy software, and whenever anything was wrong, Microsoft's general position was that it was our fault. Our engineers were forced to suffer daily indignities in the face of these obnoxiously arrogant programmers. One of my friends referred to them as Hitler Youth." (Hitler Youth was Adolf's brainchild to indoctrinate children into the Nazi Party; members were, in effect, programmed to be a cross between a Boy Scout and an attack dog.) Metcalfe continues, "Here's Microsoft, which has had success squared. They've become Hitler Youth. They think people who don't work there are assholes and bureaucratic jerks."

Besides dealing with the hard-core Microsoftians, 3Com got the worst of the deal from the start. According to Metcalfe, at the press conference announcing their partnership Microsoft "made it clear it was a Microsoft operation. It wasn't a joint press conference, it was a Microsoft press conference." The acrimony continued when the product hit the market. Though 3Com sold almost three-quarters of all LAN Managers, a minimum monthly royalty payment clause in the contract forced it to pay Microsoft even if 3Com didn't sell anything when Microsoft itself decided to sell its portion the program. Metcalfe not so slowly realized just how untrustworthy Microsoft was, and would be among the first people to question the legality of Microsoft's monopolistic conduct in print, comparing its licensing practices to the types of extortion schemes subject to federal racketeering laws.

Microsoft was exhaling an ill wind. Says one venture capitalist, "Microsoft is like [the hockey player] Gordie Howe. [Howe played a fierce game, and never won a Lady Byng trophy, voted to the 'most gentlemanly' player.] Competitors were complaining about getting hit with elbow after elbow, and were growing tired of being worn down." A former president of the Seattle-based University of Washington, who knew Gates and his family for decades, told Biography, "It seemed that Microsoft was always playing with two feet on the foul line."

At the time, economist James S. Henry was researching an article on how Silicon Valley perceived Microsoft. He discovered that many of the gripes Californians had about Gates & Ballmer, Inc., were well founded, not mere jealousy. Furthermore, Henry found that while it seemed everyone had an opinion of the company, almost always negative, few people would go on the record with their comments, fearing the repercussions. When his piece appeared in the November 1990 issue of *Business Month* magazine, he noted that Bill Gates was by now the Pacific Northwest's first billionaire ever, and that he was the "most successful Harvard dropout since Putzi Hanfstaengl, the German aristocrat who introduced Adolf Hitler to the German industrialists in the 1930s." Henry kept hearing stories about how Gates had gained his wealth "by being tediously technical, less innovative, a ruthless deal maker who freely 'borrowed' from partners and grew fat as a parasite on their success, and a rich kid whose main claim to fame was that he had been lucky enough to be standing there when IBM needed an operating system to launch its PC blitz." Henry quoted columnist John Dvorak as saying, "Thank goodness Gates is into computers and isn't a mob boss or a preacher." A software executive told him, "Microsoft's secret is that it is not an innovator. Bill is just a systems guy who's been able to fund a wide range of me-too applications on the basis of one extremely lucrative product practically given to him ten years ago by IBM. All he's done is just hang in." An industry analyst observed, "Everyone in the industry hates Gates. He has tried to turn people away from [Apple] and GO and Novell. He raided people from Borland. Not everyone thinks he played it straight on Windows and OS/2. Most software developers would love to work with someone else, but he's the elephant in the hallway."

Henry concluded by saying that "Gates now has such a stake in the status quo that he has no choice but to hold up progress. Microsoft's huge 'installed base' has become a curse. It is not only an entry barrier that protects his handsome profit margins; it is also a barrier to innovation. Furthermore, Microsoft's size gives it the leverage to limit access to its customers in such a way as to create an effective Microsoft standard for software. Bill Gates is a smart, rather conservative, very lucky technician. He is an able business manager and aggressive, shrewd deal doer who rose to the top not because he had any particular vision of how personal computers might set us all free but because he was very good at blocking, talking, recovering fumbles, and emulating winning plays." Ballmer wasn't mentioned in Henry's study but, in fact, as was shown with 3Com, it was he, the former football player and manager, the head of systems software, who did much of Microsoft's blocking, talking, recovering fumbles, and emulating winning plays.

A lighter side of what Henry called "the Silicon Valley bully" was that Microsoft jokes started to appear. One of the better jests: How many Microsoft programmers does it take to change a lightbulb? None. Microsoft just declares the dark the standard. Another response: Lightbulb? That's a hardware problem.

Tech author and PBS host Mark Stevens, best known under his pen name Robert X. Cringely, sees March 1989 as the most important month in creating Microsoft as we know it. Cringely credits Steve Ballmer with what he terms the beginning of the Age of Microsoft. This came about that March, during Apple's "touch and feel" lawsuit against Microsoft, for violating a licensing agreement, when the presiding federal judge ruled that Apple hadn't given Microsoft carte blanche to adopt Apple's GUI to Windows. Wall Street reacted by devaluing Microsoft stock. To prop up the stock price, Steve Ballmer borrowed and borrowed and borrowed—a total of $46.2 million—to purchase 945,000 shares of Microsoft on the open market. Though Cringely proposes that this move made Ballmer rich, his 1.7 million shares from the IPO had already doubled, making him worth more than $150 million, so he wasn't hurting too badly. Ballmer had stepped in with his own (borrowed) money, which was almost unheard of for someone in his position. Maniacal loyalty. In spades. While Cringely posits this as a seminal event, others say that the next year, when Microsoft would release Windows 3.0, was when Microsoft as the Borg became fully operational, and resistance to Gates and Ballmer became futile.

The six-foot-six-inch Seattle rhythm and blues guitarist G. C. Follrich performs under the name Daddy Treetops. Treetops, Tree to his friends, talks fondly about the time he spent in Louisiana, supporting his music by taking a laborer job. One afternoon one of his co-workers said, slowly, in a drawl, "I gots ta get home. It's my wife's twenty-first birthday, and our seventh wedding anniversary." Tree was stunned. "Why," he asked, "would you marry a fourteen-year-old?" In a deep, gospel-truth tone, the husband shot back, "That way, ya gots a hand in how they raised. If ya don't get 'em soon enough, they ruined." "Ya gots a hand in how they raised" sums up much of the nascent Microsoft cult or culture Ballmer and Gates were creating, and how it relates to customers.

Publicly denouncing software piracy had been Microsoft's chant ever since February 1976, when Bill Gates wrote his legendary "Open Letter to Hobbyists," bemoaning the fact that "the majority of [computer] hobbyists . . . steal your software. Who cares if the people who worked on it get paid?" The missive was published in various tech publications. (One editor responded that the BASIC program Bill Gates wrote "was done on a Harvard computer provided at least in part with government funds and that there was some question as to the propriety if not the legality of selling the results.") At the same time Microsoft was publicly condemning software piracy Ballmer confided to Cringely, "Piracy isn't that bad. People learn how to use a computer with our software. Something's bound to go wrong and they're gonna need us. Then they have to buy it and register it." Some computer engineering students at the University of Washington were wondering if all the free software Microsoft was giving them wasn't just to get them "addicted" to it. By 2002, as the domestic market for its software became more saturated, Microsoft helped fund a trade group that encouraged employees to report piracy on their current or former companies.

Though he was head of operating systems, Ballmer continued his relentless search for people to help Microsoft not only do whatever they could to get companies to use Microsoft software, but execute the software contracts already in hand. Ballmer often reached out to his Harvard alums. Harvard has one of the most extensive alumni associations on earth, if for no other reason than to bother them for donations (as if their $18.4 billion endowment isn't enough), and freely makes available its alumni's names, addresses, and phone numbers to their brethren. Ballmer would often visit, sometimes lecture at, and almost every year recruit from Harvard—not only to try to get his pick of the best, but to help insure that his competitors didn't. This was the case with Mark Zbikowski. Soon after graduating from Harvard in 1981, he got a call from Ballmer. Zbikowski recalls, "Steve said, 'I've got this great little company here. Why don't you come out to Seattle?'" Zbikowski liked what he saw and signed up. He's now a millionaire many times over. If Ballmer came across someone like Zbikowski, he'd invite them out, all expenses paid, and show them "the campus," as Microsoft had started calling its corporate office park.

By now, Gates and Ballmer had moved the company to a group of offices they built on former farmland in Redmond, which resembled the Harvard where the dynamic duo had met: four-story buildings placed within hemlock and pines. Their hallmate from Harvard, Dr. Judith Kaplan, says, "Microsoft buildings remind me of Currier House—the same height, the underground passageways, the common areas." A former Microsoft executive says, "We figured that by making it like college, it would be easier to attract recent graduates, many of whom had never lived away from home except college. We wanted to make work a place they would want to come—the free soft drinks, the subsidized food."

Charles Simonyi, who often joined Ballmer's recruiting efforts, recalls, "We were really looking for the inexperienced people" because "they were easier to get, or more predictable to get. There was a supply and we had a mining operation. They were easier to motivate." Microsoft also "gots a hand in how they raised."

Ballmer described the Microsoft working environment as "a math camp for geeks." Few Microsoftians were married, and the work, work, work lifestyle wasn't conducive to a family life. A close female friend of Bill Gates described the growing Microsoft campus as a "kind of bachelor heaven. It was kind of like visiting the Lost Boys." An employee at the time recalls it as a sexually charged environment, with more than a few women who were looking for a rich techie husband. Ballmer was a prime catch, more so than Gates. An early programmer recalls, "Most of the time Gates was past scruffy. He never showered. The joke among the secretaries was: 'Who would you rather have sex with, Gates or Ballmer?' Answer: Ballmer, because you had less chance of getting a disease."

By 1990 the bachelor heaven was ending, and the majority of Microsoftians were now married and starting or raising families, with Gates a notable exception. Cameron Mhyrvold recalls, "In the late eighties, Steve wanted to get married. He wanted to have children. He was concerned that he'd be a bachelor all his life. He was always trying to arrange dates, calling up his buddies while we were together on the road, trying to get them to set him up. He was very focused about it, but Steve isn't exactly a ladies' man. He tried hard, too hard sometimes. He was clumsy about it, awkward. He was really, well, cute about getting dates. Personal relationships with women were not his strength." After graduating from the University of Oregon in 1984 with a degree in communications, Connie Snyder had returned to her hometown of Portland, Oregon, where she worked for Microsoft's outside public relations firm, Waggener Edstrom. Snyder and Ballmer worked around each other a great deal. Mhyrvold says, "There isn't a stuck-up bone in Connie's body. She's a lovable, warm, compassionate woman. In the decade I've known her, I have never heard one negative word about her." On March 31, 1990, Steve Ballmer married Connie Snyder in Portland. Ballmer was so overcome with emotion that he broke down and cried while giving his vows. Bill Gates was his best man.

That Ballmer married a PR staffer wasn't unusual for someone in his position. As *Wired* magazine noted, in a piece they called "Love Among the Press Releases," "It's the high-tech version of interoffice romance—high-tech execs who marry public relations representatives. 'PR people guide clients through scary experiences,' one PR veteran told *Wired*, 'and when you're helping somebody through a difficult time, you tend to bond. Sometimes, that bonding takes the form of romance." Kelli McFarland, who worked with Willie Tejada at Novell, then married him, says, "When you work on pitches, your biorhythms get in sync." The list of male high-tech execs who would marry marketers include America Online's Steve Case, who would formally couple with his vice president of communications, Jean Villanueva; Netscape's executive VP Mike Homer, who married PR exec Christina Lessing; and Jerry Kaplan of GO, then Onsale, who married his vice president of marketing and PR, Michelle Pettigrew. Certainly, the rough sides of Ballmer would benefit from bonding with a public relations pro.

Steve and Connie Ballmer bought a house valued at five hundred thousand dollars in an upper-middle-class area near Microsoft, relatively austere for a man now worth over a billion dollars. Tradesmen working on the Ballmers' house speak highly of Connie Ballmer—they really enjoy the fact that she brings them coffee and cold water and sandwiches for lunch. In fact, several years later, when a roofer working on the Ballmer homestead failed to secure his safety line and fell to his death, it affected both Steve and Connie Ballmer deeply, though they were absolutely not at fault.

"Connie settled Steve down," says one journalist who covered the Microsoft beat at the time. "She changed Steve." People familiar with the marriage told me that Connie is from a big family, and is used to not being the center of attention just as much as her husband is used to being the hub of activity. Bea Ballmer bonded with Connie, and Olga Dworkin told me that Steve's mother and his wife got along very well.

Apparently, Connie Ballmer didn't change husband Steve enough, at least in terms of toning him down. In May 1991, while shouting "Windows! Windows! Windows!" at a sales meeting in Japan, Ballmer ripped his vocal cords, which had to be surgically repaired. According to the speech laboratory at the

University of Washington, a person can't tear their vocal cords with a single incident; it's the product of years of pathological behavior, with a gradual buildup of polyps. For quite a while Ballmer's body had been telling him to take it easy, but Ballmer apparently ignored the warnings. Such dedication, or at least enunciation, inspired many on the campus.

Says one former Microsoftian, "Steve believed. He was so into Windows. Sometimes he opens his mouth way too much. Sometimes he berates people. But Microsoft needs Steve. You've got to hear one of his speeches to understand. He's like John Belushi in *Animal House*, when Belushi finds out that he and his frat brothers had been kicked out of school, and their draft boards were notified their student deferments were gone. Belushi stands up and shouts, 'Did we take it when the Germans bombed Pearl Harbor!?' 'Germans? Pearl Harbor?' says a frat brother. 'Don't stop him,' says another. 'He's on a roll.' Ballmer's always on a roll. He might get his facts wrong. but this is a guy you want to follow. He's a leader, not a manager but a leader. If [the] 520 [floating bridge over Lake Washington] was frozen and you were in an accident, Steve would somehow find a way to drive out and pull you home. He's like that. Steve believes."

When I asked the former Developer Relations Group head Cameron Mhyrvold if Steve Ballmer has an off switch, he laughed, then said, "Not that I've ever seen. I wonder how he sustains the sheer amount of energy that he brings to bear. I think he's absolutely motivated by challenge. He's a fully engaged, hands-on manager. Some people would turn their brains off when they heard his volume. But Microsoft is a big place, with a great deal of smart, fast-thinking, fast-moving people, and the human characteristics tend to take a backseat."

May 22, 1990, is one of the most important dates in Microsoft history. That day, Windows 3.0 was released; it would quickly sell almost three million copies. A decade later, during an interview with one of the better tech industry publications, *Fast Company,* Ballmer admitted that the products he had been calling "great" for many years were not-so-hot. He said, "Windows 1.0 wasn't a success. Windows 2.0 wasn't a success. It wasn't until we put out Windows 3.1 that we really had a big winner." *PC* magazine agrees. They wrote, "The great leap forward for Windows came in 1990. In May Microsoft introduced Windows 3.0, widely perceived as the first version of Windows that was ready for prime time. Technically, the major difference between Windows 3.0 and its earlier versions was that Windows 3.0 exploited [features of] Intel's 286 microprocessor, giving the environment access to 16 MB of memory. But additional factors were at work to make Windows 3.0 a success, and a critical mass had finally been reached: Windows was finally robust enough, hardware finally fast enough, and applications finally plentiful enough for Windows to be a full-time environment for most users.

"Windows 3.0 ran on top of DOS, so it offered compatibility with DOS programs. Although Windows 3.0 requires minor rewrites of just about every Windows program to date, there weren't many of them to be rewritten. Most important, almost as soon as Windows 3.0 was introduced, applications appeared, led by Microsoft's own applications division and followed by just about every other major developer." This is where Ballmer's support of the Developer Relations Group paid off. His constant recruiting convinced a talented manager, Brad Silverberg, to come aboard and take over the Windows 3.1 project, the fine-tuning of Windows 3.0. Windows 3.1 added better application integration—working better with the operating system—and more stability.

Microsoft came to dominate many more areas in computing as its Visual Basic and Visual C++ overcame big competition from Borland to dominate programming languages. And Microsoft's applications—led by its Office suite of Word, Excel, PowerPoint, and later Access—took much of the market for applications.

At the same time, Ballmer made a new friend while visiting an old one. Now serving on Country Day's board of trustees, Ballmer went back to Birmingham (a rezoning actually puts Country Day in Beverly Hills) and gave the graduation speech, talking about how good Harvard was for him and mentioning his Country Day teacher John Campbell. He also mentioned that the students should send him a résumé, if they felt like it. The prep school students were also an emerging personnel source and, again, "ya gots a hand in how they raised." By staying in the education flow, Ballmer would soon get wind of the wild popularity of the Internet on campus.

At Country Day, the basketball fanatic Ballmer met a parent who had a kid going there, the Detroit Pistons captain (and NBA most valuable player) Isaiah Thomas. Ballmer was attracted to not only his professional prowess, but to how devoted Thomas was to his mother (the subject of a book and made-for-TV movie). Ballmer later said that Thomas was a personal role model as an unselfish team player. The team Thomas captained set a league record for fouls called against them. They relished their nickname "The Bad Boys." Ballmer also talked with his former English teacher Beverly Hannett-Price. She asked him, point blank, "Steve, I've got an extra ten thousand dollars. Should I buy Microsoft?" Ballmer said, "No, it's too expensive. It's overpriced." (With just a touch of pain in her voice, she adds, "Do you know how much money I could have made?") She encountered Ballmer and Microsoft on a campaign to lower expectations about his company. Ballmer was voicing the beginning of what came to be called the beans-and-franks era. According to a former executive, "We were now a billion-dollar company, Windows was taking off, but neither Ballmer nor Gates nor anybody, for that matter, knew what was going to happen, how long it would last, what would come across the horizon and knock us out. It was time to cut expenses and economize, not have such an extravagant or at least as extensive a subsidized cafeteria. You know, push the beans and franks." What was on the horizon? A sun that would rise in the South.

Led by Starbucks, Seattle was becoming famous for coffee, a wonder when you consider that the nearest coffee beans are grown thousands of miles away. Over the horizon, down in Silicon Valley, Scott McNealy's Sun Microsystems was preparing to challenge the men behind the Microsoft curtain. He realized that, for Sun to thrive, he needed to create some sort of alternative to what he would call "the Beast from Redmond." McNealy was developing a revolutionary new way of approaching personal computers and their software. Borrowing a page from DEC computers, he convinced a twenty-five-year-old programmer, Patrick Naughton, to cobble together a small, swift, almost underground group free from some of the bureaucratic restraints, to develop a new line of "write once, run anywhere" software to compete directly with the king of coffee town. In an in-your-face move, they called the software Java.

In computerdom, when you've got a bright, bright guy who's getting tired and bored with the commercial side of the science and you fear losing him, you name him chief scientist. This is what Sun had done with their programmer extraordinaire Bill Joy. A few years before, Joy, who resembles the actor Tim Robbins, had convinced McNealy to help fund a research lab of a high-minded nature, akin to PARC. For the past few decades, the awkward name of Skunk Works, taken from a moonshine still in the comic strip Li'l Abner, was used for such a group. Joy's Skunk Works was set up in his Aspen, Colorado, stomping grounds. When Joy heard about Java, he became its biggest supporter and invited the group to Aspen, where they, as one code monkey says, "thunk and thunk."

While Sun was thinking about Microsoft, Steve Ballmer was thinking about his son. In 1992, over in Seattle, the newlywed Ballmers began fulfilling their Darwinian duties. Connie Ballmer gave birth to Samuel Ballmer, named after Steve's maternal grandfather, who had been such an influence on him back in Detroit. Bill Gates was the first nonrelative to see little Sam; Gates's fiancée, Microsoft program manager Melinda French, was the second. (In his typical warm way, Bill Gates had told a fellow Microsoftian that he considered babies "a subset.")

The same year, Ballmer was elected to the Harvard Board of Overseers, the governing body running the school. Ballmer was serving with people like Dan Morales, the attorney general of Texas, and a U.S. senator from Tennessee, Al Gore. (Morales ran against Ballmer for a committee chair. Morales won.) True to his Democratic roots, Ballmer publicly supported the Clinton-Gore ticket in the 1992 presidential election. He introduced fellow Harvard alum and overseer Gore at a fund-raiser he'd helped organize, and donated the thousand-dollar maximum individual contribution to the campaign. Furthermore, Ballmer wrote a letter to software execs in the Pacific Northwest cheerleading for Clinton-Gore and urging other executives to do the same. Ballmer denied that there was any connection between his support for Clinton-Gore and the Bush Administration's Federal Trade Commission (FTC) investigation of Microsoft. According to a family friend, Gates voted for the 1992 Clinton-Gore ticket as well. At the time, Microsoft had exactly one lobbyist in the other Washington—Kimberly Ellwanger—possibly the thinnest lobbying army of any billion-dollar American company. (One of Gore's daughters, Karenna, would come to Redmond and work for the on-line magazine *Slate,* after it was established in 1996.)

While staying true to his political roots, Ballmer also returned to his professional base, switching from overseeing systems software back to huckstering, his official title becoming executive vice president for sales and marketing. As the *Wall Street Journal* reported, he was "in charge of the eleven thousand employees who closed the deals and made the numbers that fueled Microsoft's growth" and "was concerned about losing touch with the tech side of the company." But Microsoft director Jon Shirley had told Ballmer that if he wanted to be president someday he had to take the sales job. In 1990 Shirley had retired as president (but stayed on the board), and was replaced by Mike Hallman, who lasted a little over a year. Microsoft's board knew that though Ballmer wanted the job, he wasn't seasoned enough to handle it. In a compromise of sorts, Microsoft created a three-member Office of the President, shared by Ballmer; the vice president now in charge of systems and applications, Mike Maples; and Frank Gaudette, who took care of finance, human resources, manufacturing, and distribution. Wall Street responded in the affirmative, kicking Microsoft stock up five dollars a share.

Now that he was again in charge of sales and marketing, Ballmer was in closest touch with the people who actually used Microsoft's products. Ballmer became obsessed with something he called "dollars per desktop" and had a worldview of Microsoft's markets. When interviewed by the *WSJ* he thundered, "Everything I do is global!" He developed what he called the "yellow book," a loose-leaf binder with results for Microsoft's over two dozen foreign subsidiaries. "Units! It's all about units!" Ballmer said, and it became evident he thought in terms of revenues per PC. Off the top of his head, Ballmer would later tell a reporter that Microsoft made about ninety dollars for every new computer sold in Brazil, thirty dollars in India, $135 in Australia and $110 in the U.S. Large corporate customers signed up for annual subscriptions at two hundred dollars per PC for all the software Microsoft would release, spending about eighty dollars per PC on Microsoft products for their thirty-three million computers. Small businesses, with roughly seventy million computers, spent about thirty dollars per PC. Home computer users spent only about ten dollars per PC on Microsoft software after purchasing their PCs. Gates wanted to lay the groundwork for customer subscriptions to a steady stream of upgrades. Gates's strategy was to turn "software into a utility, billed annually if not monthly." He wanted Windows to be the "digital nervous system" for the whole economy. Steve Ballmer intended to lead the charge to make international computerdom as dependent on Microsoft as possible. For some, the concept of hell would no longer be an abstraction.

CHAPTER EIGHT

PASSING GO

In 1987 Jerry Kaplan, a former Lotus executive who had founded a company named GO, had a idea to build a pen-based computer, something similar to what some years later would be called the Palm Pilot. Kaplan approached Bill Gates, who, after listening to Kaplan's presentation, said, "We have a choice. We can start to work with you now or play catch-up if it succeeds." Gates followed up, saying he wasn't interested in investing in GO but that he would have Jeff Raikes from the applications group contact him. In his book *Startup*, Kaplan relays, "After meeting with Gates, Jeff Raikes had called to begin exploring the possibility of building applications for our operating system. We negotiated a cooperative agreement in which he was to supply the people who would study our technology and evaluate the opportunity for Microsoft, and we would train them and provide technical support. The document read, 'Each party agrees to use the other party's confidential information only for the purpose of furthering this joint project. The participation of Microsoft and GO staff in joint design and implementation efforts will not create an interest or ownership on behalf of either party in the other's proprietary, confidential, or trade secret information.'" Raikes then reiterated the Chinese Wall policy so Kaplan needn't worry about GO's confidential information jumping from Microsoft's applications group to the operating systems group—which he saw as a potential competitor.

Microsoft assigned two people to work with GO, including "a talented young engineer named Lloyd Frink, who looked and acted like a junior Bill Gates." Frink took notes and spent many hours studying GO's documentation to understand how they went about things. A few weeks later, a GO executive briefed a larger group of the people in the applications division at Microsoft's headquarters. According to Kaplan, the GO executive was "thoroughly disgusted when he returned." He told Kaplan, "All they did was beat me up about why we should be using Windows [to operate the pen computer]." They insinuated that if GO didn't use Windows, Microsoft might do the application themselves. Microsoft never called GO to arrange a follow-up visit, and neither did GO.

Sometime later, Kaplan happened upon Gates and Ballmer at a Comdex convention, and they invited him to share their limousine. Kaplan says, "Ballmer looked a little embarrassed at this apparent extravagance. 'The hotel provides it for free,' he explained, 'because we rent so many rooms from them.' On the way there, to my surprise, Ballmer wasn't reticent about briefing Gates in my presence about what he learned from hanging around IBM's OS/2 booth. He listed, feature by feature and application by application, what worked and what didn't. 'They've done a better job than I would have guessed at getting Windows apps running,' he said, 'But I still contend that full Windows compatibility is virtually hopeless.' Gates agreed. 'It's only a matter of time until they can't keep up,' he said ominously.

"Ballmer turned his attention to me. 'I imagine you're going through the same things we did with IBM.'

" 'Probably.' I kept a poker face

" 'We were ultimately forced to make a hard decision,' Ballmer said. 'Whether to build the right product or do what they wanted. It was very emotional for us.'

"After a brief silence, Gates spoke up. 'I hear your system is quite bigger than you thought.' "

Kaplan says, "I was amazed that he knew this well-kept secret . . . virtually no one outside our shop knew of the problem, except for a few of our most important [Internet service providers]." As investigative author Scott Armstrong told me, "Microsoft has an incredible intelligence network, much of it coming from its clients because the company is so close to them."

After working over a year on Penpoint, Esther Dyson asked Kaplan to show it at her "Beyond the Desktop" computer conference in 1991. Dyson also asked Microsoft to show its application-in-progress, Pen Windows. As Kaplan sat in the audience, looking at the stage, he said to his seatmate, "It looks like Jeff Raikes, the guy who signed Microsoft's confidential cooperation agreement with us, is going to make their presentation." His seatmate looked up, then shook his head, saying, "But that's not the worst of it. Look at who's doing the demo." Sitting in front of them, about to demonstrate Microsoft's competitive entry into the pen computing market, was Lloyd Frink. Kaplan said, "So much for their Chinese Wall." Where was Ballmer in all this? As Wallace and Erickson reported, "Steve Ballmer was involved in every strategic move Gates made."

Kaplan felt that the audience knew that the incredible similarity between their demo and Microsoft's couldn't be a coincidence. He thought it had to be a premeditated attack. But virtually everyone in the audience depended on Microsoft in some way, shape, or form for their business and they weren't about to endanger themselves by being the first ones to cry foul. One observer told Kaplan, "You got fucked, plain and simple. They just figure that you don't have the wherewithal to go after them." Resistance is futile.

Soon afterward, the *New York Times* ran a piece in their business section calling into question the legality of Microsoft's business practices. Kaplan was accurately quoted for the piece when he said, "People should think twice before showing their confidential ideas to Microsoft." That got Bill Gates's attention. He called Kaplan and released his toxins. Kaplan was concerned that Gates would file a preemptive suit. But what could he do? As he noted in *Startup,* corporate law is designed for large companies—it protects only those with deep enough pockets to finance a protracted legal battle. Compared with Microsoft, "GO could barely afford the car fare to the courthouse." Kaplan knew that a lawsuit could tie him up "forever, with discovery requests, endless depositions, and baseless counterclaims." He felt that if GO so much as threatened to sue Microsoft, "it would rain lawyers in our offices like the plagues of Egypt." GO was later sold to AT&T.

Who would stand up to the Microsoft bully? That question was being debated at the Federal Trade Commission in Washington, which had received complaints about Microsoft's business practices. The FTC asked Jerry Kaplan to come to Washington and tell them what had happened. Microsoft confirmed that the company was under investigation. According to Wendy Goldman Rohm, Ballmer was questioned by the FTC about Microsoft's alleged use of "sneaky code" to disparage competing products. Yet it was another small company that would call Microsoft's bluff several months later.

In 1990 an enterprising company in Carlsbad, California,

named Stac Electronics created a program that would compact data on a hard drive, in essence doubling its usable space. On May 14, 1991, Stac received a patent for their "Data Compression Apparatus and Method." Naming their product Stacker, it became an immediate hit, on which *PC* magazine bestowed a 1991 technical excellence award at the fall Comdex convention.

Stac's president, Gary W. Clow, happened to run into Bill Gates at the conference. According to court records, Gates told Clow that Microsoft was considering including a data compression capability for the next release of MS-DOS, and he was interested in Stacker. Gates had Brad Chase, head of Microsoft's Group Products Division, contact Clow. They began negotiations. Chase repeatedly told Clow that he believed Stacker was the best data compression program in existence. Problem: Microsoft refused to pay Stac any royalties for incorporating Stacker into MS-DOS. In fact, Chase presented Clow with "a spreadsheet analysis purporting to detail the adverse impact of sales of Stacker in the event Microsoft and Stac failed to reach an agreement and Microsoft incorporated a different data compression utility in future versions of the MS-DOS operating system." This kind of negotiation had traditionally been done in the American West wearing a face mask and holding a pistol.

Wondering what was in the deal for Stac, Clow turned it down. Microsoft went ahead and incorporated a disk compression program, DoubleSpace, in their MS-DOS 6.0 release. As a developer, Stac needed a copy of the new release to have its application interface with the operating system. Microsoft delayed in getting Stac a copy. In late November of 1992, Chase contacted Clow and told him that Microsoft had discovered that it had "unwittingly" infringed on Stac's patent with DoubleSpace. Clow asked Chase to make a written licensing proposal for Stacker, and again requested an advance copy of the 6.0 release. Chase finally sent Stac a copy, along with a letter saying, "Don't worry about the patent stuff. We are just going to keep with our changed code which does not infringe [on Stac's patent]." When Stac's engineers had a chance to see Microsoft's DoubleSpace code it became clear that, surprise, surprise, Microsoft had, to be nice, infringed on Stac's patents; to be blunt, Microsoft had stolen their code. Clow lamented, "A lot of people make the analogy that competing with Bill Gates is like playing hardball. I'd say it's more like a knife fight." When he was head of systems software, Ballmer was responsible for any substantial changes to MS-DOS, such as adding DoubleSpace.

After the release of MS-DOS 6.0 Stac's revenues were cut in half, forcing it to lay off about forty of its two hundred employees. Given that some 85 percent of Stac's thirty-seven-million-dollar annual revenues came from Stacker, which retailed for between a hundred dollars and $150, Stac's only hope to remain in business was to sue. In January 1993, Stac filed suit in a San Jose federal court against Microsoft for patent infringement. Describing the case, journalists grew fond of using the term David and Goliath, with Goliath being one of the nicer names given Gates and Ballmer.

Gates took the stand and repeatedly claimed that Microsoft's programmers had not copied Stac's product. On February 23, 1994, the jury disagreed, and awarded Stac $120 million in damages; it also awarded Microsoft $12 million on a counterclaim against Stac. Microsoft immediately announced it would appeal, but had second thoughts and agreed to settle with Stac for $83 million—about a day's worth of Microsoft's revenue. Clow said, "We're a small, innovative, entrepreneurial company that invented a technology that turned out to be important to the industry. The money can't compensate for what happened to the company. I'm not sure it can establish the momentum we once had." Microsoft was forced to recall MS-DOS 6.0. Ballmer didn't have any public comment on the case, yet on March 16, 1994, Gates ripped off his microphone and stormed out of an interview with CBS journalist Connie Chung when she brought up Stac and Microsoft's reputation as a bully. Living up to that reputation, Gates shouted, "Connie, I just can't believe how fucking stupid you are!" before running away.

The success of Windows 3.0 and Windows 3.1 put Microsoft in the operating systems driver's seat, but the way they did business continued to stink up computerdom. In 1991 the FTC opened a formal investigation, in part because of the suspected collusion with IBM, in another part because of a complaint filed by Sun Microsystems. Sun produced powerful workstations—hardware and software for businesses. Given Microsoft's stranglehold on operating systems, Sun was unable to compete. Microsoft had implemented a scheme by which original equipment manufacturers (OEMs) like Dell and Compaq were required to pay a royalty to Microsoft for each unit they shipped, whether or not it operated with Windows. This became known as the Microsoft tax, and stifled anyone else from bringing another operating system to market.

Probably Microsoft's biggest challenger at the time was the Utah-based Novell computers, headed by Ray Noorda. Noorda and Novell had brought a competing system to market, an updated version of Gary Kildall's CP/M called DR-DOS. While Microsoft had a lock with OEMs, DR-DOS had started to surpass Windows in retail sales. Gates and Ballmer sniffed around DR-DOS. Ballmer invited Noorda to breakfast, where he claimed that they were interested in merging Novell with Microsoft. Noorda and Gates and Ballmer explored such a marriage before Microsoft suddenly pulled back. Pondering why Microsoft would come courting and then grow cold, Noorda came to believe that Gates and Ballmer simply wanted a closer look at DR-DOS so they could steal parts of it. This is when he called the dynamic duo "the Pearly Gates and the Em-balmer: one sets you up for heaven and the other prepares you for death." Gates and Ballmer reminded him of World War II. Noorda told Wendy Goldman

Rohm that he was convinced his mission in life was to stand up to "Gates's atrocities" and that he "could not get over the similarities between Gates's methods and the propaganda campaigns of the Third Reich." Gates wrote to Noorda that he was offended that Noorda would say that Microsoft had people "who are the equivalent of 'Hitler and Goebbels and Goering.'" Novell would sell DR-DOS to Caldera Corporation, which would later file a private antitrust suit against Microsoft.

Steve Ballmer's commitment to stay close to his schools paid off big in December 1993. While at Harvard for an overseers' meeting, the students Ballmer talked to were all abuzz about something called the Internet. Years before, Gates had dismissed cyberspace as not being all that important. Instead, Gates and Ballmer concentrated on making or utilizing compact discs with read-only memory or, as they came to be known, CD-ROMs. Returning to Seattle from Harvard, plopping down in front of his PC, Ballmer pounded out an e-mail to Gates and other top execs in a language closely resembling American English. About this thing he called the "greta internbet," Ballmer typed, "I sense an opportunity could/should someone look inot this i was at harbard talking to studnets Mon theya ll have a view of what would be cool lw ant to sell mail and chicago [Windows 95] somehow this way what think." So began Microsoft's exploration of what would become their next battleground. Microsoft's strategy for winning the Web would form the basis for the Department of Justice's antitrust suit several years later.

While Ballmer was writing about the internbet at harbard, a young, gifted programmer, Marc Andreessen, was getting ready to graduate from the University of Illinois. At Illinois, Andreessen had taken a part-time job, for $6.75 an hour, on a project that came to be called Mosaic, a software package that would comb the cyber data banks looking for whatever a user wanted. As time went on this would become known as a search engine. Within several months, Andreessen would hook up with a founder of the billion-dollar Silicon Graphics, Inc. (SGI), Jim Clark, who'd resigned from the company after growing tired of SGI's internal wars. Andreessen and Clark jointly established Netscape, its powerful search engine an outgrowth of Mosaic to the point that the University of Illinois threatened to sue. ("For what," Clark would remark, "taking knowledge with him? That's what you're supposed to do at college.")

According to author Paul Andrews, Ballmer "asked his sales staff to 'coordinate a drill-down on Netscape's browser revenues to understand where they make their money.'" Ballmer boasted to *Forbes* magazine "I've had my whole group of guys—finance, marketing, product development—here around this table. And we pore over [Netscape's] 10-K and financial statements. We know exactly where they make their money." Netscape's CEO Jim Barksdale responded, "Oh, he's the biggest bag of wind. I wish he'd tell me [where we make our money]!"

Microsoft's response to the Netscape threat was its usual "let's be partners/we're thinking about buying you" approach, which it had taken with Novell and others. At the same time, Microsoft was plotting to "cut off their air supply," as infamous testimony at the subsequent antitrust trial would reveal. The strategy was that, by integrating an Internet search engine into the Windows operating system, Microsoft would give its product away for free. But Microsoft would be in charge of how you entered the Internet, guiding you to as many Microsoft-friendly Web sites as possible. And Netscape would go broke. The technical term is bundling. If you want Windows, you have to take our search engine. Ballmer was well aware that IBM had been prevented from bundling and had signed a consent decree with the government promising not to. In fact, the move created the independent prepackaged software industry in 1968, eventually giving birth to companies such as Microsoft. Simply put, if you've got a monopoly in one area, you can't use that monopoly to force a consumer to buy another product in another area. What was Microsoft thinking? It was simply doing what it had always done, protect its raging revenue river, which by now was over ten billion dollars a year.

Though the FTC branch of the monopoly police had deadlocked against filing suit, the Department of Justice had taken up the case. For almost two years Microsoft worked with and around the DOJ to settle, Microsoft slowly chipping away at the charges until they hammered out an agreement. Among other things, Microsoft would stop charging the Microsoft tax to OEMs no matter what operating system the OEMs enclosed. But this wasn't much of a restriction now that they'd successfully stomped out almost all of their potential rivals. What Microsoft didn't count on was Federal Judge Stanley Sporkin.

Judge Sporkin had been randomly assigned the Microsoft and monopoly police case. He was limited to approving the consent decree required under the Tunney Act, created post-Watergate to get public comments on such cases to prevent too cozy of a settlement by regulators with whom the offenders were chummy. The act was prompted by the infamous Dita Beard memo, which detailed how ITT had donated four hundred thousand dollars to President Nixon's reelection campaign in return for the monopoly police overlooking some of ITT's shady actions. Sporkin's son-in-law recommended that he read a recent book called *Hard Drive* that described many of Microsoft's business practices. Sporkin was enraged at what he read, and demanded to know why the Justice Department hadn't looked into the charges of vaporware and the fictitious Chinese Wall that the authors, James Wallace and Jim Erickson, had fairly well proved. Anne Bingaman, head of the DOJ antitrust division at the time, pounded her fist on the prosecutor's table in Sporkin's courtroom, shouting, "I decide what makes out a winning case, and if I don't want to file it, nobody can make me!" Sporkin took Microsoft to task as well, saying they were "lawyers looking for loopholes," chiding one of their attorneys, "You can stand on your head. I cannot accept your word anymore. You have lost your credibility. This is a trusting judge but you've lost your credibility."

Sporkin wasn't about to rubber-stamp a settlement he thought was "simply telling [Microsoft] to go forth and sin no more" because it "does little or nothing to address the advantage it has already gained. If I approved this, the message would be that Microsoft is so powerful that neither the market nor the government is capable of dealing with all its monopolistic practices." Steve Ballmer closely followed the case, and was in the courthouse when Sporkin refused to sign off. He told reporters that the problem wasn't with his company, but that "the judge needed a brain."

Like a couple agreeing that their marriage counselor stunk, Microsoft and the monopoly police jointly petitioned the court of appeals to get rid of Sporkin. As it would five years later, and to the same court of appeals, Microsoft used a book as evidence. They claimed that Sporkin had been tainted by the book *Hard Drive*, about Gates and Microsoft. They attacked the messenger, not the message. And they won. A few months later, a three-judge federal panel kicked Sporkin off the case. They said Sporkin had contaminated the judicial process by considering *Hard Drive* in his decision, had tried to force the monopoly police into action, and had bad-mouthed Microsoft's lawyers. Microsoft had really pissed off Sporkin. Could it be that angering Sporkin was at the core of Microsoft's strategy? Is that what they'd planned? Recall that when Ballmer was at Stanford Business School it was often said that "it's better to know the judge than to know the law." One federal judge down, how many more to go?

Judge Thomas Penfield Jackson was randomly assigned to the case and, after a seventeen-minute hearing, signed off on the settlement. His timing was great. Three days later, computerdom felt the deluge—Windows 95 was released.

CHAPTER NINE

WINDOWS 95!

On January 1, 1994, the world's most eligible bachelor, Bill Gates, married his former co-worker Melinda French in Hawaii. (There are numerous reports that Gates dispatched Ballmer to have French sign a prenuptial agreement, which Gates and Ballmer have repeatedly denied and the now–Mrs. Bill Gates refuses to comment on.) Of course, Steve Ballmer was Bill Gates's best man. And Gates had decided that Ballmer was the best man to head up one of the most extensive marketing campaigns in American history, the release of Windows 95, a few days before Labor Day 1995. His strategy was brilliant. Working with a budget estimated at $250 million, more money than the health care lobby mustered at the same time to stifle reform, he focused on turning a press release into a news story, multiplying its advertising like fruit flies in a well-funded lab. It worked. As one participant said, "It was what God would have done to announce the Ten Commandments, if only he had Bill Gates's money."

One of Ballmer's tactics mimicked many small-town celebrations, with a Ferris wheel twirling above tents pitched on trim exhibitionist lawns, where twenty-five hundred people mingled and a band played and a clown jested. The only difference was that, at Microsoft's celebration, the band was the Rolling Stones, on tape, and the clown was Jay Leno, in person. It seemed everybody knew about Windows 95; the release was the lead story on newscasts nationwide. Microsoft was out to remake the computer world in its own image, and you'd better not get in its way.

But IBM got in Microsoft's way. As Garry Norris, IBM's primary negotiator with Microsoft in the mid-1990s, would later testify, IBM was pressured to stop shipping OS/2 and a series of business programs which competed with Microsoft as it was preparing to release Windows 95. In March, Gates sent an e-mail to Joachim Kempin, the top Microsoft exec in charge of OEMs, wondering if IBM's SmartSuite "should become an issue in our global relationship with IBM?" Kempin wrote back, "I am willing to do whatever it takes to kick them out." Kempin said that Microsoft's relationship with IBM as a computer maker "should be used to apply some pressure." IBM had bought Lotus and, on July 17, announced it would make the Lotus SmartSuite its primary desktop offering. On July 24, Gates called Norris, who says, "Gates was complaining about SmartSuite, the audit, and competing with OS/2." At the time an accounting firm was conducting an audit because IBM had underpaid Microsoft for software and both sides wanted to know how much IBM owed. Kempin told Norris that Microsoft would settle the underpayment problem if IBM would agree not to compete with SmartSuite for a while. IBM refused to stop shipping its own product. Microsoft responded by not supplying IBM the Windows 95 code until fifteen minutes before the August 24 release. As Norris testified, "We missed the initial spurt of demand, we missed the back-to-school season. And we were late to the Christmas market as well, which is our biggest quarter. It was hopeless for IBM to try and go it alone with its operating system. We would lose 70 percent to 90 percent of our volume. There was no place to go without Windows 95. We couldn't be in the PC business without it." Norris's primary Microsoft contact, Mark Barer, told him, "Where else are you going to go? This is the only game in town." In an interview with CNBC, Ballmer later said, "We didn't try to push out OS/2 in any sense in the negotiations we had with IBM."

What most of the world saw on August 24, 1995, was clips of Jay Leno bantering with Bill Gates as the Rolling Stones' "Start Me Up" played in the background. Microsoft paid the Stones a reported twelve million dollars to use the tune. On television, you saw and heard Leno and the Stones, interspaced with clips of the "midnight madness" news story Ballmer had created by encouraging computer stores to start selling Windows 95 at midnight. Checking out how well the "Midnight Madness" marketing was going, Ballmer rode around Seattle software outlets with Jeff Raikes in the latter's BMW with a tape of the Stones tune blaring in the Beemer's cassette deck. Ballmer said, "We spent all this money for this song, we might as well enjoy it!" As author David Kaplan wrote, "All this . . . for a $109 software upgrade (suggested retail price, prices may vary, some assembly required). The ballyhoo worked. In many stores, people stood in midnight lines to get their Windows 95. *Stood in line?* Wouldn't it be available the next day? . . . The Windows 95 show left little doubt that Microsoft could generate a tidal wave."

One Houston attorney, Charles Storer, got caught up in the hype, saying the midnight madness was "sort of a happening [and] someone who grew up in the sixties should be familiar with a happening." What was happening was an upgrade from the wildly successful Windows 3.1, which had sold many tens of millions. Microsoft kept saying that a new release would be out "soon" to fix some major problems Windows 3.1 had—mainly that, for some reason or another, the program would stop run-ning at times. To those lucky few unfamiliar with the stoppage, more commonly known as crashing, a user would suddenly find themselves looking at a frozen screen with an all-too-often virtu-ally indecipherable error message, commonly called the Blue Screen of Death. Like the original Windows, the upgrade was slow in coming, over six months past its first announced release date. Some people's financial lives depended on running Windows 95. Software developers coding Windows 95 applications needed it right away. Besides, many of the midnight shoppers were noc-turnal tech geeks. They were up and around anyway. But Microsoft made the news positive even though it was, yet again, way late with a delivery that many people depended on. Shortly after, when Scott McNealy found out that Bill and Melinda Gates were going to be parents, he quipped, "It's a good thing Melinda's going to deliver the baby, then it'll be on time."

By now, McNealy and company had released their revolu-tionary Java software with the hope that it would live up to the promise that you could "write once, run anywhere" (which it does much of the time). Developers could write an application using Java and have it run on Windows or Apple or almost any other operating system. By the time of the Windows 95 release, tens of thousands of programmers were using Java to write appli-cations. But for Java to really take hold, it needed to work well with Windows. With Microsoft's if-you-can't-beat-them-buy-them strategy, attorneys from Microsoft and Sun spent four months negotiating a licensing agreement. One of Sun's negotia-tors, Alan Baratz, says that Sun was operating "under the assump-tion that Microsoft is going to behave like a law-abiding corporate citizen, [so] licensing to them was and is the right thing to do." Sun's head attorney, Mike Morris, notes, "We went into this agreement with our eyes open. We wrote the agreement as tightly as we could." But Morris wondered, "Were we naive because we thought Microsoft would follow the contract?" The question would form the basis of a breach of contract lawsuit that Sun would file against Microsoft in federal court two years later, a month ahead of the feds' antitrust case.

Around the same time, Microsoft was facing some internal problems from employees who felt they were working on the uncomfortable side of right and wrong. One of the biggest and saddest jokes in corporate America are the four qualifying words accompanying many a financial report: generally accepted accounting principles (GAAP). In a recent example of the flexibility of GAAP, according to its accountants, Arthur Andersen, Enron was a sound company up until moments before it crashed. Journalist Rob Walker, writing about accounting and accountability in a so-titled article in Microsoft's own *Slate* magazine, detailed the hundreds of millions of dollars the top five American accounting firms would pay in settlements and fines for "cooking the books" around the turn of the millennium.

By now, Microsoft was, in a way, a prisoner of its tremendous success. Wall Street expected it to maintain its huge profits. For the past ten years of publicly reporting their profits, Microsoft's operating income had risen fast and steadily, from forty-one million dollars to over ten billion dollars. Its stock had already split five times. To paraphrase W. Somerset Maugham, only a mediocre company is always at its best, and the ebb and flow of commerce has to do with ebb and flow. Microsoft committed itself to smoothing out its financial statements by putting hundreds of millions of dollars on its books in reserve funds. Through various schemes, Microsoft would release these funds and call them profits—when it chose. Even with its phenomenal success, Microsoft was cooking the books, and some of its employees were looking and not at all liking what they saw.

One, Charles Pancerzewski, brought his concerns about this fudging to his boss, who promptly dismissed them; a little while later, the company dismissed Pancerzewski as well, even though his pre-complaint performance reviews had been excellent. Under federal law, anytime a company retaliates against a whistle-blower, the company is liable for specific damages. Pancerzewski sued. Once a Seattle judge ruled that there was enough evidence for the case to go ahead to trial, Microsoft settled. According to the Rainy City's alternative newspaper, the *Village Voice*–owned *Seattle Weekly*, Microsoft paid over four million dollars to make Pancerzewski go away, an amount that presumably wouldn't be paid out without the Office of the President, the trio to which Ballmer belonged, signing off on it.

While Ballmer and Microsoft would often be shown to intimidate people, usually rivals, Ballmer is well aware that his size and manner can put people off. Once, while twiddling a baseball bat in his hands at a company meeting, it came loose from his grip and flew across the room, rolling to a stop inches in front of a female employee. She stared at Ballmer and said, "It is a good thing that didn't hit me." As Ballmer often does when he unintentionally offends someone, he got a hurt-hound-dog look on his face. But sometimes Ballmer does hit people, sometimes accidentally, sometimes not. In a favorite story Ballmer tells, he was down in Columbia, talking to a group of customers, playfully throwing baseballs into the crowd. One of the hardballs bonked a customer on the head and knocked him out. According to Ballmer, "I begged, I pleaded, 'Bring that customer to life.'" The customer regained consciousness. Or, as Ballmer put it, hopefully in hyperbole, "And from the ashes he rose up again. And to this day, this is the most important thing that ever happened at Columbia in IT [information technology]." (Ballmer gave his victim a free copy of Microsoft Office.)

By now many Microsoftians were rich, and many were rich

with an attitude. By the late 1980s, the golden handcuffs started paying off. People were making, literally, millions of dollars as their stock options finally became theirs. More than a few Microsoftians took to wearing buttons with an abbreviation of "Fuck You! I'm Fully Vested!"—FYIFV. Says one rich, respected former Microsoft executive, "After working there five years, they were hooked. They were addicted. To the hours, to beating everyone else. They can't not work twelve-, fourteen-hour days." Another ex-exec says, "In human resource terms, the vested employees were called volunteers."

Within two months, Windows 95 sold over seven million copies. Within four years, with Ballmer as head of sales, Microsoft had sold many millions of copies of its operating systems, riding the crest of the huge explosion in personal computer use. Windows 95 was a mega hit, even though, as usual, it was late and didn't do everything Microsoft claimed it would. As with every Microsoft product, Windows 95 had its critics. A big gripe was that it wasn't totally compatible with all past Windows and MS-DOS programs, which was seen by some as a programmed obsolescence. Others complained that it wasn't easy to install, crashed too much, and needed a more powerful machine than they had to run well. One of the inventors of the Internet wondered why you had to stop a program by clicking on the Start button. Another user said, "The 95 in Windows 95 is the number of hours needed to install it, the percentage of existing Windows programs that won't run under it, or how many times it will crash in an hour." Microsoft had come to so dominate operating systems that, by 1995, there were few alternatives; Microsoft had some 90 percent of the market.

It was in Washington, D.C., that Windows 95 faced its most powerful critics. Responding to complaints, Ralph Nader and his associate James Love wrote President Clinton a letter asking him to prevent federal agencies from buying Windows 95 because

Microsoft had bundled Windows with its new Microsoft Network (MSN) Internet access, and that the Registration Wizard, an antipiracy feature programmed into the release to make it easier to register the program, actually provided Microsoft with information on files located on a customer's hard drive, a charge that would be echoed six years later with Windows XP. A few days prior to the Windows 95 release, the DOJ agreed not to seek a restraining order (a consent decree) preventing Microsoft from bundling Internet access with Windows. Little did they know, but the way Microsoft went about Internet access was, in part, by preventing other ways of getting to the Internet from working well on Microsoft software. It's as though Microsoft had gotten a contract to pave most of the American roads, and did so in a way that only the cars Microsoft made would ride best on it, if they could ride at all. The game theory Gates and Ballmer had learned at Harvard, increasing odds by decreasing competitors, was at work again, until the DOJ realized what was happening and brought suit two years later. More than a few critics would argue that the DOJ hadn't gone far enough. Bob Metcalfe openly wondered in a magazine column if and when the feds would charge Microsoft with racketeering, under the RICO act normally associated with the Mafia.

When Michael Kinsley headed out to work for Microsoft and establish its on-line magazine, *Slate*, *Newsweek* put his picture on its cover, with him wearing a yellow raincoat. Kinsley had graduated from Scott McNealy's Bloomfield Hills prep school, Cranbrook Academy, in 1968. After Harvard, he studied at Oxford University on a Rhodes Scholarship before getting a degree from Harvard Law School. A former editor of both *Harper's* and *The New Republic* and for seven years the liberal talking head on CNN's *Crossfire*, Kinsley spent five years as *Slate* editor before signing off to deal with his Parkinson's disease.

When Kinsley read that Microsoft was thinking about starting an on-line publication, he wrote Steve Ballmer, whom he knew slightly from Harvard, who passed the idea of him starting *Slate* around the food-for-thought chain. *The New Yorker* reported that Kinsley—known as a professional contrarian—showed up for the first day of work in Redmond wearing a Department of Justice baseball cap. Kinsley told me it was actually a Halloween party, and nobody thought the hat was funny.

In June 1996, Kinsley set up a *Slate*-sponsored on-line debate entitled "Does Microsoft Play Fair?" He called in a few Harvard guys he knew to give it their best shots. Among them were Steve Ballmer and James Fallows, a fellow Harvard graduate and Rhodes Scholar, who were joined by author and Microsoft critic James Gleick (who graduated from Harvard a year before Ballmer). They and a few other commentators went back and forth for a week in an intelligent, spirited, and dead-on accurate discussion about the good, the bad, and the ugly about Microsoft. According to *Slate*'s associate publisher, Jodi Sternoff, "*Slate* has not asked Steve to participate in any debates since then."

Economist Herbert Stein, the moderator of sorts, put five hard questions on the table that went to the core of what should be done about Microsoft, if anything. The panelists talked amongst themselves in cyberspace while the public listened in. Stein asked:

> *Can and does Microsoft use its present dominance to prevent the development of new and possibly better operating systems and applications?*
>
> *Does the method in which Microsoft licenses its operating systems to manufacturers keep other producers of operating systems from competing?*
>
> *Does the bundling of Microsoft applications with the Microsoft operating systems give these applications an advantage and inhibit the development of superior applications?*

Does Microsoft's dominance as a provider of operating sys-tems enable it to neglect the interest of consumers in the most efficient and reliable use of their equipment?

Is there a possibility that Microsoft's present position and resources will enable it to dominate the future world of com-munications as AT&T once did?

Ballmer dove right in, talking in a voice that sounds pasteur-ized. Checking his grammar and spelling, hitting the send button, Ballmer began by saying, "It's ironic in 1996 to see all these old questions about why Microsoft is 'too' successful being trotted out once again. We've spent much of the past year answering the opposite question: 'Can Microsoft even survive The Internet Tidal Wave? Microsoft software is very very popular with con-sumers. Some of our competitors say Microsoft is 'too' successful, and somehow we hurt the industry. Yet I can't think of any sector of the economy—not one—that is more competitive, dynamic and innovative than software for PCs. . . . All of *Slate*'s questions boil down to one: 'Who should determine success in the software industry? Millions of consumers making individual purchasing decisions? Or government regulators?' "

James Gleick said that he uses Microsoft Word, Microsoft Exchange, Internet Explorer, and Microsoft Excel, along with "a few non-Microsoft programs—Intuit's Quicken, for example, that hasn't been swallowed up, thanks to government intervention. . . . I've given up software from companies with fine toll-free support so that I can put on my blood pressure cuffs and enjoy Microsoft's notorious customer service—the (206) [area code telephone] numbers, the labyrinthine phone menus, the Orwellian-trained staff forbidden to admit the existence of Bug[s] . . .

"Why have I lain down before the steamroller from Redmond? Because life is short. Because I need all my software to work together. Because I need it to work with the software everyone else is using. Because there's really no choice. I'm a true believer in free-market economics. Once in a while, the Government has to find ways to protect free markets—that's what antitrust law is for. You may not have noticed, but competition has vanished in huge areas of the software business. There hasn't been a significant entry into (for example) word processing—not because the word processor has been perfected, but because Microsoft has locked up the space. In 1996 America, it's far easier to start an airline than a word-processing software company. . . . Does Microsoft play fair? No, of course not. It is known throughout the industry—and has been cited definitively by the Justice Department—for its unethical and sometimes illegal gamesmanship. . . . If you own the operating system that runs the world's PCs, and if you're allowed to leverage that power in entering new businesses, you have an advantage that the great monopolists of the 19th century could only dream of."

Ballmer ignored most of what Gleick said and responded, "Microsoft stands accused of making all its software products 'work together' and 'work with software everyone else is using.' Guilty as charged!

"Last time I checked that's what we're supposed to do. I want to pick up on Jim Gleick's point about customer support. Microsoft's customer support is the best in the industry. For two years running, Microsoft has won *PC World*'s World Class Award for Best Service and Support. No wonder, since wait times for customers are on average under a minute, and we spend more than $500 million on support to make sure we get you the right answers right away! . . . Windows is an open platform, based on published specifications, and Microsoft provides a lot of support for developers writing Windows applications."

Gleick struck back, "In fact, while Microsoft does publish huge amounts of information about how to make programs work with Windows, it also withholds much essential information, making it available only to inside programmers and to friends of Microsoft. It uses the information to make deals, doling it out in exchange for other specific benefits and services.

"Steve, when I interviewed you for my [*New York Times*] article 'Making Microsoft Safe for Capitalism' you made [it] clear that Windows was 'open' only as and when that suits Microsoft. You said, 'We could say hey, we're not publishing any APIs to our operating system. Or we could pick five guys and tell them what's in the operating system—we're not going to tell other people.' Do you support that view now? Or will Microsoft commit to a policy of true openness where the Windows operating system is concerned: agree to publish and document all its APIs, and to make the information freely available to outside programmers as soon as it is available to Microsoft's programmers? Not just sometimes-always?"

James Fallows entered the fray, writing, "To Steve Ballmer . . . I hope that the points you start with are official posturing rather than what you really think. To wit: 'Yet I can't think of any sector of the economy—not one—that is more competitive, dynamic and innovative than software for PCs.' What the fuss is about, of course, is not 'software for PCs' in general but 'operating systems software for PCs.' When it comes to operating systems, it is hard to think of another sector of the economy as dominated by one company's products as OS's are by Microsoft." Fallows went on to question Ballmer's contention that the debate boiled down to the question of who should determine the success of the software industry, millions of consumers or government regulators. "Donnez-moi un break, Steve. A few weeks ago I listened to Bill Gates beg for stiffer government action to penalize software pirates based in China. Suppose some Chinese buccaneer had stood up at the meeting to say, "All your complaints boil down to one question: Who should determine success in the software industry? Billions of consumers making individual purchasing decisions, buying their CDs for the equivalent of $4 US? Or government regulators trying to enforce unfair trade laws. I can't believe that someone as sophisticated as you can really believe" that government regulators are trying to make customers' purchasing decisions. "From Dick Armey, yes . . . or maybe a character in an Ayn Rand novel, but not someone who knows how the agreed-on rules of competition affect corporate strategy.

"Civilian competition of every sort involves rules. Adam Smith knew it. Teddy Roosevelt knew it. You know it. The question is not whether rules will exist, and it is of course not whether 'government regulators' are going to make purchasing decisions. It is whether the rules of the game now are the best ones for the vigor of business in the long run. . . . Roosevelt obviously loved the muscularity of competitive capitalism—but he also loved it best when those animal spirits were contained by certain rules. These rules preserved certain land for national parks (even though market forces would have dictated otherwise), they forbade companies to compete by hiring children and so on. TR would no doubt say 'Bully! Bully!' about the business you have created. But he would not have thought, as you are suggesting here, that therefore it was vulgar to even talk about competitive rules."

Fallows then brought up a disruptive personal experience he had using IBM's OS/2 operating system. He relayed, "I recall the charming way that whenever I load some kind of Microsoft application on my OS2 computer, it detects an alien operating system, warns me about the grave danger this creates to my computer, and helpfully offers to reformat my disk." Fallows rails less about the edge Microsoft has by owning the operating systems standard than about how it uses that edge to get ahead. He compares it to what would happen if President Bill Clinton controlled the distribution of money from the Federal Election Commission, that Clinton "might be tempted to see this as an edge—or at least his ambitious underlings would."

James Gleick pointed out that there are some benefits to having all software provided by a single company, that "Microsoft forestalls disorganization among hardware companies who cannot agree on standards. Redmond just tells them what to do. And it is correct to say that customers get value for their dollar in a rich feature-laden product like Windows 95. These benefits are genuine if slightly distasteful, like the advantages that come from totalitarian governments (In Singapore, the trains do run on time)."

Fallows noted, "To butter up Steve B for a moment, he is a good sport to participate in this kind of debate—you don't see comparative big shots from, say, R. J. Reynolds or AT&T going online to answer questions about their company." Fallows would later call Bill Gates the greatest American business strategist of the twentieth century. He says, "What made the company powerful and what should impress observers is the business vision of its leaders—in particular, the idea becoming the standard mattered more than anything else. Even before there was a VHS/Beta drama, Gates, Ballmer, et al. understood the importance of being VHS. They clearly did this for their company's benefit but it had an historic effect on the industry by creating a standard for [application] makers to use when programming.

"Weirdly, the public still seems not to get this. When they see Bill Gates they think of some Albert Einstein/Gary Kasparov counterpart. No doubt the guy is smart, but I contend that there are more people as smart as he is (in the IQ sense) than there are business strategists as capable and relentless."

Fallows relayed a personal anecdote: "At this moment, I am typing these words on a laptop using Win95. Did I choose this interface because I was convinced of its superiority over all alternatives? No. I 'chose' it because I HAD NO ALTERNATIVE. My old laptop blew up; I needed a new one . . . simply becoming the standard makes a lot of other 'quality' comparisons meaningless. Do millions of customers 'choose' the QWERTY keyboard above all alternatives? No—it's just there. Do I choose to fly USAir when I go from DC to Boston? No. There is literally no alternative. And so with DOS/WINDOWS. You can rightly use the 'millions of customers' as evidence of the brilliance of your business strategy. As evidence of the brilliance of the products themselves . . ."

Ballmer took after James Gleick. "Jim G., you need to go back and check your facts on the outcome of the DOJ investigation of Microsoft because every time you refer to it you get it wrong.

"Between 1990 and 1994, not one but two federal agencies exhaustively investigated the raft of competitors' complaints that you and Jim F. are dredging up once again. In the end, the FTC made no claim against Microsoft. The DOJ determined to challenge only certain narrow aspects of the way we licensed operating systems software to computer manufacturers. In fact, the DOJ specifically told the courts there were no grounds to file suit against Microsoft other than those contained in the resulting settlement. . . .

"Your claim that the DOJ 'proved the illegal tactics by which Microsoft killed the last remaining operating-system competition' is just flat-out false.

"First off, the DOJ didn't prove a thing. All it did was allege. . . . Second, the DOJ didn't even allege that the initial success of MS-DOS and Windows was due to any unlawful act. So what was all the fuss about? It's hard to say. We always said that the reason computer manufacturers pre-installed Windows on most of their machines was because most of their customers wanted to buy Windows machines (not because of particular contract language.) It isn't that complicated. So we made a business decision to settle with the DOJ, and modify our licensing practices in certain ways. We've been operating under that settlement for two years now. And guess what—customers still want Windows machines, and computer machines are still making them."

James Gleick set Ballmer in his sights. "Steve Ballmer wrote 'Jim G., you need to go back and check your facts . . .' Oh, no. You're not really going to dispute these facts, are you, Steve? OK, let's see: 'Between 1990 and 1994, not one but two federal agencies exhaustively investigated the raft of competitors' complaints that you and Jim F. are dredging up once again. In the end, the FTC made no claim against Microsoft.'

"To be precise the commissioners deadlocked on pursuing the FTC staff's recommendations; and the Justice Department took over the investigation. [You then go on to say] 'The DOJ determined to challenge only certain narrow aspects of the way we licensed operating systems software to computer manufacturers.'

"Your word is 'narrow'? Let's see . . . The DOJ determined, among other things, that Microsoft over a period of years had violated Sections 1 and 2 of the Sherman Antitrust Act, using (to quote from court papers) 'exclusionary and anti-competitive contracts to market its personal computer operating system software. By these contracts, Microsoft has unlawfully maintained its monopoly of personal computer operating systems and has unreasonably restrained trade.' In summary: 'illegal monopolization and unlawful restraint of trade. . . .'

"As I'm sure you recall, the U.S. District Court [Judge Sporkin] that should have approved this settlement found it distasteful and refused, stating, 'The picture that emerges from these proceedings is that the U.S. Government is either incapable or unwilling to deal effectively with a potential threat to this nation's economic well-being. It is clear to this Court that if it signs the decree presented to it, the message will be that Microsoft is so powerful that neither the market nor the Government is capable of dealing with all of its monopolistic practices.' An appellate court then approved the settlement. I won't waste more space on this. It's history and can't be undone. I hope you aren't giving us a preview of the *Encarta* version." The debate soon ended.

The *Encarta* Gleick referred to is an encyclopedia Microsoft purchased and changed, an example of what can happen when the company becomes a content provider. According to *The New Yorker*, "after Microsoft bought *Funk & Wagnall's* encyclopedia and turned it into *Encarta,* the entry on Bill Gates changed. The line that Bill Gates is 'known as a tough competitor who seems to value winning in a competitive environment over money' was changed to read 'known for his personal and corporate contributions to charity and educational organizations.'" In fact, if you use the on-line version of *Encarta* and type in the name Bill Gates, you still get this entry. As Orwell famously said, "He who controls the past, controls the future." If you type the name *Steve Ballmer* into the same version of *Encarta,* you have to look very closely to see that his entry is actually a handout from Microsoft's propagandists.

CHAPTER TEN

GRIEVING SON

April 1997 was one of Steve Ballmer's cruelest months, in what would be a tumultuous year for both him and Microsoft. As Microsoft negotiated with the Department of Justice over antitrust complaints, Ballmer was hit with personal tragedy: within a month both Fred and Bea Ballmer were diagnosed with lung cancer. Ballmer brought his parents out to Seattle so he could care for them and Microsoft, in that order. Bea went quickly. Steve took three months off, allowed under the Family Leave Act, but there's no doubt Gates gave his best friend all the time he needed to deal with the shock. Either Steve or his sister, Shelly, was at Bea's bedside in twelve-hour shifts for over two months at the University of Washington Medical Center. Bea died of a heart attack, as a consequence of her cancer, on the afternoon of April 20. Steve Ballmer was devastated. He gave a passionate eulogy while putting her to rest back in Detroit.

Says a former Microsoft exec, "Steve was real quiet for a while.

We knew something was wrong." Says another former employee familiar with the situation, "Ballmer wanted to quit. Gates talked him out of it, some say by promising him the presidency," a move many people considered a natural progression. Steve and Connie Ballmer built a house very close to theirs for Fred Ballmer. In addition to his lung cancer, Fred had almost totally lost his hearing. Shelly Ballmer had also moved to Seattle, and put aside part of her social work practice to care for her dad.

In August, commenting about Microsoft's market capitalization, Ballmer told the *Wall Street Journal,* "Is our company worth $180 billion? It's beyond my imagination spectrum. I don't think it's true. . . . This is a fine company and a fine business and we're doing a fine job. But we're maybe not worth $180 billion." Wall Street reacted accordingly, and the stock took a temporary dive. Steve Ballmer, husband of former Microsoft press flack Connie, was made well aware of the effect his public statements could have on the price of Microsoft's stock, if he wasn't already.

According to *Journal* reporter David Bank, Gates told aides there was little chance Ballmer would become CEO because the role of a CEO at a large software company simply required somebody with a deeper technical knowledge than Ballmer. But there was no doubt about Ballmer's organizational and operational skills. Since he joined the company Ballmer had tinkered constantly with Microsoft's organizational chart to get the right people working on the right things.

Six months after Bea Ballmer died and son Steve had returned from her Michigan funeral, his suburban Detroit schoolboy rival Scott McNealy would become even more of a thorn in Ballmer's side. In the first week of October, Sun Microsystems filed suit against Microsoft in the San Jose federal court, charging what McNealy had taken to calling "The Evil Empire" with breach of contract, trademark infringement, false advertising, unfair competition, and interference. It was Cranbrook against Country Day all over again, only with much higher stakes; the once-relatively-poor Country Day's now decabillionaire Ballmer and his $180 billion company against the former Cranbrook rich kid, now relatively poor, "only" a few hundred times a millionaire, and the fourteen-billion-dollar firm he headed. After filing suit, McNealy wrote an op-ed piece for the *Wall Street Journal,* arguing that Microsoft altered Java, then offered a "polluted version" to "subvert the growth of a new software industry that's not dependent on the Windows operating system." When using the Microsoft version of Java to write programs a developer would find that, surprise, surprise, many times they were only compatible with Windows.

In his usual way, Ballmer was still a behind-the-scenes guy, with Gates the company's public face and lightning rod. In fact, one ex-Microsoft exec told me, "Ballmer's management style can be summed up in three words: the hidden hand. He doesn't need to get the credit for a project, he's way beyond that. So he makes things happen with his hidden hand." And while Ballmer doesn't often make Microsoft's battles with competitors personal, with Sun and McNealy he would make an exception. Ballmer told *The New Yorker* about how "Sun is just a very dumb company," how "those sub-50 IQ people at Sun who believed we and Sun had this sort of wonderful dovetailing strategic interest are either uninformed, crazy, or sleeping." Ballmer went after the Cranbrook boy, saying, "It makes me mad at McNealy that he takes part in that kind of corporate character aspersion," and how McNealy "is monomaniacal about us. He's two standard deviations away from reality in what he says." Commenting on Sun and the suit, Ballmer went into typical Microsoft denial mode, saying, "Our goal in signing the contract was not to neutralize Java," but at the same time admitted, "We are not 'write once, run-anywhere' kind of guys." Internal Microsoft documents offered as evidence in the trial would show that Microsoft's strategy was, in fact, to "get control of" and "neutralize" Java, reminiscent of Netscape and the Chinese Wall fiction.

McNealy gave as good as he got, and took to calling the dynamic duo "Ballmer and Butt-head." When he testified before Congress the next year, McNealy quipped, "The only thing I'd rather own than Windows is English, because then I could charge you two hundred and forty-nine dollars for the right to speak it, and I could charge you an upgrade fee when I add new letters." McNealy calls Windows "a hairball" and once, during a presentation at the Moscone Center in San Francisco, he tried to get his dog to pee on a Microsoft logo he'd brought onstage. When *Forbes* ran a cover story on Ballmer many months later, McNealy told the *San Jose Mercury News,* "Ballmer is the reason Microsoft is so successful" and sent Ballmer a note saying, "Finally, credit where credit is due." But when John Heilemann asked McNealy how he felt about accusations from Microsoftians that he was on a religious anti-Microsoft crusade, McNealy said that "tells me that I'm getting through." Harking back to his days as a jock at Cranbrook, McNealy said, "In a hockey game, you try to get under the skin of the best players, to try and get them off their game. That's why, if you get booed in an opposing arena, it doesn't bother you—it charges you up. When Steve Ballmer says I'm wacko, I consider that a compliment."

Sun's suit against Microsoft would seemingly become only so much background noise when, two weeks later, on October 20, the Department of Justice filed suit in Washington, D.C., charging Microsoft with contempt of court for violating the 1995 consent decree that Judge Thomas Penfield Jackson had signed off on to end the earlier antitrust proceedings.

Bill Gates, the son of a prominent Seattle attorney, has always had an interest in the law. Kelly Corr, the attorney who represented Seattle Computer Products in its 1986 trial, was surprised that Gates showed up every day of the trial just to watch. It's been said that one of Microsoft's greatest strengths has always been its tightly written contracts. Beginning in the early eighties, author James Fallows would contact Ballmer for background information on a series of computer-related articles he scribed for *The Atlantic Monthly*. In 1986, Fallows wrote, "One of the reasons there is so much software piracy is that so many software developers are pirates." Fallows pointed to Microsoft's terms of sale, which are similar to those of some used cars. Its disclaimer specifically stated, "The program is provided 'as is,' without warranty of any kind. The entire risk as to the results and performance of the program is assumed by you." That its contracts also restricted competition is one of the main reasons the monopoly police went after Microsoft.

As Bob Metcalfe notes, "There are three monopolies in the computer industry—Cisco [on routers], Intel [on computer chips], and Microsoft. Only one of them has antitrust problems." Indeed, Cisco has an employee training video on how to comply with the law. And when the feds let Intel know they were investigating it for possible antitrust violations, Intel fully cooperated and made some slight changes in its operations. As Cameron Mhyrvold said, "Microsoft doesn't know a goddamned thing about how to deal with the government. Their problems came about because of the personality of Bill and Steve." Microsoft's trial strategy was simple. Deny, decry, and delay. Tell the big lie. Claim that it is not a monopoly, even though it's just fine to be a monopoly in American capitalism. Computer software itself is granted a monopoly, called a patent or copyright, so its creators or owners can profit from their labor or management. And, of course, there are public monopolies like water and sewers so we don't have the insanity of five or six sets of pipes laid in five or six sets of ditches dug to provide the same service. It's okay to be a monopoly. You just can't harm consumers. You can't stifle innovation, set a monopolist's price rather than a market price, demand that customers buy other products which they may not need to get an operating system, actively seek to unlawfully eliminate competition, and stuff like that. Yet the big lie was to never admit Microsoft was even a monopoly, let alone a good one. That's their story and they're sticking to it. And nobody told the big lie any better than Steve Ballmer.

Recall that Gates and Ballmer had discussed the Wonder Bread antitrust case twenty years before at Harvard, that Ballmer, like much of Detroit, was well aware of his father's employer, Ford, and its 1971 antitrust trial, that the section of the Nuremberg trials his now-ailing father worked for centered on antitrust, that Procter & Gamble was in an antitrust suit when he worked there, and that he was riding what he called the IBM bear when IBM settled its antitrust suit in 1982. Despite this history, Ballmer's big lie defense was tenacious ignorance. Even after seven years of litigation, during which nine federal judges had found Microsoft to be an unlawful monopoly, and it was in the courtroom of a tenth federal judge on the same charge, in August 2001 Ballmer told conferees in Brazil that "I still don't know what a monopoly is." As actor Kevin Spacey said in the film *American Beauty,* "Never underestimate the power of denial."

Ballmer told author John Heilemann that "Microsoft had had 'antitrust audits, antitrust training' since the mid-1980s. 'Now,' Ballmer said, 'do we train every Tom, Dick, and Harry in the company? No. But it's not every Tom, Dick, and Harry that's making the decisions.'" In dozens of interviews with current and former Microsoft executives, Heilemann found few who could recall having received antitrust training, and even fewer who remembered anything they'd been taught, beyond the vague instruction to "obey the law." But Microsoft doesn't obey well. Some think that Microsoft, like Richard Nixon, sometimes thinks that it is above the law. A few days after the Department of Justice filed its antitrust suit in 1998, Ballmer didn't help matters much when he stood onstage at a conference in San Jose for small-business owners and bellowed, "To hell with Janet Reno."

Steve Ballmer will never become secretary of state. The Defense Department couldn't afford it.

Before Ballmer's proclamation, Microsoft took its story into the same courtroom where Nixon's big lie had begun to unravel. Its lawyers told Judge Thomas Penfield Jackson that Microsoft couldn't follow his order not to bundle its Internet browser (Internet Explorer—IE) with Windows because it would break the operating system. We, the smartest, most sophisticated, most technically competent software company in the universe, can't figure out a way to remove the browser from Windows. A couple of days later, Judge Jackson ordered Microsoft into his courtroom, the same one in which the Watergate burglars had been convicted twenty-six years before. Jackson told the gathered mass a story. Since their last hearing, he had instructed a technician to run the "uninstall" process on Windows to try and make Internet Explorer go away. "Less than ninety seconds later," Jackson relayed, a message came up on the screen saying that IE was no longer operative yet Windows was functioning, in Jackson's words, "as flawlessly as before." He continued, "If the process is not that simple, I'd like to have it refuted by any evidence Microsoft wishes to introduce." Pause. Pause. Nine-months-pregnant-with-quadruplets pause. "I want to know whether to believe my eyes." Pause. Microsoft couldn't provide any evidence to prove Jackson wrong.

Not surprisingly, the press had a field day. Like Judge Sporkin, Judge Jackson didn't trust Microsoft. Could this have been the company's goal? On December 11, Jackson issued a preliminary injunction ordering Microsoft not to bundle Internet Explorer as a condition for licensing Windows. Stanford law professor and cyberspace guru Lawrence Lessig told author Ken Auletta that "Microsoft was convinced that Jackson was an idiot, and he's not." A Microsoft insider told him that Gates was acting like a kid who thinks he's smarter than the rest of the class. And during the ten hours in which Auletta interviewed Jackson, Jackson judged Microsoft's courtroom conduct as "very sophomoric, arrogant," that they were proud to operate outside of business norms, that "they didn't think they were regarded as adult members of the community," that "they don't act like grown-ups." Bob Metcalfe echoes that observation: "Gates and Ballmer are like huge teenage boys who don't know how big they've gotten, and they keep knocking things over." But there's at least one other explanation.

During Microsoft's courtroom machinations with the monopoly police, I was talking with a well-placed member of the Seattle bar. We were sitting on his classic forty-eight-foot wooden boat in Lake Washington, which was resplendent in several shining new coats of prime Dutch varnish, a spoil of his successful litigations against huge corporations. I mentioned to the lawyer that the press was really giving Microsoft a hard time for the apparently inept way it was running its antitrust defense. Did he think the press was right? The attorney looked me in my eyes and said, firmly, "No. [Microsoft's head lawyer] Bill Neukom is a smart guy. His strategy is to piss the judge off so that he'd make a reversible error. Then they'd have to start over again at square one."

Deny, decry, delay.

Microsoft denials are to be expected, and there are people who believe them. Microsoft's decrying often mimics Captain Renault in *Casablanca*, who is Shocked! Shocked! to find out gambling is going on at Rick's as he pockets his winnings. And Microsoft's frequently underhanded delays to avoid a final antitrust judgment brilliantly keep the raging revenue river running through Redmond racing on undammed—but not undamnable.

As has been widely reported, at one Microsoft board of directors meeting, Bill Gates broke down and cried. The philosopher Archimedes said, "The gods make mortals pay for arrogance with their tears."

On December 11, 1997, Judge Jackson ordered Microsoft to stop its practice of licensing Windows on the condition PC makers also license and install a Microsoft Internet browser software. Jackson was saying that you can't require a customer to take something they don't want. Bill Gates's response was, in effect, We'll break Windows. We'll give consumers a product that simply doesn't work. Given that angering the judge was Gates's strategy, it was brilliant, but Ballmer instantly realized the downside. He told the *Wall Street Journal*'s David Bank, "We're going to look terrible. We're going to look terrible. We're going to look terrible. . . . We agonized over that, looking bad." Bank reported, "Microsoft employees visiting home for the holidays were suddenly forced to defend the integrity of what had long been one of the country's most respected companies. 'It's very painful when you go home and your son asks, 'Daddy, why is the government suing Microsoft?'" said Anthony Bay, one Microsoft manager. "Ballmer acknowledged the damage: 'It left us in a position where a lot of people are questioning our company, whether it's a moral company, a proper company, [a] respectful company . . . the number of people enthusiastic about the company, the products, who would recommend, or would buy them, has clearly taken a dip. It's not cataclysmic. But it's clear.'" Ballmer was like Sancho Panza, dealing with the practical side of his Don Quixote. Ballmer would later take the breaking-Windows strategy even deeper.

With the monopoly police, many competitors, and more than a few customers pummeling the Napoleonic Bill Gates in various courts and the court of public opinion, he clearly needed help. Gates could relate to Napoleon when the emperor said, "Four hostile newspapers are more to be feared than a thousand bayonets." Gates was spending more and more mental time away from

Redmond. His attention was being diverted to other things, such as testifying before Congress. As he had for the past eighteen years, he turned to his Chauvin, his General Grant, Steve Ballmer, to get things done. No matter what his title, ever since Paul Allen resigned in 1983, Ballmer had been the number two guy at Microsoft. Or, as author Mark Leibovich writes, number one point five. As Gates would later say, Ballmer took on "about 20 percent" of his workload. Actually, it was a lot more.

On July 28, 1998, overlooking his spoken contempt for Janet Reno and the belief of some members that he was a loose cannon, Microsoft's board gave Ballmer what some say Gates promised him to stay on after Bea's death: the company presidency. Bea Ballmer would have been proud. According to board member Jon Shirley, it was Gates who cleared the way for Ballmer's promotion by making sure that each of the executives who would report to him was satisfied with the arrangement and by convincing the board that he could modify his behavior. Ballmer passed his worldwide sales and marketing vice presidency off to his longtime lieutenant Jeff Raikes.

While total sales were rising, Ballmer became aware of the simple fact that much of the American market was becoming saturated; foreign markets were where he needed to concentrate his energies; over 50 percent of Microsoft's sales now occurred outside of the United States. He spent two months of the year away from Connie & Sons (she had given Sam two brothers, Peter and Aaron) checking out Microsoft operations worldwide. According to the *Wall Street Journal,* on one European trip to review sales operations, he claimed to have put in 130 hours of work in 168 hours on the ground. As Microsoft's president, Ballmer would run the company while Gates ran the antitrust defense.

Ballmer was up to the task. Like any good general, he inventoried what he had to work with and went to the front lines to review his troops. He immediately scheduled one-on-one interviews with the top hundred of Microsoft's now thirty-five thousand employees, asking them what they thought was wrong with the company and how it could change. At the same time Ballmer became president, Windows 98 was launched. Though Ballmer kept saying in public that Windows 98 was "great," the internal buzz on the advantages of Windows 98 over Windows 95 was that it was "less shitty." The excremental nature of Windows 98 became a theme others both inside and outside the company would voice.

I was having drinks one evening with a former Microsoft programmer on his sailboat at Seattle's Shilshole Bay Marina. He was, in his words, "fully vested and free." Rummaging around the dock he came across a Windows 95 disk, laughed, and threw it overboard. When the disk rose to the top of the water and stayed there, he looked at me and deadpanned, "Shit floats." He then said, "Over three thousand programmers have worked on Windows. Can you imagine what a novel would read like if it had three thousand authors?" A wealthy ex-Microsoft exec expands on that thought. "Imagine," he says, "if you had three thousand authors working on a book. Now imagine that one writer would be in charge of all periods, another all commas, another all colons, another chapter headings, another first sentences, another closing sentences, another every 'and,' another every 'the,' ad infinitum. Now imagine this happening over fifteen years. It isn't the fact that Windows is so clumsy that's the story. The fact that it works at all is an unmitigated miracle." In fact, Ballmer looked at what he had inherited and was appalled. Before their release, Windows 2000 and its sister, Windows Millennium Edition (Windows ME) had grown like a self-inflating lifeboat to over forty million lines of code. He ordered it pared. When Windows ME was released, it had about twenty-nine million lines of code; the hectoring Scott McNealy would call it "Windows More Errors." Windows was Bill Gates's baby, the shrine to which Microsoftians had been trained to genuflect, the reason the sun rose every morning in Redmond. Yet Ballmer realized that Windows was becoming somewhat passé. He needed to revector the company. He saw Microsoft's future being tied to the "greta internbet." He invested his energies into developing his Internet-based strategy, called .Net.

The ensuing internal struggle over .Net versus Windows would see Microsoftians break into two camps: "Bill guys" and "Steve guys." As author David Bank relayed in *Breaking Windows*, "Like Gates, Bill guys are apt to want to do everything without trade-offs. Like Ballmer, Steve guys think they know how to prioritize ruthlessly and sacrifice the non-essentials. Bill guys think winning is mostly about strategy. Steve guys rely more on operational execution. Gates's favorites tend toward technical absolutism. Ballmer loyalists are likely to be more savvy about revenues, marketing, and customer concerns."

Ballmer also worked yet again to rally the troops. Not everybody who got the pitch was pleased. One, Chief Technological Officer Nathan Mhyrvold, decided it was time to take a break. The older brother of Developer Relations Group head Cameron Mhyrvold, Nathan had a Ph.D. from Princeton, his dissertation involving plasma physics, and had studied under Stephen Hawking at Cambridge before establishing a software company in Berkeley that Microsoft bought in 1986. The Mhyrvold brothers came along in the deal. But after working at Microsoft for a dozen years, Nathan Mhyrvold had grown tired. Rather than outright quit, he decided to take a year-long sabbatical and follow his hobby of digging up dinosaur bones. Ballmer said, "If a guy wants to go study paleontology, that's what he should do." More than a few Microsoftians were deciding it was time to leave, a trickle that, within a year, would turn into a flood.

Ballmer had taken the job before the monopoly police of the

feds and those of twenty states had filed a broad antitrust suit against Microsoft in Washington, D.C. As Ken Auletta reported, the Department of Justice charged that Microsoft broke the law in two ways. First, it was a monopoly that tried to crush or coerce competitors and sometimes allies, thus harming consumers. Next, Microsoft tried to preserve its Windows monopoly and to use this as leverage to enter and control new markets, thus harming competition. Joel Klein, the head of DOJ's antitrust division, said, "What cannot be tolerated—and what the antitrust laws forbid—is the barrage of illegal, anticompetitive practices that Microsoft used to destroy its rivals and to avoid competition." Ballmer had managed to avoid testifying at the previous Microsoft trials; that was Gates's job. But as president, he knew he would be called by the monopoly police to swear under oath what had happened. Surprisingly, in the millions of pages of documents the Justice Department obtained during discovery, there was nary a Ballmer memo that could be used by the Department of Justice against the company. (In a private antitrust case in 2000, a former Microsoft executive testified that, like Nixon's White House and later Enron's Arthur Andersen, more than a few company executives' e-mails had been destroyed.) The Department of Justice was already complaining that Microsoft's execs "claimed an astonishing lack of recall" during the depositions they gave. Ballmer responded to his impending deposition with humor. When tech writer Steve Hamm asked him what he planned to say, Ballmer told him he would take his cue from Sergeant Schultz of the 1960s sitcom *Hogan's Heroes* and, in a fake German accent, said, "I see nothing! I know nothing!"

The affable Ballmer's well-developed sense of humor is one of the reasons many of his subordinates, and even some of his critics, have good things to say about him. Sometime during the 1980s more than a few Microsoftians let off steam by throwing Nerf balls around, to the point that the halls seemed to be, as one observer noted, invaded with Star Trek Tribbles. Ballmer put his foot down and banned the balls before heading off on one of his journeys. While he was gone, the Tribble defenders built a fake wall several inches away from the glass in Ballmer's office and filled it with Nerf balls. When Ballmer returned and saw the display, he let out what listeners call the loudest laugh they ever heard. In November 1988, on a dare, he swam across one of the artificial ponds on campus. And in 1997, he and Gates spoofed a Volkswagen television ad by driving around in, reportedly, a Ford, because Ballmer had refused to get into a foreign car, and picking up a Sun Microsystems workstation from the side of the road only to throw it out after they noticed a stench. (Microsoft's propaganda department was unable to find a copy of the video when asked.) Ken Wasch, executive director of the Software Publishers Association, of which Microsoft was a member until it realized the SPA wouldn't march to the Microsoft drummer, says, "I find Ballmer refreshing. There's a joy and love of life about him."

But Ballmer's downright ornery side would sometimes take control. When he found out that Pacific Bell had made a deal to distribute rival Netscape's browser rather that Microsoft's, he shouted at Pacific Bell's CEO, David Dorman, "You're either a friend or foe, and you're the enemy now!" Just as one treats a playground bully, Dorman stood up to Ballmer and scolded him, reminding him that Pacific Bell had some thirty-four thousand PCs running on Windows. Ballmer backed down. Around the same time, a temporary Microsoft employee was having a snack in a break room when, she told me, "This big, mad-acting guy came in and started banging pans around because he couldn't find something. It was scary. The guy was deranged. I was going to call security until someone told me the guy was the company president, Steve Ballmer." That employee was better off than a permanent Microsoftian whose office Ballmer ran into, shouting, "You fucking idiot! How could you make [such a] fuckin' stupid decision?! What the fuck were you thinking?!" The employee quit, and founded a successful Web site. According to the cure for insomnia called Microsoft's official history, *Microsoft: Inside and Out,* Jeff Raikes is quoted as rationalizing that Ballmer would shout, "How could you make such a so-and-so decision" because he liked his employees.

Three months into his presidency, on October 19, 1998, the antitrust trial began in Washington, D.C. *Business Week* would name two books about the trial, Ken Auletta's *World War 3.0* and John Heilemann's *Pride Before the Fall,* among its top ten books of 2001; either book is worth reading for an in-depth, blow-by-blow account of how Microsoft successfully carried out its plan to anger Judge Jackson, though neither author mentions that strategy. How did the trial affect Steve Ballmer? Just as important, how did Steve Ballmer affect the trial?

Ballmer's "to hell with Janet Reno" statement certainly did not sit well with either the monopoly police or Judge Jackson, though it played just fine on campus. Says one Microsoftian, "Many of us were thinking exactly what Steve said. After her Waco debacle, and especially the Ruby Ridge murders, Reno wasn't the most popular person around Seattle to begin with. Most of us just wanted to write cool code. The word came down to watch what you wrote in e-mails, to watch what you said to the press, to clear all press contacts with the PR department. The company line was that the trial was 'white noise.' " Yet Microsoftians were very concerned about the trial, and it consumed more than a little of their verbal intercourse. As evinced by the Windows 95 blitz, one of Microsoft's strengths is its public relations machine. Yet Ken Auletta reported, "For a prominent, powerful company in the throes of a life-threatening lawsuit, Microsoft could be surprisingly inept in its dealings with reporters. Bill Gates or Steve Ballmer would decide not to talk to certain reporters, perceived as critical (as opposed to avowed enemies)." Auletta noted that Microsoft kept dossiers "much like a raw FBI file" on reporters. Auletta gained a copy of his file. Auletta told me, "My sense from reading the dossier that Microsoft compiled on me was that it was like many FBI files in that it was filled with gossip and hearsay. I did not sense at all that it involved a serious investigation because the information was comically wrong."

CHAPTER ELEVEN

THE TRIAL

Since October 19, 1998, when the federal antitrust trial began in Washington, D.C., it's easy to picture Steve Ballmer sitting in front of the *New York Times*, singing the Beatles' lyric "I read the news today, oh boy." Ballmer likes to sing Top 40 songs, and it seemed that one of Microsoft's documented dirty deeds after another kept exploding onto the front pages worldwide. The *Washington Post* would term Microsoft's bullying "corporate thuggery." In his book, *Pride Before the Fall*, John Heilemann reported that, while testifying, one Microsoftian, Dan Rosen, "uttered such patent falsehoods that [government lead attorney David] Boies felt no compunction about calling him a liar outright." Another Microsoft witness, Senior Vice President Bob Muglia, "prattled on so incessantly and nonsensically that . . . he drove Judge Jackson into a blind rage." Jackson shouted, "No, no, stop!" and took a ten-minute recess. A third Microsoft witness, MIT economist Richard Schmalensee, said, "To be honest with you, Microsoft's internal accounting systems do not always rise to the level of sophistication one might expect from a firm as successful as it is. They record operating system sales by hand on sheets of paper."

At the outset of the antitrust trial, some observers estimated that it would take about six weeks. Yet Microsoft's delaying tactics—challenging every possible point, and not admitting that they were even a good monopoly—would extend the trial for over a year. Many of Microsoft's witnesses followed Gates's lead when he seemed to purposely confuse even simple questions. In one exchange with David Boies Gates was asked if he had typed "Importance High" at the top of an e-mail. "No," responded Gates.

"No?"

"No, I didn't type that."

"Then who did?"

"A computer."

"A computer. Why did the computer type in 'High'?"

"It's an attribute of the e-mail."

"And who sets the attribute of the e-mail?"

"Usually the sender sets that attribute."

"Who is the sender here, Mr. Gates?"

"In this case, it appears I'm the sender."

"Yes. And so you're the one who set the high designation of importance, right, sir?"

"It appears that I did."

Over the year of the trial, just about the only major point Microsoft would win was when Judge Jackson found that, because the Netscape browser was still available, Microsoft wasn't guilty of "exclusive dealings." Ken Auletta wrote, "It was as if Microsoft, down 20 to 0 in the ninth inning, sent a batter to the plate who then smacked a home run."

Just as fellow federal judge Harold Greene had done in the same courthouse with the AT&T antitrust case nineteen years before, Judge Jackson repeatedly attempted to get the parties to settle; he would eventually appoint a mediator, Richard Posner, to work at that goal. Some people close to the settlement talks have said that they were not only another delaying tactic, but a way for Microsoft to ferret out what evidence the government had against it. In Seattle, Ballmer had to deal with the fallout from the on-going trial. The employee hemorrhaging continued. Indeed, Cameron Mhyrvold, one of the Microsoftians who testified, was said to have walked off the stand and out of both the courtroom and Microsoft. Mhyrvold joined a Belleview, Washington, venture capital firm, Ignition Corporation, along with a few other ex-Microsoftians, what one computer executive calls "The Billionaire Ex-Microsoft Boys' Club."

As part of its broad case against Microsoft, the Department of Justice had included Scott McNealy's charge that Microsoft had altered Java so that its version would only run on Windows, tanking its "write once, run anywhere" concept. One internal memo showed that a powerful group at Microsoft considered Java's "cross-platform issue a disease within Microsoft." Two of Sun's executives testified at the trial. But the real question was, Where was the normally quite vocal McNealy? In fact, when the government concentrated on the remedy phase of the trial—what to do to curb Microsoft's illegal behavior—many in Silicon Valley acted out the venerable story about the Lone Ranger explaining his plan of attack to Tonto, only to have his sidekick reply, "What you mean 'we,' kemosabe?" Testifying against Microsoft might tend to raise the ire of the unsleeping giant. (*Los Angeles Times* syndicated political cartoonist Jeff Danziger drew a cartoon showing an attorney sitting in a Department of Justice office, saying, "My client agrees to testify against Microsoft . . . if you can put him in a witness relocation program.") But a huge stage was set for Scott McNealy, who has a son named Maverick, to literally take the stand against what he called the Evil Empire, the Beast from Red-mond. McNealy could be like Gary Cooper in the film *High Noon*, or Luke Skywalker in *Star Wars*. Finally, rather than simply hamming it up for customers or mugging for the press, the trash-talking Cranbrook boy would have his day in court against the company run by his prep school rival. And it would take place on the largest media stage possible. He could make his biggest impact ever. McNealy strapped on his legal pistols, pulled himself up to his full six-foot-two-inch build, stood tall, looked toward the shoot-out at the Microsoft-is-not-okay corral, soaked in the lay of the lawyerland, took stock of the courtroom gulch, stared the predatory monopolist in the eye, and blinked. Rather than walk the walk after talking the talk, he balked and balked. McNealy backed down.

"What the fuck are you talking about!" Sun's head lawyer, Mike Morris, screamed at McNealy when he saw his client's uncharacteristic silence. "We've been over this a million times! Our position is public!" One observer told John Heilemann that "Scott had himself a little epiphany. Today, Microsoft is the number one operating system company and Sun is the clear number two. But if Microsoft is broken into three operating system companies, Sun immediately drops to number four. And if Microsoft is broken into six operating system companies, Jesus, Sun falls into seventh. The more McNealy thought about it, the more keeping Microsoft in one piece seemed like a pretty good idea to him."

Throughout the yearlong wrangling, the Department of Justice would play excerpts from the twenty hours of videotaped deposition Bill Gates had given earlier in Redmond. Recall that Gates had eagerly taken the stand at many other Microsoft trials, including the Stac Electronics and Seattle Computer Products suits. But Gates didn't take the stand in Washington. Why? Says one San Francisco–based corporate trial lawyer, who went to Harvard with

Gates and Ballmer, "Gates is what lawyers call a 'bad client.' [We] often use the term 'bad client' (other than one that doesn't pay) to mean a client that can't be prepared, that doesn't listen to the lawyer's advice, and that thinks he's smarter than all the lawyers on both sides of the case; someone who doesn't have at least a little respect for the opponent, or at least the opponent's ability to make him look bad. From the outside, Gates looked like a bad client.

"I find it hard to believe that Microsoft's lawyers could have prepared Gates to give videotaped testimony that was so bad. There is always the possibility that Gates's lawyers screwed it up, because they seemed to be surprised, over and over, by David Boies. Of course, Boies is a phenomenal lawyer, and every bit Gates's equal in smarts, if not his superior." The attorney continues, "A bad client in this sense presents tremendous risks in litigation and trial, because a good lawyer on the other side can use the overconfidence (and lack of preparation) to trip him up, get harmful admissions, and simply [like Boies did with Gates] make him look evasive and not credible. If you can't be sure what the bad client will do or say, it's often better to try to settle."

Gates would later brag to the *Washington Post* that the government didn't even call him as a witness. "Why," says the same attorney, "would the government call Gates as a witness? He could only have done better than he had done in the videotaped deposition. A deposition of a party can be freely used at trial, so the government did exactly the right thing by using the most embarrassing and damning excerpts. Of course, Microsoft could have called him as a witness. Its failure to do so suggests to me that its lawyers either feared what might happen, or that they didn't want to give the government's case credibility by calling in the big guy, or that it would have made it more difficult to complain about the result—or all of the above."

While Judge Jackson considered the case, Steve Ballmer flew with his family to Boston to dedicate the twenty-five-million-dollar Maxwell Dworkin computer center he and Gates had donated to Harvard. On the way he stopped by Detroit to pick up his aunt Olga and uncle Irving Dworkin and two of his cousins. Fred Ballmer was too sick to attend. Gates, presumably concentrating on the trial, sent his father in his stead. Says Olga Dworkin, "Steve and Bill spend time on one thing, then go on. They debated back and forth over whether to put a hyphen in the name of the computer center, couldn't reach a decision, and so it went without [the hyphen]." Olga Dworkin laughs when she says, "Steve is so focused that when he and Connie and the kids returned to Seattle, they found that the lights were out in their house. They went downstairs and checked the circuit breakers, which were all in place. A few minutes later they realized they hadn't paid the electric bill."

Steve Ballmer's philanthropy is modest, at best. There isn't a Ballmer foundation akin to Gates's and the company line is that he makes his donations anonymously. Surprisingly, Gilda's Club, the cancer support groups set up around the country that were named after his second cousin Gilda Radner, couldn't provide a record of a Ballmer contribution, though Olga Dworkin volunteers with the club's Detroit branch. Ballmer told *Newsweek*, "I'd made a gift to our class at Harvard before Bill and I did [Maxwell Dworkin] together. But I'd done it completely anonymously because I'm embarrassed. It just seems so wild. I've got a job. I've got kids. We live a normal life. The notion that you run around giving away money . . . I enjoy doing it but at the same time, I really don't enjoy all the fallout from it. But at the end of the day, both [Bill and I] have more money than anybody ought to have or certainly can ever spend." Gates interjects, "Or that would be helpful to your children to pass along to them." Ballmer picks up the thought, "Yeah, that's not exactly a productive chain. If you pass it along to them, you want it to be when they get to be super-old so that they don't get screwed up in advance."

Ballmer does work to ensure that his family lives as normal a life as possible for a decabillionaire. The Ballmers live in a relatively modest house, the children go to public schools, they don't own a yacht, and they drive Ford cars (Steve, a red Lincoln Continental, sans chauffeur). Of course, there are security systems in place in their home, including what's termed a "safe room," where they can run to if they are threatened.

Whatever pains Ballmer, and to a lesser extent Gates, take to have a normal life in their billionairehood were shaken up two weeks after the Maxwell Dworkin building was dedicated. On November 5, 1999, Judge Jackson made the unusual move of handing down his stinging 207-page, 421-paragraph findings of fact in the case. Jackson hoped both sides would see what his ruling would probably be, and work to settle. Microsoft lost, and lost badly, on virtually every point. (The findings of fact, as well as Bill Gates's deposition and many other trial documents and exhibits, can be found on the Web sites of either microsoft.com or the Department of Justice, doj.gov). Ballmer would later say that in the days after the release he felt "under siege." No wonder.

Jackson wrote, "Viewed together, three main facts indicate that Microsoft enjoys monopoly power. First, Microsoft's share of the market for Intel-compatible PC operating systems is extremely large [95 percent]. . . . Second, Microsoft's dominant market share is protected by a high applications barrier to entry. Third, and largely as a result of that barrier, Microsoft's customers lack a commercially viable alternative to Windows." Jackson listed numerous demonstrations of Microsoft's predatory tactics, including giving away its Internet Explorer to cut Netscape off at the knees and forcing original equipment manufacturers like Dell and Compaq to use Microsoft icons on the all-important start-up page, not allowing these OEMs to offer either an operating-system-free or Internet-access-free computer so that consumers could purchase their choice rather than being forced to buy Microsoft's products. Jackson cited an internal Microsoft study which showed that Microsoft could have made healthy profits by charging consumers forty-nine dollars to upgrade their system from Windows 95 to Windows 98 but instead forced the "revenue-maximizing price" of eighty-nine dollars on them, another clear indication of its monopoly. Being an income statement guy, Ballmer was far more interested in the short run, in keeping that raging revenue river running through Redmond. Jackson found that if a personal computer owner was happy with his or her operating system but bought a new computer, they couldn't transfer the operating system they had. Nor could one purchase a computer without any operating system. This is somewhat similar to being forced to buy new CDs every time you buy a new CD player. Then Judge Jackson relayed the facts he'd found concerning the king of the coffee town's brewing of Java.

Jackson found that Microsoft had sabotaged Sun's system, that "incompatibility was the intended result of Microsoft's efforts," noting that a tool developers needed in order to have Java work best on a non-Windows platform was hidden in an obscure location on Microsoft's developer Web site and not listed in the site's index. As Jackson noted, "a Microsoft employee wrote to his approving manager, 'They'll have to stumble across [the needed tool] to know it's there. . . . I'd say it's pretty buried.'" Jackson detailed how Gates pressured Intel and others to use the Java which Microsoft had altered to work only on Windows, and various other underhanded ways they worked to undermine the "write once, run anywhere" promise Java offered. It was a slam dunk.

Life looked rather bleak in Seattle. The wet season had started, when Seattleites would endure over one hundred straight days of measurable precipitation, but it was Judge Jackson, not Mother Nature, who would rain the most on Microsoft's profit parade, though not immediately. The next month Microsoft's stock would reach a recent-record $119.75 per share. With 5.5 billion shares outstanding, Microsoft's market capitalization (market cap) would reach over six hundred billion dollars. Microsoft was worth the equivalent of a hundred dollar bill held by every one of us six billion people currently living on earth, or six bucks for every one of the estimated hundred billion human beings who've ever lived. For the next year, both Microsoft's market cap and profits would slide down a slope that Ballmer, to his immense credit, would be up to the Herculean task of stopping.

As one co-worker says, Steve Ballmer "likes guys who get shit done." *Shippers* is his term. Thinking was nice, and needed, but doing was what mattered most. The Steve "guys" had realized that for Microsoft to stay competitive, they needed an Internet-based product, what would become the Net program. Ballmer yet again reorganized the company by creating the Business Leadership Group, a dozen top executives who got together weekly to mull over strategy. James Fallows later noted something that his friend Steve Ballmer had known for many years. In Fallows's first-person *Atlantic Monthly* article, "Inside the Leviathan," he said that the company understood exactly who their most important customers were, that their revenue river ran from the business applications of Windows and Office—everything else, be it Hotmail, Flight Simulator, *Slate*, MSNBC, mice and keyboards, Expedia, or Encarta, is "financially meaningless." Microsoft's target market "is large-sized organizations ('LORGs' in tech speak) which might buy thousands of copies of Office or Windows at hundreds of dollars apiece."

The Borg concentrates on the LORGs.

To better concentrate on the LORGs, Ballmer changed the organizational chart into five groups organized around customers' needs, showing another of Microsoft's strengths, its flexibility. As one Microsoft manager told me, "The people I hire will probably not be doing the job I hired them for within six months. So I look for broadband people, who are both wide and deep in their knowledge and abilities, multitaskers. It matters far less to me where they went to college or how unbelievably smart they are than how quickly they can brake and turn and reverse, and then floor it when a shipping date is near."

While he still publicly championed Windows, Ballmer privately realized that it was the Internet, not the desktop, that would rule the future. Yet his best friend was married to a Windows-based strategy—Windows Everywhere, it was called. How could Ballmer be loyal to Gates at the same time that he realized that Gates's vision was guiding the company on a collision course with reality? And how would Ballmer deal with the fact that Judge Jackson might very well accept the government's recommendation and order the company he loved broken up? If you're supersalesman Steve Ballmer, the solution was simple. By promoting the concept that Internet-based services were the future, and moving the company in that direction, the thing Gates and Ballmer feared most—the breakup—would not be necessary. After all, if their monopoly wasn't fixed, why break it?

To that end, Ballmer wrapped his hopes and his dreams, as well as those of his company, around what came to be known as "Dot Net." Under .Net, software wasn't going to be prepackaged, it was going to be a service, like cable or the telephone. But under Ballmer's strategy, rather than sell you millions of lines of code all at once and leave it at that, with .Net Microsoft would, in essence, rent you its software, with constant upgrades. Microsoft had set the PC operating systems standard, had conquered the GUI, and had taken away Netscape's air supply. .Net was the fourth big bet that Microsoft would make, but the first under the nongambler Ballmer. .Net wouldn't be detailed to the public until June 2000.

CHAPTER TWELVE

THE AVALANCHE

Thursday, September 23, 1999, began as a usual rainy Seattle morning. The fifty-degree drizzle muted the horn of the commuter ferry from Bainbridge Island, announcing its 9:10 A.M. arrival at the downtown Washington Street terminal, carrying many late worker bees toward their high-tech hives. Clouds, like gray and white cotton balls, covered the sky in all directions, obscuring views of Mount Baker to the northeast, Mount Olympus to the west, and Mount Rainier to the south. That morning Mike Mailway, the *Seattle Post-Intelligencer*'s trivia columnist, posed the question: "Can a yodeler really cause an avalanche?" His answer was "It's not impossible."

Five blocks up the hill from the ferry terminal, in the Emerald Ballroom of a luxury hotel, Ballmer had just finished a speech on "Technology in the New Millennium." That morning *Forbes* magazine had released its list of the four hundred wealthiest Americans, and Ballmer was number four, with a net worth of about twenty-one billion dollars. (With Bill Gates, Paul Allen, and Oracle chairman Larry Ellison ahead of him, though Ballmer was the fourth-richest American, he was only the third-richest resident of his county. Given that Gates, Allen, and Ellison had all dropped out of school, Ballmer was the country's wealthiest college graduate.) Ballmer fielded questions from the assembled scribes. The proceedings were aired on the Investor Broadcast Network. A journalist asked if he thought there were any underreported stories in the computer industry. Ballmer roared with his booming voice, "There's such an overvaluation of tech stocks, it's absurd. And I'd put our company's stock in that category." That Thursday was also the autumnal equinox, the beginning of fall. Ballmer's words started another one.

Twenty-eight hundred ninety-four miles to the east, it was a beautiful day in the heart of New York City's financial district: clear and sunny, seventy-one degrees and little wind. The noon Staten Island Ferry was halfway to Whitehall Terminal in lower Manhattan. Five blocks from the terminal, up Whitehall Street, the NASDAQ stock index was edging higher after a weak start. Formed in 1971, when Ballmer was a junior at Country Day, taking college math classes, the index had hit a record high of 2,887 two weeks before, boosted mainly by tech stocks. The Dow Jones industrial average was at 10,520, up 15 percent since January. Ballmer's remark shot through cyberspace, hitting Wall Street like a tech stock virus.

The NASDAQ abruptly reversed course. Trading volume surged. The plunge spread to the Dow. Contacted to clarify his words, Ballmer echoed them, adding, "I love our company and I don't sell my stock." (Over twenty years, Ballmer has sold less than two hundred thousand of his 240 million shares.) Trading increased. The market dive continued. By the end of the day the NASDAQ was down 108 points, a loss of 4 percent. Microsoft shares lost nearly five dollars. The Dow was down 205 points, a loss of 2 percent. Asian stock exchanges followed suit: Japan's Nikkei index fell 3 percent; the Hong Kong exchange slid 2 percent.

When the markets closed on Friday, the Dow was down 524 points, up until then its worst weekly point decline ever. Two hundred eighty of those points came after Ballmer spoke. Ballmer himself lost $1.17 billion, Microsoft as a whole was trimmed by twenty-eight billion dollars. With 40 percent of Microsoft stockholders living in the Seattle area, within twenty-seven hours the Rainy City found its collective net worth down over eleven billion dollars, more than three thousand dollars for every man, woman, child, and dog.

A yodeler can cause an avalanche, but why would they want to?

The ensuing debate over Ballmer was fierce. His market influence was compared to that of Federal Reserve Board Chairman Alan Greenspan. One analyst said, "That tech stocks are overpriced is obvious on its face. But it's an emperor's new clothes situation. Everyone knows, but nobody's supposed to say." Another opined, "Maybe what we heard was the sound of a bubble bursting. There's always a watershed event that triggers it. Maybe we found one honest man." Seattle businessman Ted Kartes rued, "For someone in his position to say that, it's irresponsible. Someone should take him to task." Four months later, Microsoft's board would instead name Steve chief executive officer. The financial weekly *Barron's* noted, "Cynics wondered if Ballmer's remarks were prompted by the issuance of a new round of [stock] options to Microsoft management. A lower stock price means a more attractive options [purchase] price."

That Friday morning the trading company Goldman Sachs was taking public the stock of a new high-tech company, NetZero, for the first time—an initial public offering (IPO). Goldman Sachs had underwritten Microsoft's successful IPO fourteen years before; NetZero's would raise far less capital than expected. As *Vanity Fair* reported, "The market opened, as it does every weekday, at 9:30. Right away, technology stocks started tumbling. On the electronic ticker tape was Cisco Systems' stock symbol, down three percent; Microsoft, down one percent. For the second day in a row the market was tanking, and it was all the fault of Steve Ballmer. People were outraged, especially people trying to take their companies public. 'It was just a stupid remark,' said one Net-Zero executive. 'He was just listed number four on the *Forbes* list of richest people, so why does he care?' said another. Ballmer was ruining it for everyone. 'I can't understand what he was thinking,' added NetZero's CEO Mark Golston. 'Why did he say that?'"

Consider this: Maybe Ballmer's words weren't as casual as they appeared. After Ballmer's previous comment that he didn't think his company was worth $180 billion hit the *Wall Street Journal*, Microsoft's stock took a similar dive, so he was well aware of the effect his words could have. Given that Microsoft then had over twenty billion dollars in the bank, it didn't (and doesn't) need to enter a capital market for funds, while its current and potential competitors did and do. By lowering all tech boats with the financial tide, Ballmer made it more difficult for competitors to gain ammunition to bring to bear in their market share battles. Brilliant. Ruthless, but brilliant.

As the antitrust trial moved slowly along in Washington, D.C., another suit against Microsoft in another federal court in the other Washington was nearing conclusion. In 1992, seven temporary employees filed suit charging that Microsoft's calling them temporary workers was, in effect, a dodge to avoid paying them full compensation. Ballmer was instrumental in setting up the temp system in response to an IRS ruling that many of their independent contractors were, in fact, employees. In the suit, these temps also claimed the company was not letting them share in the employee stock-purchase plans. It was not unusual at Microsoft for temporary employees to work there for years, leaving many wondering what the word *temporary* meant. In fact, this practice prompted the invention of the term *permatemp*.

Microsoft had been using a two-tier employee system since Ballmer joined the company in 1980. And the Harvard at which Ballmer was currently an overseer was paying more than a few of its lower-level employees less than a living wage, prompting a strike a few years later. As many as one in three people working at Microsoft were permatemps, most of them actually employed by temp agencies. As the suit was coming to a close, Microsoft yet again found a unique way to anger another member of the federal judiciary.

In July 1999, the federal judge presiding over the permatemp case in Seattle, John Coughenour, was stunned when he read an article in the *Seattle Times* that Microsoft had altered their temporary employee contracts to require that the workers forfeit any potential gains from the lawsuit or terminate their employment. Judge Coughenour called the usual suspect into his courtroom and demanded to know at what level in Microsoft's corporate hierarchy the new contract language was approved. Before Microsoft's attorney Jim Oswald could open his mouth, Coughenour said, "Before you respond, let me suggest that there might be Fifth Amendment [self-incrimination] implications." Oswald said that the language applied only to future judgments, not previous rulings. Wrong answer, one that angered Coughenour even more. He said, "I thought maybe I might hear that this was done by somebody without the advice of counsel, and upon reflection of counsel it was realized that it might be charitably described as ill-advised. I confess that, of all the thoughts I had, never did it occur to me that you would feel that it was a defense to this conduct that it was prospective only. . . . The language is outrageously arrogant."

As though he were scolding a slow-witted child, Coughenour

continued, "We're going to recess this question for about a week to give the lawyers an opportunity to suggest to their client that they do the right thing, and then we'll discuss it again in the event that the court doesn't feel the right things have been done. All right." He adjourned the hearing. Microsoft removed the unlawful language from the contract.

By December 2000, Ballmer and company would agree to a ninety-seven-million-dollar settlement with the permatemps. The court had ruled that Microsoft improperly restricted long-term temporary employees from the stock-purchase program. Stephen Strong, one of the permatemps' lawyers, said they accomplished two of their goals in bringing the suit—to eliminate the idea that people can be temps forever and to get Microsoft to change its practices. Earlier in the year, Microsoft began strictly enforcing a policy that puts a one-year limit on temporary employees working through employment agencies. The temp would then have to take a month off before starting a new contract.

Getting and keeping people was a major concern of Ballmer's—even more so during this time than usual. With an economy on full employment, a dearth of high-tech workers, dot-com start-ups offering good salaries and stock-option candy—even sweeter when they are pre-IPO options—there was great competition. Microsoft had become a big company, employing almost forty thousand people, some of whom felt they were getting lost. The antitrust trial was putting a damper on spontaneity, and while the recent downturn in stock prices might turn around anytime, Microsoft stock options were becoming worthless. This was still the most sustained period of economic growth in American history, and other grasses looked greener than those on the Redmond campus. Ballmer's big problem was that Microsoftians were leaving in droves. Some estimates put the hemorrhaging as high as 150 people per week, including about half of the higher-level executives.

Ballmer found that one way to deal with the dire need for skilled employees was to import them. He was all for the expansion of immigration quotas under what's termed an H-B1 provision, allowing highly specialized foreign workers into the country. In fact, in 2000 he would donate five thousand dollars to the reelection campaign of one of Michigan's U.S. senators, now the energy secretary in the George W. Bush administration, Spencer Abraham, who was leading the regulation change. The opposition to expanding H-B1 pointed out that it took jobs away from Americans and gave an employer nearly total control over the worker; if they quit or were fired, the now-former employee was subject to immediate deportation.

Working through Ballmer, James Fallows was a consultant for Microsoft at the time, in an attempt to improve Microsoft Word. (If you've ever been bothered by Clippy, that annoying little paper clip icon that pops up while you're writing a letter on Microsoft Word and tells you that you're writing a letter when you obviously know that you're writing a letter, Clippy stays in Word because it was developed by Melinda Gates when she was Melinda French.) Fallows observed that "people of every skin color work in Redmond. The difference is that the dark-skinned people who work in high tech are nearly all non-American. They are from India, perhaps Malaysia, sometimes from Kenya or Ethiopia. American blacks have about the same representation in software development that American Jews have in pro basketball." Clarence Page told me that he thinks there are so few blacks in high tech because they don't tend to concentrate on the needed math and science classes in high school.

One black employee, Rahn Jackson, a member of Ballmer's sales force, confronted Ballmer at a meeting with the fact that less than 3 percent of Microsoft's managers are African-Americans. Jackson told me, "Ballmer listened, then said that there wasn't anything he could do about it. I thought, If he can't do anything about it, who can?" Jackson accepted a better offer from Sun, and is the lead plaintiff in a five-billion-dollar class-action lawsuit filed a year later. Through the luck of the draw the case would be assigned to Judge Thomas Penfield Jackson, who removed himself after giving a blistering verbal attack on the defendant. Judge Jackson would say, in open court, "Microsoft's senior management is not averse to offering specious testimony to support spurious defenses to claims of its wrongdoing." He said that he'd formed an impression "of a company with an institutional disdain for both the truth and for rules of law lesser entities must respect." To Judge Jackson, it seemed that Microsoft was acting out the Michael Dukakis statement "Some people say I'm arrogant, but I know I'm better than that."

When it comes to race relations, Steve Ballmer doesn't have a bigoted bone in his big body. ("Have you checked them all?" asked Clarence Page.) Recall that rumor has it he provided the scholarship money for the black NBA star Chris Webber to attend Country Day. He was also rumored to have helped prompt Bill Gates to set up foundation grants designed specifically to fund scholarships to promising blacks who want to go into computerdom. It would be difficult to love professional basketball and not admire African-Americans, and one of Ballmer's heroes is Isaiah Thomas. While blacks reach a glass ceiling at Microsoft—and it's easier for a black American to become a secretary of state or a Supreme Court justice than be a member of Microsoft's elite Business Leadership Team—Ballmer's view of black subordinates resembles Vince Lombardi's. When one of Lombardi's African-American players was asked if he was handled differently by the coach than white players, he responded, "Lombardi treats us all alike—like dogs."

One of Ballmer's biggest problems was that many Microsoftians' bags were packed and they were ready to go, including about half of the higher-level executives. Why were Microsoftians jumping ship? Some reasons can be seen in a probing nine-page good-bye letter sent by one such employee, a Wharton M.B.A. named Brandon Watson, who e-mailed his reasons to Gates and Ballmer and the rest of the executive committee. Watson wondered, "At what point did Microsoft lose its passion, fun and impact at the heart of its leadership team? I wanted to have impact, freedom to think and innovate without being constrained by the cash cow business." Watson was voicing the concern of many frustrated Microsoftians, who thought the company was more concerned with protecting its installed base and was run by managers who could care less about the work they were doing. Watson asked, "What is the next jihad that is going to delight our customers?" To fire up the troops, Microsoftians often talked in terms of jihads—Islamic religious wars. Ballmer's top lieutenant, Jeff Raikes, told *Fortune* that "Microsoft is at its best when it's on a jihad."

Watson continued, ". . . we are going to lose many people because we are no longer being innovative. Yes, Windows is a key to Microsoft's core business, but the problem is that it is too big, too chaotic. The change agents that you wish to attract/retain want to do something new and exciting, not something that has been in the works for five plus years. . . . I hope you can all understand that this is a very distressing and frustrating thing to see when you want nothing more than for the company you love to succeed."

Watson then raised another problem that was on the minds of many a Microsoftian: the review system. Every six months or so, Microsoft managers were required to rate each employee under them on a scale from one to five, with five being tops (and with fractional assessments allowed). Using a bell curve, the lower 10 percent would be highly encouraged to find work elsewhere, if not outright fired. Furthermore, when you gave an employee a high mark, they would become a target for other, more powerful managers to try and steal away. This is very similar to the employee review system used at General Electric, where Ballmer's cubicle mate from Procter & Gamble, Jeff Immelt, was being groomed to take over the top job when *über*-chairman Jack Welsh retired. The system carried the flaw that, rather than help those struggling, managers were encouraged to let them go. Watson picks up on this and says, "Being told by my manager that even if someone was doing 4.5 work, they could still get a 3 because he 'has to fit the curve' is just about the most backward, frustrating, and de-motivating thing I have ever heard in my entire life."

As the *New York Times* reported, the practice of ranking or grading employees is common at technology companies like Cisco Systems and Hewlett-Packard, but as more companies turned to grading on a bell curve, employees pointed out that the system favored some groups of employees over others: white males over blacks and women, younger managers over older ones, and foreign citizens over Americans. Lawsuits questioning the fairness of the so-called rank-and-yank procedure were filed against not only Microsoft but Ford and Conoco as well.

Using the review system, Ballmer once showed Cameron Mhyrvold another side of his Ballmerness. Mhyrvold relates, "My boss decided that our developers group was going to concentrate on just one Internet service provider (ISP). When Steve heard that, oh, my God, he went through the roof. He was screaming, 'That's your plan!? That's your plan!? If that's your plan, you've got a 1.0 plan. You go with that plan and you'll get a 1.0 performance review.' But the whole time Steve was doing that, he would look at me and grin on the side. It [his anger] was just show. People don't look past his show, his hyperbole."

Even though Watson had spent over an hour talking with Ballmer about the issues his exit letter raised, no action resulted from the meeting. Watson told me, "He has always been, in my opinion, very accessible. He's just a busy man." Incidentally, Watson is also an African-American but is not joining the racial discrimination suit. He says, "If you are smart and talented and African-American at Microsoft, you will do well. Those employees at Microsoft who are or were claiming bias have a difficult situation, and I feel bad for them, but for me and my close friends, to my knowledge, race never figured into our careers at Microsoft." Not content to simply say what he found wrong, Watson offered an inspired solution to keeping people in the Redmond fold. "How do you create jihads?" he asked, then suggested a way. Rather than keep buying companies, which Microsoft was doing in the hundreds (being bought by Microsoft was a dream of many a start-up), Watson recommended Microsoft grow its own. "If you took just 20–30 people internally (of the 35,000 you already have), give them $10 million and say, 'here, go make your dream happen' you would solve many problems at once. Looking behind you is fine to see what is sneaking up on you, but if you persist in looking behind you too long, you'll hit the wall that you didn't even know was coming." Alas, Watson's concerns and suggestions fell on ears deafened by the background noise of the trial. He left.

The actor Wallace Shawn, a son of fabled *New Yorker* editor William Shawn, could have been talking about Microsoft when he recalled his father telling him, "If you let yourself get too comfortable, you start converting creative energy into defensive energy, and you spend all your time just protecting what you've got." Ballmer knew that, and worked for change. He e-mailed another former employee who had left for a job at Amazon.com, "I, too, am part of the problem. Hard to know what to do."

Of course, knowledge workers are Microsoft's stock in trade. Cameron Mhyrvold says, "Microsoft does a great job in teaching you how to hire people. Hiring decisions are the most important decisions for a tech company producing intellectual property." In fact, by 1992, Microsoft was visiting over 130 college campuses a year, some of them up to four times. Brad Silverberg said, "It's a machine, the way Microsoft is set up in the universities." Ballmer's lieutenant Jeff Raikes says, "You can't hire bad programmers and get good software." Ballmer's technique for testing people is legend. Before he hired John Neilson to be regional general manager of Microsoft's New York office, Neilson went jogging with Ballmer in Central Park. Ballmer suddenly turned to Neilson and said, "How many gas stations do you think there are in the United States?" Neilson spent the next twenty minutes puzzling it out. Ballmer told *Business Week,* "They don't have to get the right answer. But I want to see how they go through the process. If they're good, I make the game harder."

Since the success of Windows 3.1, the company had been receiving some twenty thousand résumés a month, winnowing out the vast majority before bringing the remaining few candidates to Redmond for interviews. Two of those jobs were filled by Joe and Cathy Jo Linn. The Linns, who both have Ph.D.s, were working at a military think tank in Washington, D.C., and were considering an offer from Microsoft. They didn't look forward to moving across country, they didn't want to live more than a mile from work and in a certain-size house, and they were taking karate classes they didn't want to miss. Microsoft recruiter Carrie Tibitts offered them flexible hours, found a suitable house within a half-mile of the campus and faxed them a picture, and even found them a karate instructor. Hiring people was one thing, keeping them was another, and how to let them leave was a third.

By 2000, Ballmer faced a different problem most managers never have to deal with. The *Harvard Business Review* estimated that about 30 percent of the forty thousand Microsoftians were millionaires—about twelve thousand people. How do you motivate millionaires? Or, as Suzy Wetlaufer, a senior editor at the

Review, asked, "Who wants to manage a millionaire?" (Wetlaufer will neither confirm or deny that she interviewed Ballmer for the piece, but James Cash, the head of Harvard Business School publications, sits on Microsoft's board. Wetlaufer would later gain notoriety for having an affair with the recently retired Jack Welch, much to the consternation of Mrs. Welch, and to a few members of the *Review* staff.) Wetlaufer found that millionaires force companies to be far more creative and entrepreneurial about their products and services. Microsoft wasn't. They push companies to keep beating their targets in the marketplace. Microsoft did. And they compel their bosses to build a productive, healthy culture, a plot Ballmer has followed for the past twenty years. She found the working millionaires to be "demanding and fickle," but that having them on the payroll means that the culture of the company is intolerant of mediocrity. She noted that millionaires tend to be individuals who want to create a legacy, who want to build a dream, to make a difference, to even change the world. Wetlaufer observed that they require freedom: "You cannot micro-manage someone who, for all intents and purposes, is an independent agent." Finally, she found that it was very important to have an exit strategy.

At this point, the rest of the article could have been written by Ballmer. As he knew, at some point, individuals will outgrow a job—or the company will have exhausted every opportunity for redesigning it. Wetlaufer recommended that a manager handle the exit "in a way that the individual feels so good about the company" they are leaving. She said that one way is to offer them a sabbatical—a tactic Ballmer had used for years—or a part-time advisory position. One person she interviewed said, in words that sound like Ballmer's, "You've got to give people opportunities to pursue their passions. If they leave, our people treat them as valued alumni—and perhaps they will return." Microsoft has a formal alumni association where, for $130 a year, former Microsoftians can stay in touch with each other via regular events, a newsletter, and, of course, job postings, just like the Harvard alumni association. The brochure for Microsoft's alumni association asks, seriously, "Is there life after Microsoft?" The same question was being considered in Washington, D.C.

CHAPTER THIRTEEN

MILLENNIUM'S END

The last year of the last millennium truly began for Steve Ballmer on January 13, 2000, when he became CEO. Some observers wondered if Ballmer's appointment was just a public relations move to deflect attention from Judge Jackson's findings of fact, but it was a true shift of power. Hemingway wrote, "The world breaks everyone, and afterward, many are strong at the broken places." The trial had broken Bill Gates. Steve Ballmer became Gates's strength at the broken places. By the end of the year and the millennium, Ballmer would bury his father, Fred, carry most of the huge weight of managing the beleaguered Redmond beast, settle a few major lawsuits against his company, see Judge Thomas Penfield Jackson take him to task before ordering his company bisected, throw out his lifelong Democratic politics and support the Republican George W. Bush for president, and gain the conflicting honors of simultaneously being voted the best American CEO by his peers in the same poll that also named him the second-worst American CEO, following only the head of Bridgestone, with its fatally exploding tires.

On January 7, as Ballmer was getting ready to officially take over as CEO, Microsoft announced that it had settled a one-billion-dollar private antitrust case brought by the Utah-based Caldera, Inc., that had been set to go to trial in early February. Ballmer had already announced that he would testify at the trial, but apparently had second thoughts. Microsoft announced it was taking a three cents per share charge against the settlement, which caused the *Wall Street Journal* to estimate Microsoft paid about $275 million to Caldera. One effect of the settlement was to have the court records sealed. Albert Foer, the president of the American Antitrust Institute, said, "The rumor was that Caldera had amassed a lot of information that was very, very negative for Microsoft. It may have been very, very important for Microsoft to keep this information, whatever it was, from going public."

Caldera had purchased the PC operating system DR-DOS from Novell in 1996. As noted earlier, Novell had purchased the CP/M operating system from Gary Kildall's DRI—the system Kildall claimed Gates had stolen part of MS-DOS from—and turned it into DR-DOS. DR-DOS was making a run at Windows, and had captured almost 10 percent of the American market, surpassing Windows in some retail venues. Overseas, DR-DOS had fared much better, especially in Germany. The federal judge presiding over the case, Ronald Boyce, responded to applications by various media organizations and released some of the sealed records. Though Ballmer's deposition wasn't released, one deposition by a former Microsoft account manager in Germany, Stephanie Reichel, was made available; it provided a smoking gun. Reichel said, under oath, that she had been pressured to destroy hundreds of e-mails that could have proved to be incriminating in the case going on in Judge Jackson's Washington courtroom. Reichel's supervisors physically removed her hard disks and "dumped them in graveyards in East Germany that no one knows about." The problem for Ballmer was that the major German original equipment manufacturer Vobis, who Reichel worked with, preferred DR-DOS to MS-DOS. In fact, Vobis was the leading computer manufacturer in Europe in 1991, and all of the computers it sold used DR-DOS. It was as though the ghost of Gary Kildall had come back to haunt Microsoft.

The only way that Microsoft could persuade Vobis to change was by agreeing to pay Vobis the cost of the DR-DOS copies that Vobis had and give them a sweet deal for MS-DOS. According to a released Bill Gates e-mail, Steve Ballmer was very concerned about Vobis. Another e-mail by Microsoft vice president Brad Chase said, "Steve [Ballmer] told me to eat, sleep and drink Vobis." After the sweet deal with Microsoft, within a year Vobis was selling some 90 percent of its computers with MS-DOS. No wonder Microsoft wanted to keep the records sealed. Ballmer had a company to run, not another antitrust trial, and probably pushed for the settlement.

It's said that a son only becomes a man after his father dies. Five weeks after Steve Ballmer took control of a six-hundred-billion-dollar company he personally discovered the truth of what author Clark Blaise meant when he wrote that middle age is the final orphanage. At exactly noon on February 21, his father, Fred Ballmer, passed on, at home in the house Connie and Steve Ballmer had built for him. Death was attributed to respiratory failure, a consequence of renal failure, which itself was a consequence of non-small-cell lung cancer. Fred Ballmer had not gone gently into that good night, and his deafness hadn't stopped him from raging against the inevitable. For some reason, the home health care nurse whom Ballmer had hired was injured tending to Fred, and filed a complaint with the Washington State Labor and Industries Division. It's not unlikely that Fred's death was a relief of sorts for Steve Ballmer. He wouldn't talk about Fred's death much, yet author Mark Leibovich reported that when an executive told Ballmer he was leaving, "Ballmer closed the door of his office and the two men shared a cry and a discussion of their [dead] fathers, ending with a bear hug." (A problem is that Leibovich reported that the incident took place in January 2000, when Fred Ballmer was still alive.) Fred Ballmer was buried next to Bea back in Detroit.

In April, speaking to students at George Washington University in Washington, D.C., Ballmer said, "Microsoft did not break antitrust law and has a very strong set of factual legal arguments. Values are super-important to Microsoft. It matters to me that we're a company of fine integrity. It matters to me a lot. It matters to me when I address my kids." Two hours later Attorney General Janet Reno also spoke to the students; Reno did not talk about the antitrust case, nor did any news reports mention that she'd spoken to Ballmer.

Ballmer told a reporter, "We have spent the past twenty-five years thinking of ourselves as a small, aggressive company playing catch-up to large companies, even though at some point along the way we became a large company." Ballmer insisted that this was merely an image problem; "our passion for being the best has sometimes been misinterpreted." In *World War 3.0* Ken Auletta wrote that "Microsoft was sometimes immature, Judge Jackson was suggesting, not brazen or brutal or unethical. Once again, the conclusion that perhaps Ballmer and Microsoft are afflicted by a disconnect from reality, unable to fully comprehend the consequences of their own behavior, was inescapable."

Auletta continued, "When Judge Jackson picked up his copy of the *Washington Post* on April 19, 2000, he read of a visit Ballmer had made to the paper the previous day. To a roomful of reporters and editors, Ballmer said, 'I do not think we broke the law in any way, shape, or form. I feel deeply that we behaved in every instance with super integrity. I'm not saying we don't talk tough, that people don't get a little 'grrr' in their e-mail and all that.'" According to Auletta, "Judge Jackson was livid and interpreted what Ballmer had said as 'We're a little rough around the edges, but you have to be tolerant!' To this day, Microsoft continues to deny they did anything wrong." Gates then told PBS, "It's important to understand that Microsoft is very clear that it has done absolutely nothing wrong." Probably the most stringent of state attorneys general, Iowa's Tom Miller, said, "To see Ballmer say that they did nothing wrong, that did bother us. We [state attorneys general] talked about that. It looks like they missed the whole point. It fed our concern that they would try and do it again." Judge Jackson prepared to have the case taken directly to the Supreme Court under the Antitrust Expediting Act because, he told Auletta, "What I really don't want is for Microsoft to have the advantage of a two-year delay and continue what they've been doing."

In late May, Judge Jackson asked Microsoft attorney John Warren if Steve Ballmer was quoted correctly in a software association brief in which he was said to declare, "Forty percent of the functionality of the desktop version of Windows 2000 is useless without a Windows 2000 server." Jackson was truly puzzled why Ballmer might make such an incriminating statement when such behavior was at the core of the government's case. Warren had his cohort Steven Holley answer. Holley said that the brief was written by competitors, and he could neither certify what Ballmer said nor what he meant and that the question was irrelevant since Windows 2000 wasn't at issue in the trial. Jackson then let it be known that he wasn't contemplating a hearing for the remedy phase of the case. Microsoft bristled, and responded with a thirty-five-page brief containing proposed remedies and said that both Bill Gates and Steve Ballmer would be among the sixteen witnesses it would call at the hearing (both could have testified at the trial, but chose not to). They said that in "the brief time available" they had gathered valuable information and more time would allow Microsoft to better address the remedies. "In 'the brief time'?" questioned Jackson. "That is correct, Your Honor," said Holley. An irritated Jackson responded, "This case has been pending for two years, Mr. Holley."

On June 7, Jackson issued his decision and ordered the company broken up. Jackson took aim at Gates and Ballmer, writing, "Microsoft as it is presently organized and led is unwilling to accept the notion that it broke the law or accede to an order amending its conduct. Microsoft officials have recently been quoted publicly to the effect that the company has 'done nothing wrong.' Microsoft has proved untrustworthy in the past." Jackson refused to rely on Steve Ballmer to appoint a compliance officer, as the government had proposed. Displaying more disdain for Ballmer, Jackson gave Microsoft directors ninety days to establish a compliance committee consisting of no less than three board members "who are not present or former employees of Microsoft," and empowering this committee—not Ballmer—to appoint a chief compliance officer to report to both the committee and the CEO.

When the decision was handed down, Ballmer was on a European tour and told a group of Norwegian computer reps, "The pace of innovation in the computer industry would be slowed if the breakup went ahead." In fact, as has often been pointed out, very few computer innovations originate within Microsoft.

Wall Street reacted sharply to Jackson's ruling and Microsoft stock plunged over fifteen dollars a share, effectively fining Bill Gates more than eight billion dollars and Steve Ballmer three and a half billion dollars, which they could easily absorb. What's a bullying predatory monopolist to do?

Spin like a top.

Gates and Ballmer almost immediately hit the broadcast airwaves, appearing in television ads wearing fuzzy warm sweaters (in June), making nice, claiming that "the best is yet to come," attempting to defend their "freedom to innovate." Of course, Microsoft arguing for the freedom to innovate is like when Mahatma Gandhi was asked what he thought of Western civilization; Gandhi replied, "I think it would be a good idea." Judge Jackson had specifically convicted Microsoft of illegally stifling innovation. Microsoft announced it was appealing—the decision, that is.

Most people weren't buying Microsoft's television appeal or crocodile tears, including *Advertising Age* columnist Bob Garfield, who wrote of the ad's phoniness and opined that rather than trying to talk their way out of the problem, Gates and Ballmer would do better to follow the court's opinion and make their company "a little more Micro, a little more soft." Cartoonist Jeff Danziger was a little more harsh. He ran a six-panel sequence of Gates taking off a black overcoat, revealing an Iron Cross, removing a Nazi SS cap, taking off his uniform, mussing up his hair, sitting down at a desk, and saying, "Vicious monopolist? Me? I'm just a harmless little computer nerd."

Ballmer rushed back from Europe and worked on damage control. He reminded employees that Judge Jackson had been overturned on a previous ruling concerning the consent decree. He recognized that, with a falling stock price, halved over the past six months, stock options held little value. He authorized managers to pay their people 100 percent of market. And he knew that, by announcing his .Net strategy, he would get some good press. So, on June 20, 2000, Ballmer did just that. To the reporters and analysts assembled in Redmond, Ballmer said, "Windows isn't going away. But to take advantage of this new software trend in technology, we need the .Net platform." He pounded his fist into his hand and said, "The bet is on .Net! We don't yet know all the specific potential sources of revenue, but we do see lots of opportunities here."

Ballmer then laid it on rather thick to the *Seattle Times*. He said, "We will be working with third parties to insure interoperability," denying, of course, that the move was motivated by the government's antitrust case. "It's just the right strategy for us to pursue. One of the great travesties of the trial is that people have painted Windows as somehow not open." Great travesties? Given that it was repeatedly shown at trial that, using the hidden APIs and sabotaging Java, among other things, Windows is open only to Microsoft's friends, one wonders why the *Times* didn't call him on the phony claim. The paper did point out that "developers who turn their backs on .Net run the risk of missing out if Microsoft succeeds on evangelizing the platform. [Yet] doubts also have emerged about Microsoft's ability to execute on strategy, given the departure of numerous veteran high-level executives in recent months, many to dot-com startups. Ballmer dismissed 'brain drain' talk, however, saying only a handful of departures made him 'really sad. A half-dozen to a dozen (key executives) don't break the bank.' "

Recall that one of the "half-dozen to a dozen" executives who left was Cameron Mhyrvold. Mhyrvold told me, "Leaving was very hard, very emotional for me after working there for thirteen years. Steve offered me a great job. I left because my wife and I had just had our first child and I was never good at balancing my personal life with work at Microsoft. And I thought it would be more interesting to do something outside the company rather than sign up for my fourth or fifth tour of duty." While offering the longtime Microsoft millionaires more money didn't keep many on the farm, there was one other, major battleground on which the mighty Microsoft money would make noise and get respect: the presidential election. And Microsoft voted with its dollars.

In Washington State, the 2000 race for the U.S. Senate saw the Democratic high-tech executive and highly telegenic candidate, Real Networks vice president Maria Cantwell, edge out the Republican incumbent, Slade Gordon, by a mere six thousand votes. Exhibiting either blatant demagoguery or delusional behavior, both ran as the "Senator from Microsoft," insinuating that they would, somehow, prevent the federal courts from carrying out Judge Jackson's ruling; they were apparently hoping voters would forget that they would be part of the feds' legislative branch, not the judicial branch, which would ultimately decide the fate of the leviathan Microsoft.

Indeed, such thinking extended to the presidential election. Many people thought that if Bush the Younger was elected, his Justice Department wouldn't aggressively pursue the antitrust case; to more than a little extent, they were right. But such reasoning negated the nineteen state attorneys general joined in the suit; though after Bush's election ten states would peel off from the pack, and Microsoft would pay their legal costs, nine states remained in the fold, including the tech centers Massachusetts and California.

The 2000 presidential election showed a sea change in Steve Ballmer's politics. Winston Churchill is often misquoted as saying, "If at fifteen a man isn't a liberal he has no heart; if, at thirty-five, a man isn't a conservative he has no brain." (Churchill himself was conservative at fifteen and liberal at thirty-five.) On the other hand, John Stuart Mill once corrected a reporter, "I never said that all conservatives were stupid people. What I said was that most conservative people were stupid." Democratic presidential candidates generally receive over 70 percent of the Jewish vote. Of course, Gore's running mate was Senator Joseph Lieberman, a practicing Jew who talked almost incessantly about his religion while stumping. Seventy-nine percent of Jews would vote for Gore-Lieberman. And not only were Ballmer's parents loyal Democrats, but son Steve himself had actively campaigned throughout his life for Democrats, from his prep school teacher John Campbell to the Clinton-Gore ticket in 1992. Yet in 2000 Steve Ballmer turned his back on his lifelong personal beliefs and supported the Republican. The Democrats couldn't countenance the foul play of Ballmer's game. It was as though Ballmer were saying, "It's our basketball, we'll play by our rules." When Ballmer heard that George W. Bush was to be president he was riding in a car in Boston. Immediately, his fisted hand punched the air, punched the air, punched the air as he shouted out, "Who-op! Who-op! Whoop!" the seat restraint locking, the car bouncing from side to side. The enemy of his enemy was his friend.

When I asked Sam Verhovek, the *New York Times* Pacific Northwest reporter, if the Microsoft antitrust trial affected the national election, he said, simply, "No, Gore won the popular vote." During the 2000 presidential election, much was made of Al Gore's claim that while in the senate, he "took the initiative in creating the Internet." Gore was instrumental in passing legislation paving the information superhighway, and is a staunch supporter of Internet access for all. Gore worked to woo high-tech voters, not an easy task since high-tech workers—techies—are, as a whole, libertarians who don't want the government telling them what to do. But they liked Gore.

The on-line magazine *Upside Today* published the presidential voting results for Silicon Valley, south of San Francisco; Microsoft's King County, Washington; Austin, Texas, where Dell computers reigns; North Carolina's Research Triangle; New York City's Silicon Alley; and Boston's Route 128 Corridor. Their verdict: Gore, by a two-to-one landslide.

Austin's Travis County and Williamson County, Texas, voted 206,173 (52.4 percent) for their hometown boy Bush, 152,013 (38.6 percent) for Gore, and 34,705 (8.8 percent) for Nader.

North Carolina's Durham, Orange, and Wake counties cast 201,859 (52.1) votes for Gore, 185,609 (47.9) for Bush.

Seattle's King County voted 319,262 (61 percent) for Gore, 178,976 (34 percent) for Bush, and 24,304 (5 percent) for Nader.

Silicon Valley's Santa Clara and San Mateo Counties went a whopping 440,126 (73 percent) for Gore, 134,737 (22.4 percent) for Bush, and 25,715 (4.3 percent) for Nader.

New York's Silicon Alley, in New York County, went a more whopping 409,257 (79 percent) for Gore, a measly 77,614 (15 percent) for Bush, and 28,202 (5 percent) for Nader.

Finally, Boston, in the only state to vote for McGovern in 1972, went 72 percent for Gore (129,861) and 7 percent for Nader (13,301), with a mere 20 percent (35,931) for Bush.

Total Tech Vote: 1,649,378 for Gore (63.6 percent) 818,880 for Bush (31.6 percent) and 126,227 for Nader (4.8 percent).

Though Microsoft likes to pose as a company that can't be bothered with the machinations of Washington, D.C., the reality now was just the opposite. While Gates and Ballmer wisely refrained from personally donating money to either presidential candidate, the company spent over $2.2 million on soft money gifts and targeted contributions between 1999 and the first quarter of 2000, making the company third, behind Philip Morris and AT&T, for such funding, along with shoveling two million dollars to help underwrite the Democratic and Republican presidential conventions. In fact, through the connection of his family's friend Senator Brock Adams, from July 17 to August 18, 1972, Bill Gates had served as a page in the U.S. House of Representatives. According to authors Paul Andrews and Stephen Manes, "Gates apparently learned most of the classic page scams, such as pouring soup down the four-story mail slots in the

House and Senate Office Buildings, and sending people on bogus errands to the numbered rest rooms there." Gates even bought thousands of McGovern-Eagleton buttons in the hope of "making a killing" after Eagleton withdrew on August 1. After pointing out that there were hundreds of thousands of such buttons, Andrews and Manes conclude that Gates's claim of big profits "does not compute."

By the late 1990s, Microsoft's D.C. lobbying staff had gone from one to seventy-three and included former Republican representative Bill Paxton and Ballmer's former *Harvard Advocate* cohort Grover Norquist. Another Microsoft advisor was former Newt Gingrich staffer and Christian Coalition executive director Ralph Reed. While working for Microsoft, Reed was also a Bush campaign advisor who, on the recommendation of future Bush White House Chief of Staff Karl Rove, was hired as a consultant by Enron Corporation. When the *New York Times* broke the story that Reed was working for Microsoft while advising Bush, the candidate was publicly embarrassed, and explained that Reed hadn't let him know of the conflict. Reed probably sought forgiveness from a higher power. Microsoft was simply exercising its First Amendment right of buying access.

In a sworn affidavit filed with the district court as part of Judge Colleen Kollar-Kotelly's Tunney Act review, Washington, D.C.–based investigative reporter and campaign finance expert Edward Roeder noted:

> I am struck by the similarities between Microsoft and the current scandal involving Enron Corporation. While Enron, of course, is in an entirely different business, it seems that the core issue—from a public disclosure perspective—is its campaign contributions and its ability to influence the nation's energy policy. Microsoft's campaign contributions significantly surpassed those of Enron. During the 1999–2000 election cycle, Microsoft and

its executives accounted for some $2,298,551 in soft money contributions. This was two-thirds more than the $1,546,055 in soft money donated by Enron and its executives. . . . In a campaign unprecedented in its size, scope, and cost Microsoft used campaign contributions, phony front groups, intensive lobbying, biased polling, and other creative, if not possibly unethical, pressure and public relations tactics to escape from the trial with its monopoly intact. Microsoft spent tens of millions of dollars to attempt to create an aura outside the courtroom of what it could not prove inside—innocence. According to *Business Week*, "Even seasoned Washington hands say they have never seen anything quite as flamboyant as the Microsoft effort." From 1995–96 through 1999–2000 the funding for Microsoft's political action committee (PAC) increased by more than 2,500 percent, an unparalleled increase. A *Business Week* commentator said, "There's something quite disturbing about watching the world's richest man trying to buy his way out of trouble with Uncle Sam. . . . Gates' actions undermined the legal system itself."

In spring 1998, the *Los Angeles Times* received a package of confidential materials created by Microsoft's prime propagandist, Waggener Edelman Public Relations. Among the documents was a media-relations strategy for a "multimillion-dollar" campaign aimed at stemming the states' antitrust case. The paper reported that "the elaborate plan hinges on a number of unusual—and some say unethical—tactics, including the planting of articles, letters to the editor and opinion pieces to be commissioned by Microsoft's top media handlers but presented by local firms as spontaneous testimonials." Groups like Americans for Technology Leadership and the Association for Competitive Technology had the veneer of independence, but were actually founded by Microsoft, launched with Microsoft dollars, and work on few other issues than the defense of Microsoft. Grover Norquist, head of Americans for Tax Reform, received over fifty thousand dollars to lobby for Microsoft, even authoring a piece for the *Detroit News* supporting the convicted monopolist without revealing that he was on the company's payroll. Microsoft's lobbying strategy was brilliant—the company hired so many major lobbying firms in key states that the opposition couldn't find any.

Roeder went on to suggest that, so that his contributions wouldn't be reported until after the elections, Steve Ballmer waited until a few weeks before the presidential voting began to donate fifty thousand dollars each to the state Republican parties of Michigan and Washington, the latter supporting Senator Slade Gorton. Microsoft itself donated $131,160 to Gorton, who lost his senate seat, as did Spencer Abraham. Microsoft as a whole donated nineteen thousand dollars to the failed reelection campaign of John Ashcroft. (Ashcroft was defeated by a man who died three weeks before the election.) Of course, Ashcroft is now Attorney General, overseeing the antitrust case. And a senior Ashcroft aide, David Israelite, was the political director of the Republican National Committee, which received more than a million dollars from Microsoft during the 2000 presidential campaign. The web became even more tangled when the *New York Times* reported that Israelite called America Online lobbyist Wayne Berman, asking, "Are you guys behind this business of the states hiring their own lawyers in the Microsoft case? Tell your clients we wouldn't be too happy about that." (The Bill and Melinda Gates Foundation donated ten million dollars to the U.S. Capitol Visitors' Center.) After Bill Gates visited presidential candidate George W. Bush in Austin, Texas, in what *Newsweek* called "part of a delicate political dance between the software giant and the Republican Party," then-Governor Bush was quoted as saying he was "on the side of innovation, not litigation." Though Roeder reported that Steve Ballmer was a technology advisor to then-Governor Bush, it was in fact Microsoft's chief operating officer,

Bob Herbold, who counseled Bush the Younger on tech issues. Interestingly, Microsoft employees themselves gave $222,750 to what are termed Democratic 527s, groups independent of the political campaigns, and only fifteen thousand dollars to such Republican groups. Democratic political action committees received $222,100 from Microsoft employees, while just $42,875 went to Republican PACs.

During the campaign, one target of Microsoft's mouthpieces angered many Washington observers, including *New York Times* columnist Thomas Friedman. He reported that the Beast from Redmond had lobbied hard to have some nine million dollars cut from the Department of Justice's antitrust division budget. He compared it to someone being arrested, then attempting to eliminate funding for the chief of police, the mayor, and the judge. When Friedman confronted Bill Gates about this in January 2000 at the annual World Economic Forum in Davos, Switzerland, Gates glared at him and called it an "outrageous, untrue" story. They had only sought to limit the antitrust division's public relations budget, said Gates. Given that the antitrust division had no public relations staff, and throughout the trial had only a single press officer and an assistant, this is, to be kind, disingenuous.

Though he had balked at walking the walk, Scott McNealy still talked the talk. McNealy told *The New Yorker*, "Washington, D.C., is my least-favorite town in the world. I see all these unbelievable monuments to government, agencies that have no reason for being on the planet—the Department of Agriculture, Transportation, FEMA, Health, Education, Commerce—all these huge erections of brick and mortar with their masses of people running around redistributing wealth. The whole thing drives me into a freaking funk." McNealy said we should "shut down some of the bullshit the government is spending money on and use it to buy all the Microsoft stock. Then put all their intellectual property in the public domain. Free Windows for everyone! Then we could just bronze Gates, turn him into a statue, and stick him in front of the commerce department."

San Jose Mercury News columnist Dan Gillmore thinks that Steve Ballmer is very adaptive, a gifted field marshal, and that Microsoft would be a very different place without him. Gillmore told me this in late October 2000 in Camden, Maine, a locale familiar to anyone who saw the recent film *In the Bedroom*. As tech author and Camden, Maine, resident Tom DeMarco notes, the five thousand people who call that moving-picture-perfect seaside town home point to the fact that it's "a special place which something inside of each of us knows is the way a town is supposed to be, full of gracious trees and lovely sea captains' houses and Victorian public spaces, with a breathtaking harbor full of windjammers and pleasure craft and working Maine lobster boats." Looking at Camden, it's about the last place one would think of as influencing computerdom, until you discover that former Apple chairman John Sculley and 3Com founder (and Ethernet inventor) Bob Metcalfe moved close by when they did what they call retiring. For the past five years Sculley, Metcalfe, and DeMarco have had a hand in putting on the world-class Camden Technology Conference, attended by techies, tech executives, and writers who were lucky enough to get in, discussing the something inside of each of them that knows the way the computer industry can be, should be, and possibly and probably will be. It seemed to be a life without Microsoft.

Steve Ballmer stayed three thousand two hundred miles away in Seattle, dealing with the fallout from the antitrust suit, the falling tech stock prices, and some of his less politic comments, but Ballmer dispatched Microsoft's vice president in charge of corporate and industry initiatives, Linda Stone, to represent the company. Stone, a very bright, quite charming woman, was scheduled to be the company's presence at the conference but, at the last minute, backed out, claiming illness, though she later intimated she dreaded Camden because, as she told me dismissively, "they're all Apple people."

It's worth noting that Stone is one of the very few female Microsoftians with much internal clout (and the only one outside of their propagandists who would talk to me on the record). When *Fortune* listed the top fifty most influential businesswomen, not one worked for Microsoft. (There is a class action gender discrimination lawsuit pending against the company.) Stone does more than parrot the company line when she says, "People like Steve Ballmer because he's passionate, committed, brilliant, energetic, caring, authentic, and thoughtful." Even many of Ballmer's critics would agree with most of her adjectives. Of course, they'll add a few of their own.

The five hundred participants at Camden filled every seat in its splendid opera house and listened to speakers from around the world talk about Being Human in the Digital Age. The tone was set when one of the first speakers noted that computerdom is peopled by "white men with high math SAT scores who can't dance." Computer guru and gadfly John Perry Barlow, credited with creating the term *cyberspace*, is a self-described "technomad" and a founder of the Electronic Freedom Foundation. At Camden, he spoke of being "the eye of his own hurricane" as he works to protect the Internet from becoming too corporate and from censorship. John Sculley noted that technology advances in a tautology of sorts, from novelty to necessity. A leader of the Tiananmen Square protests, Li Lu, the living embodiment of the spirit of Steinbeck's Tom Joad, put much of the audience in tears as he talked about his harrowing escape from China, and how the Internet is offering the average person in his birth country unparalleled freedom from official Chinese news sources. Adam Clayton Powell III demonstrated how Internet access in African villages raised the aspirations of students from wanting to be better farmers to hoping to become teachers and scientists. Sun

Microsystems' encryption genius Whitfield Diffie spoke at length about security on the Web. As he did, some Maine teachers were picketing outside the opera house, protesting government-mandated fingerprinting. (One participant offered a compromise, that the teachers submit to the fingerprinting but get to choose the finger.) The director of MIT's artificial intelligence lab, professor Rodney Brooks, talked of a not-so-distant future where the same rebellious young folk who pierce themselves now will probably have cell phone implants. Brooks noted how, with the advances made in artificial hearts and limbs, the human body is becoming like a B-52 bomber, working just fine with few of the original parts but lasting far longer than anyone initially thought (his Web site, iRobot, is amazing). ACLU executive director Ira Glasser told why, due to one vote in an obscure court case many decades ago, it isn't illegal for someone to read your e-mail. But, like a Hemingway novel, what wasn't said at the conference was many times as important as what was. The word *Microsoft* was rarely heard and even more rarely mentioned in positive terms, though it was the beached whale in the opera house.

The better one understands computer software, the less one respects the Beast from Redmond. One MIT professor wondered why people allow Microsoft to "get away with producing crummy software that crashes." A former Microsoft programmer told me, "Microsoft is like McDonald's. McDonald's doesn't make the best hamburgers, just the most. All my clients have Windows, so that's what I have to work with," thoughts most attendees would agree with. One programmer openly wondered if Frankenstein had been programmed by Bill Gates.

The four-day Camden Conference worked up to the final lecture by Steve Ballmer's fellow Farmington Hills–raised Bill Joy. Before his speech, Joy told me that "Gates is over the top, but Ballmer's mad, he's insane." (Robert Cringely told me, "That's Joy. He's so cerebral, so intellectual, so dispassionate, he's

Ballmer's opposite.") While the conference was going on, CNN reported that someone from the former Soviet Union had hacked into Microsoft's computers. Joy quipped, "The irony: someone from the former Evil Empire hacking into the current one." (*Personal Computer World* reported that the Russian could have been hacking inside Microsoft for three months, not the twelve days the Microsoft propagandists claimed.)

Joy stood up in front of the enthralled crowd and talked about his provocative, some say alarmist, but in any event much-talked-about April 2000 cover story in *Wired* magazine entitled "Why the Future Doesn't Need Us." Joy wrote of his fears that, with the advances in genetics and nanotechnology involving biologically based computers, and the advent of self-repairing and self-replicating robots (not unlike the Borg), robots could easily become a kind of unstoppable technological kudzu, with poor programming replicating poor programming, similar to the information age truism of GIGO—garbage in, garbage out. Joy also wrote about his Michigan roots, how he as a schoolboy, like Ballmer, had become interested in advanced mathematics. Unlike Ballmer, Joy wanted to be a ham radio operator, ham radio being "the Internet at the time, very addictive and quite solitary," but his mother thought he "was antisocial enough already" and nixed the idea. Joy grew up watching *Star Trek,* and says he accepted the *Star Trek* notion that humans had a future in space, western-style, with big heroes and adventures and strong moral values, embedded in its code like its Prime Directive: to not interfere in the development of less technologically advanced civilizations. Joy thinks that ethical humans, not robots, dominated *Star Trek* creator Gene Roddenberry's dream of the future. Such people don't seem to dominate Joy's current thinking.

Without specifically stating that Microsoft was the Borg, but well aware that Microsoft has over twenty thousand employees based in Seattle, Joy revealed that a professor from the University of Washington had written that, by his estimate, there were "at least twenty thousand people exhibiting delusional behavior in the Puget Sound area."

Delusional behavior. Authors independently interviewing Gates and Ballmer after Judge Jackson's ruling openly wondered if the diabolical duo is delusional. Of Gates, John Heilemann asked himself, "Is this man hallucinating? Or does he glimpse a reality that I'm too blind to see?" The *Washington Post* wrote that Gates insisting that the government was not successful in vilifying him at the trial was "a notion that most people who followed the trial would find laughable." Another wrote that it was "downright loopy." In his seminal work *Civilization and Its Discontents,* Freud observed that "no one, needless to say, who shares a delusion ever recognizes it as such." He notes that "each one of us behaves in some respect like a paranoic . . . a protection against suffering through a delusional remolding of reality." Microsoftians have been known to say the company's work ethic involves "constructive paranoia." And it wasn't for nothing that Andy Grove, the former chairman of Intel, entitled one of his books on the computer industry *Only the Paranoid Survive.*

In 1949, the clinically paranoid first secretary of defense, James Forrestal, jumped out of a window at the Bethesda Naval Hospital, shouting, "The commies are out to get me! The commies are out to get me!" Though Secretary Forrestal died, for the next four decades the profits of many manufacturers and the platforms of numerous politicians, including Richard Nixon, would come alive by invoking the Red Scare. Indeed, the decade-long national nightmare that Americans call the Vietnam War was based on a flawed theory that if another Asian country became communist, others would fall, like dominoes, a point refuted when America lost the war and not one other Asian country joined that collective. Like the vast majority of computer executives, Steve Ballmer didn't serve in the military—the draft lottery ended and the military became all voluntary the month he graduated from prep school. The draft-free, relatively war-free last quarter of the twentieth century is one reason so many young American men were freely available to work in computerdom, with the huge amount of defense spending helping fund their pursuits, along with the G.I. Bill for those who served.

Of course, Bill Gates viewed any reason that Microsoft couldn't have 100 percent control of personal computer operating systems as a threat. During one meeting with a well-known computer CEO attended by Ballmer, Gates, and a few other top Microsoft executives, the CEO explained that, when you attack a market, you shouldn't kill the competition, you should leave the companies wounded, walking wounded. You don't get rid of them. Corpses look bad and attract attention. Gates couldn't understand that. Ballmer was quiet. Gates wanted 100 percent of any market he could get. That was Gates's interpretation of the American way. As for Ballmer, a few years before he had told *CNET News,* "I think what we're doing is right, lawful, moral, proper, and competitive. I might even say it's the American way. We're innovating, adding value, driving down prices, competing, serving our customers, and we're doing it well. A lot of companies in the United States are benefiting because they're building on top of our platform and thriving. I might start playing 'The Star-Spangled Banner' if I went [on] too long."

Add to that feeling the mood of Detroit when Ballmer was being raised, one where a "Be American, Buy American" marketing tactic tied products to patriotism. Chevrolet wrapped Americana together in their slogan, "Baseball, hot dogs, apple pie and Chev-ro-lay." While Ballmer managed over forty thousand employees worldwide, he also managed to tie the Red Scare together with American boosterism and a faint blip on Microsoft's OS monopoly radar screen. Wrapping up Microsoft's annual financial analysts' meeting in Seattle, he said, "Linux is communist." Ballmer also said that he wanted "to emphasize the competitive threat, and in some senses the competitive opportunity, that Linux represents. Linux is a tough competitor. There's no company called Linux, there's barely a Linux road map. Yet Linux sort of springs organically from the earth And it had, you know, the characteristics of communism that people love so very, very much about it. That is, it's free." (An editor pointed out that Microsoft's Outlook Express was free, and also sometimes lets strangers share your hard disk.)

Linux is a free computer operating system programmed in Finland by the twenty-two-year-old Linus Torvalds. Linux is what computer operating systems would have been if Bill Gates hadn't acted like Jabba the Hut and thrown his MS-DOS, then Windows, obesity into the free software stream and jammed up the flow. Before Gates entered the computer software scene, many programs were written in a geek's spare time and passed around in a situation called shareware. In that famous 1975 "Open Letter to Hobbyists," the Bill Gates who had stolen time on both his prep school and Harvard computers, and would steal code from Gary Kildall and Stac Electronics, demanded that those programmers who copy the work of others stop so that the efforts of software creators be financially rewarded. But the hacker ethic wasn't geared toward making money, it was how to make cool, useful code. Thus was born a free software movement and a Free Software Foundation, headed by MIT programmer Richard Stallman, to champion that cause. (Stallman's firm belief is that proprietary software prevents computers from living up to their full potential.) Linux is not only free but it freely lays out its source code so any programmer can go in and adapt it to their needs. (During the antitrust trial, Ballmer toyed with the idea of opening Windows source code, a move David Boies said would "significantly change the case." But Ballmer backed down, and Windows code isn't open.) Linux is available under what is called a General

Public License, in essence giving the copyright away, asking in return that users make their changes to the code known to others. Linux requires one to have some programming skills to best install and use, which is the reason most non-techies tend to stay away. By portraying Linux as a threat to Microsoft, Ballmer could keep the fiction going that Windows had competitors and his company wasn't a monopoly, at least in his mind. But by saying Linux is communist, Ballmer lifted a big middle finger to the 1.25 billion Chinese already officially angry at Bill Gates.

Microsoft had historically done fairly well in Chinese computers. In fact, one of Microsoft's former managers in Beijing, Wu Shihong, speaks poetically about not only the company but Ballmer as well. Shihong told *China Online* that Ballmer is "the marshal of Entrepreneurs, the leader of Leaders, and the Soul of Microsoft." She says that Ballmer "seems to know every employee of Microsoft. People at the company's sales and marketing branches love, respect and revere Ballmer." However, with the bad luck of poor timing, Microsoft filed a copyright suit against a Chinese software manufacturer just after NATO planes accidentally sent a dumb smart bomb into Belgrade, blowing up the Chinese embassy and killing four diplomats. Bill Gates's well-publicized suit inadvertently put his somewhat human, definitely greedy imperialist's face on the tragedy on which the Chinese could vent their official five minutes of hate. Wu Shihong said she blamed Microsoft for taking such a stupid action, that offending one billion angry Chinese people was "idiotic." She "wasn't about to be the scapegoat." So she quit. Then Ballmer says Linux is communist. (Later, Ballmer would change his tune and say that "Linux is a virus.") Around the same time, Microsoft removed the words *idiot, fool,* and *nitwit* from Word's thesaurus; they were not replaced with *Steven Anthony Ballmer.* Author Mark Goldblatt called Bill Gates to ask him why words that were in the thesaurus of Word 97 had been deleted from Word 2000. Goldblatt was transferred to someone at Microsoft, who looked into the matter, then e-mailed an explanation to him: "Microsoft's approach regarding the spell checker dictionary and thesaurus is to not suggest words that may have offensive uses or provide offensive definitions for any words." As Bill Gates might say, "That's the stupidest fucking thing I've ever heard."

In any event, Ballmer probably regretted taking the stance. There's a perpetual optimist in Ballmer, the "we're golden—we're screwed" guy, and sometimes he almost sounds like Annie singing about the sun coming out "tomorrow." Well, almost, anyway.

CHAPTER FOURTEEN

SUNSHINE IN SEATTLE

To many people Seattle and Microsoft are synonymous, and the Microsoft powers that be are the ones who set the city's tone, driving its demeanor, some say making it meaner. But, like other people or companies, neither Ballmer nor Microsoft could control the weather. Thursday, June 28, 2001, started as an atypically overcast Seattle summer day. Normally, by this time of the year, the seemingly constant progression of clouds rolling over the city would have cleared. Though the clouds had come in the winter, the usual amount of rain hadn't, nor had the mountain snows, which, after thawing, run off to the rivers that race through the hydroelectric turbos that spin spin spin to produce the region's low-cost electricity. Seattleites were concerned that, by the end of summer, the turbos would be thirsty and the city would face a power shortage similar to the one Southern California was experiencing, forcing rolling blackouts, producing a textbook example of how not to deregulate public monopolies.

Halfway into the year, Seattle was on a roll; the problem was that it was downhill.

Seattle's image had taken a big hit two years before, when its truly inept police force incited rather than quelled well-organized protests at the World Trade Organization's annual meeting, turning it into a riot known worldwide as the Battle in Seattle. Then the dot-coms' instant-wealth-producing promise turned out to be more of a fad, their business models going bad, their many trusting employees left feeling they'd been had.

Since the Battle in Seattle and Judge Jackson's release of his findings of fact, Microsoft's stock had dropped from $119 a share to half of that. As the country, the stock market, and the city were adjusting to the George W. Bush administration and the third millennium came Seattle's February Mardi Gras riots, where gangs of blacks carried through on their vows to "beat up some white guys," killing one. These were pretty much ignored by national media when, twelve hours later, the city was rocked and rolled by a 6.2 earthquake. Even the Earth was bashing Seattle. Then Boeing announced it was leaving. Sinatra wasn't singing "It Was a Very Good Year."

Shortly thereafter, a suicidal woman, perched atop a 160-foot-high interstate highway bridge spanning a canal during morning rush hour, forced police to stop traffic, both ways, because passersby shouted things like "Go ahead and jump, bitch." And this in a city where honking a horn is considered bad form. Three hours later, rather than continue talking with Seattle police, the woman jumped. (Fortunately, she lived.) That summer, a weird statistic was revealed: Washington State ranked number one in the nation in sales of sunglasses. As the manager of a Seattle Sunglass Hut, Phil Nuygen, explains, "It's thought that since the sun disappears for long stretches, when it comes out again, people forget where they've put their sunglasses so they just go out and buy another pair."

That late June morning Steve Ballmer was taking his annual summer camping trip, as he had most summers since he was a kid. The only change was that now, at forty-five years old, Ballmer took along Connie and their three sons. This year, the Ballmers chose to camp in the Shasta National Forest, just above Redding, California. Ballmer interrupted his vacation to take a call from Bill Gates. Gates told him that the U.S. Court of Appeals in Washington, D.C., had just handed down its unanimous 7–0 ruling on Microsoft's antitrust case.

Just as Gates and Ballmer had hoped and planned and connived, the court really took to task Judge Jackson and stopped his order to bisect the company. Many Microsoftians described the ruling as a victory. Gates held a press conference a few hours later, with Ballmer booming in from a California Red Roof Inn. According to *Time* magazine and local newspapers, "Ballmer gloated, 'A cloud has lifted over the company. The sun was definitely shining today, all the way from Seattle down to Lake Shasta.'" The sun was definitely shining in California, but back home it simply teased in a dance Seattleites call "sun breaks." That day, sales at Phil Nuygen's Sunglass Hut were 69 percent below normal.

It's as though Gates and Ballmer had started reading *The Old Man and the Sea* but had stopped when Santiago tied the marlin to his boat. For the court of appeals just as unanimously found that Judge Jackson had shown no actual bias in his ruling, that Microsoft was an illegal monopoly, that it had acted in an anticompetitive manner to maintain its monopoly, that it had violated at least one, possibly two, provisions of the Sherman Antitrust Act, and that it was sending the case back down to another judge to decide what was needed to correct Microsoft's corporate crimes, up to and including a breakup. They totally upheld Jackson's ruling on how Microsoft sabotaged Java. But you wouldn't know any of that listening to Gates and Ballmer and the Microsoft propaganda machine, all spinning faster than western Washington's water-deprived turbos, masterfully protecting Microsoft's raging revenue river, pumping out more economic power than Seattle's ever known. The same day Slobodan Milosevic was arguing his case in the International Court in the Hague, as part of the Yugoslavian war crimes trials based on the law Supreme Court Justice Robert Jackson, with the help of Fred Ballmer, had set in place at Nuremberg. The *New York Times* reported that Milosevic "denied the reality of his situation."

The court of appeals ruling set Wall Street vibrating and sent Microsoft stock up a few points before investors soaked in the full ruling and the stock settled down below its pre-decision price. Weeks later, and with a straight face, Microsoft appealed its victory to the court of appeals. The court quickly rejected the company's he's-an-idiot argument that Microsoft's "witness knew more about software than the government witness did," saying the company "misconstrued our ruling," and sent the case down to another lower court, the judge to be chosen, at random, by a courthouse computer, using a Windows operating system.

A short while later, Ballmer's Monkey Boy video appeared on the Web. One observer wondered if the release of the video was timed as a misdirection play, to take focus away from the Court of Appeals ruling. The Monkey Boy video was first reported by Thomas Greene, of the British tech publication *The Register*. The reaction to the video shows the range of how people feel about Ballmer and Microsoft. Greene wrote, "I think the video shows the real Ballmer. In observing his public appearances I've often detected a volcanic, unthinking ego which he struggles to contain." A chat room on the Web site NetSlaves.com pondered the question "Is Steve Ballmer bound for Bellevue?" [the New York hospital—Ballmer lives in Bellevue, Washington]. One reviewer wrote, "If I were one of the richest men in America and I got there by running a company that wasn't directly involved in polluting the environment, running third-world sweatshops, causing cancer, heart disease, lung disease, had some products that could be kind of cool sometimes and lived in a really beautiful part of the country, I might jump around like this, too." Another echoed the thought, saying, "If the company I worked for made me a multigazillionaire, I'd love it enough to make a big jackass of myself." Others thought, "Makes him seem human." "I wonder if he played any sports in high school?" "The bit where he screams 'Give it up for meee,' I guess that means give up any kind of independent thought, all your money, your private life, your wife, basically give up everything for the master of Microsoft." One critic, claiming to be a former Microsoftian, wrote, "To an extent, Ballmer's enthusiasm as well as being able to convey it upon subordinates, is one of the things that makes him a leader rather than just a manager." Microsoft wouldn't comment on the actions in the video, or even say when the event took place, but a spokeswoman told the *New York Times,* "Microsoft employees love how excited Steve is about the company and the software industry. We're glad he's leading Microsoft."

Raising three young sons, Steve Ballmer returned to his true religious roots (as opposed to his religious belief in Microsoft) and became more public with his family and his faith. Part of Ballmer's campaign to counter his court-confirmed reputation as a hard-hearted, predatory monopolist was showing his softer, family man side. While some people might think this is like the owner of a car dealership trotting out his kids in a television ad to sell his cars, Ballmer is a committed, concerned, loving father, driving his oldest son, Sam, to school every morning on his way to work, and limiting his computer use to two hours a day. Like his father, Steve plays chess with Sam—Aaron and Peter aren't old enough yet; Sam likes the game so much he regularly has matches with an on-line pal in China. And Sam's name started to pop up in father Steve's press encounters. After Judge Jackson handed down his decision, Ballmer told the *New York Times,* "I mentioned to my son there was going to be this ruling. He said, 'Well, I hope it's good for you, Dad. Dad, if they don't agree with you, you guys will appeal, right? Because what you did is all right, right, Dad?' And I said, 'That's right, Sam.' I mean, he's not our legal strategist or anything, but he does understand our view."

As part of the nice-guy campaign, Ballmer returned to his geographic roots as well. He gave a well-received speech in front of a packed hometown crowd of over a thousand people spilling out of a synagogue several miles from his boyhood Lynford Road home in Farmington Hills, which, incidentally, he still owns. The night before his temple speech, he gave a private talk at the Father and Son's Day dinner at his prep school, Country Day. And after the court ruling, Ballmer sat for an interview for a cover story in the *Detroit Jewish News* talking about his family, especially mother Bea. At the temple, Ballmer talked not about his religion, but the importance of parenthood. In fact, Ballmer isn't very religious, but his religion is a plus in the computer industry. Given that there are few barriers to entry in computerdom, and the great value the Jewish faith (and Ballmer) places on formal education, which prepares one to produce intellectual property, it's not surprising that about 30 percent of computer executives are Jewish. Compared to the auto industry, where, when Ballmer was being raised, the only Jew to reach the realm of chief executive officer was Gerald Meyers at American Motors, the opportunities are vast. Besides, the Jewish concept of chutzpah swims well in the software stream.

As Harvard Law professor Alan Dershowitz explains, "Chutzpah is a boldness, assertiveness, a willingness to demand what is due, to defy tradition, to challenge authority, to raise eyebrows," qualities perfectly matched to the computer industry in general and Microsoft in particular. Dershowitz notes, "Sometimes chutzpah can seem vulgar to a more-reserved Christian world, but that self-assertiveness in the competitive world serves Jews well.

In business, passivity is not a virtue." About 36 percent of the top fifty American billionaires, and 33 percent of all American millionaires, are Jewish, over sixteen times their numbers in the general population. Why? Long before Steve Ballmer was born and began exhibiting his staying power and vast amount of energy, Mark Twain pondered a similar question.

Writing in *Harper's* magazine, Twain relayed,

Jews constitute but one quarter of one percent of the human race. It suggests a nebulous dim puff of stardust lost in the blaze of the Milky Way. Properly, the Jew ought hardly to be heard of; but he is heard of, and has always been heard of . . . his importance is extravagantly out of proportion to the smallness of his bulk. . . . He has made a marvelous fight in this world, in all ages; and has done it with his hands tied behind him. The Egyptian, the Babylonian, and the Persian rose, filled the planet with sound and splendor, then faded into dream-stuff and passed away; the Greek and Roman followed, and made a vast noise, and they are gone; other peoples have sprung up and held their torch high for a time, but it burned out, and they sit in the twilight now, or have vanished. The Jew saw them all, beat them all, and is now what he always was . . . no slowing of his energies, no dulling of his alert and aggressive mind. All things are mortal but the Jews; all other forces pass, but what is the secret of his immortality?

Indeed.

Then came September 11. The sun was barely over the horizon in Seattle when terrorists slammed their skyjacked planes into the twin World Trade Center towers in New York, the Pentagon in Arlington, and the ground near Pittsburgh. Would the West Coast be attacked as the workday began? No one knew and, like others on the Left Coast, Seattleites weren't taking any chances. As the events played out three thousand miles away, city officials announced that the Space Needle would be closed. Microsoft, the militarylike company that often talked of its business strategies in terms of jihads, was thought to be a possible target of Osama bin Laden's. On the advice of his security people, Ballmer took a virtually unprecedented action and effectively closed down the campus, sending a compassionate e-mail letting employees know that they could take uncharged leave. (The campus wasn't even shut down seven months before, when Seattle was hit with the earthquake.) Says one former Microsoft exec, "They were probably just being paranoid." Possibly. But as the 1960s mantra noted, just because you're paranoid doesn't mean they aren't out to get you. Not one Microsoftian was reported lost on September 11. Microsoft's Reno, Nevada, office later received what they thought was anthrax in the ensuing germ warfare attacks. The sample was retested and found not to be toxic.

Computerdom brought some measure of security and stability in that the Internet still functioned perfectly. E-mail went back and forth. As if more proof were needed of Microsoft's ubiquity, at least one of the skyjackers had, like U.S. Navy pilots, used Microsoft's game Flight Simulator to help train for his mission; he and his comrades had communicated with each other, and cells in Europe and Afghanistan, using Microsoft's Hotmail. When Ballmer found out that a graduate of Detroit Country Day, interning on the ninety-second floor of the WTC's south tower, was missing, he immediately offered his condolences and help. (One can easily picture Ballmer on the scene at Ground Zero in New York, resembling George C. Scott, in the movie *Patton*, directing traffic to keep things moving; shouting, screaming, gesturing, doing whatever it takes to get the job done.) It would later be revealed that pictures of Seattle's Space Needle, a local Boeing airplane factory, and Washington State's Grand Coulee Dam were found in an al-Qaida safe house in Pakistan, yet no pictures were found of the Microsoft office park. Microsoftians no longer talked in terms of mounting jihads. Strangely, the attacks would work to Microsoft's advantage.

A few weeks later, as the national numbness wore off and we gave ourselves permission to laugh again, *Slate*'s Michael Kinsley reacted to the post-attack near-hysteria and the many jingoistic "fight terrorism, buy American" marketing campaigns launched by penning a satirical column for the *Washington Post* offering his irreverent solutions to the sagging economy. With his tongue firmly planted in his cheek Kinsley suggested his agenda for victory, including the recommendation that the Department of Justice drop its antitrust suit against Microsoft. Kinsley wrote, "As an employee and stockholder, I know the dispiriting effect this litigation is having on people at one of the U.S. economy's most important companies . . . our government should not be picking a fight with this American company with so much software to contribute to the war effort." Incredibly, the Justice Department acted as though they took Kinsley's piece seriously. The new head of the DOJ's antitrust division, Charles James, had already announced that he wouldn't be seeking a structural remedy—the breakup of the company—thus unilaterally throwing away the government's prime bargaining chip without getting anything from the guilty party in return, a negotiating technique that raised eyebrows worldwide. Reading the news, Jeff Danziger drew a cartoon entitled "Good News Received at the Microsoft War Room," showing a large Ballmer standing behind a sitting, SS-capped Gates, watching two assistants push back briefcase-holding troops from the word *monopoly*. Ballmer says, "Ha, ha! You see? The enemy is retreating." Some people thought that Bush's Justice Department was acting out the 150-year-old words of Republican businessman Simon Cameron when he said, "An honest politician is one who, when he's bought, stays bought."

On September 28 the third federal judge to preside over Microsoft and the monopoly police, Colleen Kollar-Kotelly, told both parties, "The recent tragic events affecting our nation demanded a prompt end to litigation" that had already roiled the stock market and generated economic uncertainty. Connecticut's attorney general, Richard Blumenthal, told the *Wall Street Journal,* "The world has changed, with war abroad, threats at home and a deteriorating economy, creating a powerful dynamic to settle." In fact, Microsoft and the monopoly police had scheduled settlement talks in Washington for September 11, only to have them canceled when the Department of Justice building was evacuated. Still, settlement discussions went nowhere until, on October 15, Judge Kollar-Kotelly appointed Boston University law professor Eric Green to mediate.

Several months before the Bush Administration's DOJ began capitulating, Steve Ballmer is thought to have paved the proposed settlement way when he went to Washington and had a hush-hush meeting at the White House with Vice President Dick Cheney. Cheney's office refuses to release any notes from the meeting (of course, in February 2002 the bipartisan General Accounting Office took the unprecedented action of suing the White House for notes from the vice president's talks with Enron officials and others). Microsoft propagandists were quiet about the Ballmer-Cheney meeting until that noted liberal publication the *Wall Street Journal* ferreted out the high-level hobnobbing. Then reporters were assured by both Microsoft's propagandists and Cheney's office that Cheney and Ballmer didn't talk about the antitrust case. Cheney's spokesman said that Cheney had a lawyer present and that "Ballmer and Cheney discussed a broad range of issues, including trade, piracy, education, work-force issues, tax credits for research, and visas for foreign workers." Microsoft spokeswoman Ginny Terazano said, "Ballmer's timing has nothing to do with the court of appeals and the notion of such is silly."

The silly *Washington Post* reported that, on August 17, Philip J. Perry was named acting associate attorney general, overseeing, among other things, the antitrust division of the Department of Justice. Perry is married to Vice President Cheney's daughter, Elizabeth Perry. In an article entitled "Family Ties and Antitrust Whys," the *Post*'s James Grimaldi asked, "Does this mean Perry will be running the out-of-court negotiations with Microsoft? Has he been handed the job of giving Microsoft a lenient settlement? Is Perry the White House errand boy on the Microsoft case as part of a payback for the software giant's GOP campaign contributions? [Perry declined Grimaldi's interview request.] And, of course, these probably are silly, exaggerated rumors that come when you're related to a high-ranking elected official."

Bill Gates helped out the recovery effort at Ground Zero by appearing in New York City for the Windows XP release along with Mayor Rudy Giuliani. It's probably unrelated that, a short while later, New York State would agree to settle its antitrust case against Microsoft. The big push in Redmond was that Windows XP was scheduled for release on October 25, a shipping date Ballmer absolutely promised Charlie Rose on national television that Microsoft would make. And Ballmer delivered. Within two months of release, over seven million units were sold, one of the reasons *Business Week* would name Ballmer one of the top twenty-five CEOs for 2001 (the other was Xbox). And it was good as any Microsoft operating system has ever been. For the first time in Microsoft's history, it hit the release-date bulls'-eye. For the first time in Microsoft's history, a product lived up to much of its hype. The *New York Times* gave Windows XP a glowing review, joining the vast majority of other critics. Finally, a Windows that didn't crash. The successful Windows XP release, combined with the announcement several days later of a proposed settlement with the federal monopoly police, promised an eventful stockholders' meeting the first week of November.

After beginning to write this book I bought one share of Microsoft stock—my total tech stock holdings—so I could attend the annual choir preaching called a shareholders' meeting as a part owner. (The green and white stock certificate hangs on my wall as I write this.) Technically, Steve Ballmer works for me—and the over one million other holders of Microsoft shares. And no one appreciates Microsoft more than its stockholders. For good reason. If someone had invested twenty-one dollars in one share of Microsoft stock at the IPO in March 1986, and held onto it until the 2001 stockholders' meeting, it would be worth $9,269.00. Their stock would have increased about 440 times—over 44,000 percent—during the ensuing fifteen and a half years. If a Microsoftian had held on to their initial two thousand five hundred options given at the IPO, they would be worth well over twenty million dollars. If the population of the United States had increased as dramatically over this period, there would be over one hundred billion Americans, a few billion of them probably looking for parking spaces. (In a year of stock ownership I'd lost $4.78, not counting transaction fees.)

On Tuesday, November 7, 2001, at 7:30 A.M., I entered the cavernous Washington State Convention Center for our meeting, avoiding the media registration. While being searched in the outer lobby, presumably for any guns or bombs, the screener asked what I had in my hand. "A tape recorder," I replied. "Those aren't allowed," he said, pointing to a sign saying that recording devices were banned. Incredulous, I went over to the media desk and asked why. Though streaming video of the stockholders' meeting would appear on Microsoft's Web site, and transcripts are available there, too, for some reason one couldn't tape the goings-on. The media representative couldn't give me the reason for the no-taping rule, but wanted to sign me up. I acquiesced. (And I kept my tape recorder.) I was in the world of Microsoft, and Microsoft plays by its own rules. I pondered this weirdness while standing in the convention center's huge inner lobby, reading some Microsoft propaganda about their freedom to innovate, my head down, when the air around me swooshed; a force of energy shot by, and I felt its vortex. If I was a weather vane I would have been spinning. I looked up to see Steve Ballmer almost skipping toward the stage. That's Ballmer. He always seems in a hurry (when signing his name, his attempt to cross the *t* in Steven always appears above the *n*), and co-workers say he often invades personal space (many competitors agree), but those are some of the things some of his workers like about him.

Cameron Mhyrvold told me, "Steve always had an open-door policy, where anyone could come in and talk to him about anything. While you might work for a product manager, you felt you were really working for Steve. Once, he popped into my office and started asking about something I was working on. Within five minutes Steve had reduced it down to the key issues. In two years my project manager hadn't reduced it down to the key issues. Wow, I thought, this is a guy who knows what he's doing. That's inspiring. It's been said that Gates is a guy who people tend to be in awe of whereas Steve is a guy you want to work for. That's true. I'd walk across hot coals for the man." And novelist Douglas Coupland told me that, in the early 1990s, when he was researching *Microserfs*, both Gates and Ballmer had open-door policies. Coupland said he would just walk up to Gates's door, knock, and ask him a few quick questions; the same with Ballmer. But when he visited the campus years later, around the turn of the millennium, access to Gates and Ballmer, as well as many other Microsoftians, was severely restricted.

Safely in the convention center's main room, I took a seat two aisles away from the press corral, put my backpack down, and mingled. One stockholder I talked with came "because if you get here early enough you get free Starbucks and a light breakfast." (In fact, the two cups of Starbucks coffee and a croissant I got made us even for my stock purchase, not counting the transaction cost.) Another shareholder said she "just wanted to see Bill Gates." A third wanted to try out Windows XP on the kiosks set up around the lobby. Most of us owners kept to ourselves. When the meeting began, promptly at eight, most of the chairs were empty. Why go to the theater when you can see it on the Internet?

On the dais, Steve Ballmer sat to the left of Bill Gates, with the other six members of the board of directors spaced around. Like a good general of the armies, Ballmer sat back and let Rick Belluzzo, the man he'd chosen to take over his role as president nine months before, run the meeting. In 1999, Ballmer had brought Belluzzo over from Silicon Graphics, where he'd served as CEO after spending twenty-three years at Hewlett-Packard. By taking over many of Ballmer's administrative duties—what Ballmer refers to as "administrivia"—Belluzzo allowed Ballmer to spend more time on strategic issues.

Belluzzo introduced the board members, pointed out the exhibits in the inner lobby, then said that he's "pleased to note that we are joined by the Freedom to Innovate Network . . . a grassroots and communications tool." In fact, the Freedom to Innovate Network is Microsoft-funded and is anything but grassroots. Washington, D.C., lobbyists call such groups "Astroturf" due to their phony nature. Given the great advances in computer technology, any state-of-the-art personal computer and printer can quickly turn out hundreds of letters, saying basically the same thing with different typefaces and paper, then send them off to whatever public official they want to lobby. Iowa attorney general Tom Miller wondered why many of the letters he received calling on him to drop his state's antitrust case contained the same sentences. Minnesota Attorney General Michael Hatch received three hundred identical letters, prompting him to call the campaign "sleazy." When one letter writer found out he'd unwittingly become a tool of Microsoft, the conned man hand-wrote Hatch apologizing for his previous letter, saying, "I sure was misled. It's time for you to get out there and kick butt." But these AGs were better off than Utah's, who received two letters supporting Microsoft's freedom to innovate from people long dead. True innovation.

Belluzzo continued with the election of directors. Apparently, neither Belluzzo nor anyone else in the company noticed that their CEO was called "Steven A. Balimer" (sic) on their proxy. All eight of the nominated directors were elected. After listening to, then shooting down, a stockholder's proposal that Microsoft should change its business practices in China—mentioning that Ballmer had visited China the previous fall and met with Chinese premier Zhu Rongji, not mentioning, of course, that he called Linux communist—Belluzzo ran down the year's numbers. Total revenue was up over 10 percent, to $25.3 billion, yet the company had a $4.8 billion "impairment in investments." Belluzzo's impairment to clear language was a lame attempt to avoid the word loss, the reversals coming from Microsoft's telecommunications and cable investments. While revenues in Europe, Africa, and the Middle East were down 3 percent, they were still $4.8 billion; Asia showed Microsoft's largest overseas growth, up 15 percent. Belluzzo remarked that operating expenses "were well behaved" and that they had invested over four billion dollars in research and investment—no breakdown into exactly where. He noted that, in the past year, they'd added some eight thousand six hundred employees. Most important for us shareholders, while the NASDAQ as a whole had lost over 45 percent of its value in the last year, Microsoft's stock lost a mere 13 percent. Belluzzo then introduced Bill Gates.

Gates took the podium and said, "For many years, I've hoped to be able to get up here and say what I can say this morning, which is that we have our settlement with the Department of Justice on the antitrust case." There was mild applause. In fact, what had been reached was a proposed settlement which did nothing to penalize Microsoft for any of its past predatory behavior. Much of the opposition to the deal was summed up by Real Networks general counsel Kelly Jo MacArthur, who said, "It's a reward, not a remedy. This agreement allows a declared illegal monopolist to determine at its sole discretion, what goes into the monopoly operating system of the future." Other critics called it "toothless," containing "enough loopholes here to drive the sixth fleet through." The harshest critic was Mitchell Kertzman, CEO of Microsoft rival Liberate Technologies, who noted it doesn't do anything to curb .Net. Kertzman told CNET News that the proposed settlement "doesn't address any of the forward-looking issues like Passport or HailStorm. Microsoft just got away with what is effectively corporate murder. How are they going to be after that?"

The proposed settlement moved a former Nixon administration speechwriter, conservative *New York Times* columnist William Safire, to call the second Bush administration's antitrust division "an assortment of wimps." Charles James told the *Wall Street Journal* that if companies had problems with the settlement he negotiated with Microsoft, "they can sue." In March 2002, Scott McNealy's Sun Microsystems did just that, yet again filing suit in federal court, yet again claiming that Microsoft is impeding Java's ability to write code once and have it run anywhere, this time asking for one billion dollars in damages. The more things change, the more they . . . One ex-Microsoftian told me that it seems that software business strategy has gone from "Sun Tzu to Sun sued."

MSNBC, the news service jointly owned by Microsoft and NBC, reported that former senator John Tunney, who wrote and sponsored the Tunney Act, accused Microsoft of failing to disclose all its conversations with U.S. government officials. In the months following the cozy settlement, Microsoft and the Justice Department voluntarily removed a full paragraph from the proposal which, as the *Seattle Times* reported, "may have forced software companies, computer makers and other beneficiaries of the settlement to share their intellectual property with Microsoft." Before Judge Kollar-Kotelly could accept the settlement—similar to a plea bargain—she was, like Judge Sporkin before her, required to hold a Tunney Act review, inviting public comments within a sixty-day period. During that time, over twenty-five thousand public letters were received, over five thousand them by e-mail, including one short sentence—"I hate Microsoft!" For the Tunney Act review, Ballmer gave a videotaped deposition, parts of which can be seen on Microsoft's Web site. Taped three months after the stockholders' meeting, it shows a trimmed-down, soft-spoken, sincere Ballmer, as though, compared to Monkey Boy Ballmer, he'd taken a personality pill. If nothing else, it shows the great contrast between him and Gates, at least in how they appear in court.

At the stockholders' meeting Gates continued, "We're thinking a lot about how to be an even more responsible leader in our industry." Gates-speak at its best. A few minutes later, after more mild applause, Gates gave way to Ballmer.

After introductory remarks, Ballmer said that "the thing that I think we're really focused [on] or I'm focused in on a lot these days really is how we comport ourselves in some senses as a company. The last three years, the period of the lawsuits, people ask us what we've learned. . . . We understand based upon the fact that our industry didn't rally to support us that we need to change the way we interact and relate to our industry." Given that nine federal judges had clearly and convincingly found Microsoft to have actively sought to eliminate competition, can Ballmer really be surprised that the computer industry didn't rally to support Microsoft? As Ballmer spoke, the woman next to me said, "Look at Gates, he's glued to what Ballmer's saying." And he was, total admiration on his face, looking at his best friend as if to say "job well done." Microsoft's 2001 annual report shows a picture of a smiling, pleased, genuinely human-looking Gates standing next to the seated Ballmer, looking down as though his star pupil just gave him the perfect answer. Another stockholder said, "I came, in part, to see that Bill Gates and Steve Ballmer exist, that they are real people, but I was surprised how short Gates is." In fact, Gates is three inches shorter than Ballmer, though pictures of them together inevitably make Gates look taller.

As Ballmer spoke, I kept thinking of the public statements he or Gates had made compared with what he was now telling stockholders. Ballmer continued, "There is one principle that stays constant . . . we're very honest with ourselves ["Neither of my parents ever went to college"], we have a lot of integrity about admitting, as one of our senior people like to say, what is reality. ["You're either with us or against us and you're the enemy now."] We don't confuse ourselves ["I still don't know what a monopoly is"], we don't speak incorrectly to one another ["That's the stupidest fucking thing I've ever heard"], we don't speak incorrectly to the world ["We have done absolutely nothing wrong"]. We pride ourselves on that kind of honesty ["There is a Chinese Wall between applications and operating system"] and integrity ["DOS isn't done until Lotus won't run"], in everything that we say and do." I failed to stifle a laugh. Federal Judges Sporkin and Jackson, Seattle Computer Products' Rod Brock, DRI's Gary Kildall, GO's Jerry Kaplan, Stac Electronics' Gary Clow, and Sun Microsystems' Scott McNealy would be among the first in line to disagree, in front of many, many people worldwide.

After he was finished, Ballmer sat back down next to Gates and, along with the rest of the folk on the dais, took questions. For the past year and a half I'd debated what to ask Ballmer, and concluded it was best just to observe and let the meeting play itself out. Two stockholders' questions involved women at Microsoft. One woman noted that five years ago, two out of the top twenty officers were women. Now, only one of the top twenty-three officers are women. Belluzzo answered that they were working on the situation (someone later said that, given the results, maybe they should stop working on it. Two female stockholders later told me, "I don't care who works there, I just want them to make money"). In what some observers told me was a rift with Steve Ballmer, Linda Stone resigned from the company four months later, though she would be the last person to publicly acknowledge any discontinuity with Ballmer.

While Belluzzo and others answered other questions, the diabolical duo talked. Then Gates glared at me. No, I thought, he couldn't be. I don't have that distinct an appearance, and I was twenty rows away. Recall that Thomas Friedman had received the glare at Davos. From what I saw, it's similar to something one might do in junior high school. I glanced at the woman next to me, at the woman to the right of me, at the people behind me. None of them were looking at Gates. I looked back at the dais. Bill Gates *was* glaring at me. I hunched forward, squinted my eyes, and stared back. I don't recall who looked away first. While the meeting ended soon after, many questions remained unanswered.

CHAPTER FIFTEEN

TOMB OF THE UNKNOWNS

n the early 1990s, to take into account every unidentified American who died in our various wars, not just the military folk, Arlington Cemetery unofficially renamed the Tomb of the Unknown Soldier the Tomb of the Unknowns. There are many questions about Ballmer and Microsoft and the casualties of the information revolution that will probably lie in a tech Tomb of the Unknowns until the end of time. More than a few curious minds would relish reading the entombed court records of the numerous lawsuits Microsoft has settled, in part to insure such documents would be sealed. Programmers worldwide would welcome perusing Microsoftian source codes, ranging from MS-DOS to Windows XP, to see not only how much of CP/M Microsoft stole but exactly how they made non-Microsoft applications run slower, if at all, and to make theirs run better. Such a tomb would also contain a transcript of what Ballmer and Vice President Dick Cheney talked about when they met privately in 2001. Yet some haunting questions currently in the Ballmer tomb of the unknowns are these: What will the good father Steve say to his sons when they mature and confront him with the documentation of his dirty deeds? Will Steve Ballmer's sons react like John D. Rockefeller Jr. and use their inheritance to make up for their father's excesses? The most troubling questions are: Was Fredric Ballmer's past Steve Ballmer's prologue? Is it more than a simple twist of fate that the son of a man who helped prosecute the Nazis and their supporters for illegally eliminating competition, and who admits that his father taught him about international business, would come to use business tactics that several leading computer executives, and more than a few observers, independently compare to those of Hitler and his followers? Those are dark thoughts indeed, yet questions unavoidable from the preponderance of public documents and echoed by public statements.

In that tomb would also lie the answer to many a question concerning what the future holds for Steve Ballmer and Microsoft. Like the total number of American war deaths (there are still twenty thousand MIAs from World War II), their fortunes are unknown and unknowable, save for some key factors. Many people think it's difficult to imagine a Microsoft without either Bill Gates or Steve Ballmer; AOL Time Warner chairman Steve Case told Ken Auletta that the company reflects, and is made up of, their combined DNA (and Case told David Kaplan that he calls Gates the "Hitler of Redmond"); that genetic structure alone insures a small measure of immortality. One thing is certain: Bill Gates and Steve Ballmer will be either making software, or making money off software, or making money off the money that they made making software, until they go wherever the obscenely rich go after they stop living. One person I interviewed asked if he thought Steve Ballmer might buy a National Basketball Association team. After all, he plays pickup games regularly and he reportedly had a chance to buy the Seattle Sonics but passed.

Ballmer won't buy a professional basketball team anytime soon, if at all—it would take away from his focus—even though, by putting up part of his Microsoft stock as collateral, Steve Ballmer could buy the whole NBA, lock, human stock, and dirty towel barrel. (Unless, of course, owning the whole NBA would violate antitrust law. That might be a problem.) To study under Gates and Ballmer, which is to work directly for them, is a cornucopia of mass consumer and business marketing strategy unsurpassed at any college or university on the planet. In no small part due to their mentoring, Microsoft has layer upon layer of experienced, bright, often even capable managers who, if Gates and Ballmer were to leave, could keep reinforcing, keep coming up and at you like the rows and rows of computer-generated soldiers in the films *Star Wars*, *Gladiator*, and *Lord of the Rings*. If Gates and Ballmer were to stop working there, today, Microsoft would stumble and go on. A founder is often not the best person to run a company. Bob Metcalfe told me that he thinks Gates and Ballmer have the founder's disease. One need look no further than the idiosyncratic Henry Ford to see that the talents which led him to do incredible things worked against him in his later years.

In April 2002 Rick Belluzzo announced that he was resigning as Microsoft's president. Ballmer told reporters that he was again taking on that task, in addition to being CEO, a good husband and father, and, of course, Bill Gates's best friend. Belluzzo lasted fourteen months, longer than James Towne and Mike Hallman, two of the previous presidents. Scott McAdams, head of a Seattle-based investment firm and a longtime Microsoft watcher, observed, "Obviously Bill and Steve are not real happy with the way things are going, and [Belluzzo is] taking the heat. I don't think Rick is to blame, but he's the fall guy." It seems that Belluzzo learned the hard way that just as you don't get between a journalist and a deadline, or a mother bear and her cubs, you don't get between Bill Gates and Steve Ballmer. McAdams says,

"At the end of the day, it's still the Bill and Steve show." He adds, "It sounds like Steve will roll up his sleeves and do it himself"—just like Bea Ballmer rolled up her sleeves and greased the wheel bearings for Hank Borgman back in Detroit, just like Borgman could picture Steve Ballmer doing, just like Steve Ballmer does. If you want something done right, you have to . . .

It's not generally talked about, but Microsoft is building its own satellite system to provide Internet/MSN access without having to go through cables or telephone lines owned by others. If the Boeing rockets used to propel their satellites into orbit stop blowing up—a common problem with solid rocket boosters—Microsoft expects its system to be operational sometime around 2004 or 2005. One former Microsoftian asks, "Will the United Nations check [the satellites] to make sure they don't contain nuclear weapons?"

Ballmer's nemesis Scott McNealy compares the future computer industry to the automobile business both he and Ballmer were raised around. McNealy told *The New Yorker* that computing will eventually boil down to its own Big Three: Microsoft and Intel ("General" and "Motors," he says), IBM, and Sun. This is the reason that, as the rest of the industry has coalesced around the "Wintel" dynasty—Windows software and Intel microprocessors—Sun produces its own operating systems and chips.

The fact that McNealy and Ballmer, two sons of white-collar workers at the center of the automobile age, would become involved in the natural American business progression to the information age isn't abnormal—many of their contemporaries work in computerdom. That they both went to both Harvard and Stanford Business School at the same time is remarkable. That the wealth of the relatively poor boy Ballmer, from an unconnected family, would surpass the financial worth of well-connected rich kid McNealy some fifteen times over is the stuff American dreams are made of, the promise this experiment called America extends to the tired, poor, and huddled masses of the world, even those located outside its borders. But Ballmer queers the image in the way he gained his fortune. One can picture a kid, hearing of Ballmer's success and then discovering his documented dark side, standing next to him, tugging at his shirttail, saying, "Say it ain't so, Steve."

No matter what the Supreme Court does, if and when it again receives the case, Microsoft will pretty much keep on doing things their way; they'll keep trying to dominate anything they touch, and they'll keep getting sued—winning some cases, losing others. This probably doesn't bother Steve Ballmer too much. In February 2002, Ballmer told CNET News, "We're a company that pretty much can do anything of a software nature that we set our mind to." Recall that one of Ballmer's role models, NBA coach Isaiah Thomas, captained a team proudly calling itself the Bad Boys, which set a league record for fouls. In Ballmer's mind it's probably just fine to foul, as long as you don't foul out of the game. In terms of personal computer operating systems, though, Ballmer acts like it's Microsoft's basketball and we'll play by Microsoft's rules.

The fact is that American producers and consumers are surrounded by the fruits of fair and robust competition, much of which is best produced and sold in a rigorously competitive environment. The Sherman Antitrust Law and its sister, the Clayton Act, work to ensure a fair marketplace. Indeed, the greatest fear of Major League Baseball, America's national sport, is that Congress will remove its antitrust exemption. The American system hasn't been able to prevent Ballmer and Microsoft from taking something that costs the company, after it makes back its costs, (about a buck) and selling this needed software for $179. As such, the real action against Microsoft might well take place in Ballmer's temporary childhood residence of Brussels, Belgium. There, the European Union's Competition Commission is investigating some of the same charges Microsoft faces at home. With more than 50 percent of Microsoft's sales coming outside America, if the Competition Commission would find Microsoft guilty and order it to untie Windows, among other things, it would be a blow difficult for Ballmer and his company to handle. No doubt many people would find it ironic that the country that had stopped Napoleon from dominating the world would do the same thing with Bill Gates.

And consider this: Microsoft today could stop producing software, close up shop, give away a copy of Windows XP to every one of the over six billion human beings on the planet, and still be more profitable than over 99 percent of all American companies. Microsoft could also lay off all fifty thousand of its employees, giving each of them one hundred thousand dollars in severance pay plus ten thousand shares of stock, and it would still have over twenty-five billion dollars in its coffers. A 10 percent annual return on its remaining wealth would give it two and a half billion dollars a year in income.

Imagine a true challenge for Gates and Ballmer. In negotiations with the Justice Department Gates said, "You can give me any seat at the table [at Linux, Sun, or any other tech company] and I can blow away Microsoft!" If, like Silicon Graphics and Netscape founder Jim Clark, Gates and Ballmer just walked away from Microsoft and started all over again with, say, a measly billion dollars each, they'd find a way to make another personal computer operating system and give their former company a run for the money.

What makes Ballmer run? In 1992, after Kurt Vonnegut found out that the convicted double-F.B.I.-agent murderer Leonard Peltier had reneged on a collaboration agreement with me, out of the blue he wrote this virtual stranger the nicest, most supportive letter that any nascent author would relish. In Vonnegut's typical and explicit terms, he suggested how to rearrange Peltier's anatomy. In a postscript, Vonnegut offered that Kin Hubbard, a humorist from his hometown of Indianapolis, always said, "If they say 'It ain't the money,' it's the money." Yet in Ballmer's case, it really isn't the money. He's wealthier than 99.99999999 percent of the world's population. He could spend a million dollars a day every day for the rest of his life and still have many billions left over. When is enough enough? Why does he keep going?

Ballmer's Harvard football teammate Dan Jiggitts said it best when he observed that Ballmer's a competition addict whose competition switch is stuck in the on position. Add to that the Jewish concept of the *naches* machine, achieving to fulfill parents' expectations and unactualized dreams again and again and again. Recall that Cameron Mhyrvold said that Ballmer's "absolutely motivated by challenge." Charles Kuralt noted that the Birmingham, Michigan, residents Ballmer impressed were "all in a race, where there isn't any resting place and there isn't any finishing line."

What else makes Ballmer run? The man I found would be proud to have his epitaph read: "Steven Anthony Ballmer: son of Bea and Fred; father of Sam, Aaron, and Peter; husband of Connie; best friend of Bill Gates; and a crummy basketball player who still loved the game."

Other questions for the tomb of the unknowns: Is Steve Ballmer's mendacity just the way of the big business world, an example of the 1980s maxim that if you can't dazzle them with your brilliance, baffle them with your bullshit? At a Microsoft hearing one witness was asked if he agreed with what another witness had just said. He answered, "Jim's a salesman." Advertising journalist Bob Garfield wrote a column which basically said that Americans expect politicians and advertisers to lie to them. President Kennedy said that "my father always told me that businessmen were sons of bitches." Is Ballmer just another prosaic case? Is Ballmer like the frat brother in *Animal House* who, after totaling a pledge's car, said, "You fucked up, Flounder, you trusted us"? Ballmer and Gates have made computer security—trust us—the number one issue at Microsoft, harking back to the way Ballmer's father and his co-workers at Ford removed the "Fixed or Repaired Daily" image by adopting the philosophy and slogan, "Quality Is Job One." Microsoft even headlined its press release on the subject TRUSTWORTHY COMPUTING IS JOB #1 AT MICROSOFT. Maybe they will succeed. And one school of thought says, so what if Microsoft repeatedly lied, stole, and is a convicted predatory monopolist, business is business, *caveat emptor,* let the buyer beware, and there's a sucker born every minute, and there's nothing you can do about it. Can you hear echoes of "The only thing Nixon did wrong was get caught?" Can you hear echoes of George W. Bush saying, "You can fool some of the people all of the time, and those are the people we have to concentrate on"? (Bush was only joking.)

We've seen how Ballmer's academic, geographic, temperamental, and religious backgrounds prepared him to exploit the phenomenal personal computer explosion changing life as we know it. We've seen how Steve Ballmer represents an example of the Ameritocracy. We've seen how his virtue of loyalty was taken to excess and how that tainted him. Look at part of Ballmer's dance with veracity another way: would you lie for a friend? More than a few people would answer: depends on the lie, depends on the friend. To Steve Ballmer, Bill Gates is like Elvis Presley's blue suede shoes: you can do anything, but stay off of my best bud Bill.

What lies ahead for Ballmer and the Microsoft he leads and the brave new worlds they face? An answer can be found in words well written seventy-five years ago by Aldous Huxley, about his futuristic brave new world. Huxley observed, "The machine turns, turns and must keep on turning—for ever. It is death if it stands still. . . . Wheels must turn steadily, but cannot turn untended." Microsoft's wheels are tended by Steven Anthony Ballmer, sometimes acting like John Belushi on coke, other times as though he's like other folk—part Hemingway, part Hercules, and part Attila the Hun. Steve Ballmer can remind you of many people.

ACKNOWLEDGMENTS

Bad Boy Ballmer was born out of a suggestion by Chicago biographer Carol Felsenthal and would not have happened without her; she is, in some respects, its birth mother. The project evolved with the help of a bookbinder's daughter, Marly Rusoff, a goddess of a literary agent, who tenderly guided the proposal and drafts while stifling my campaign to rename a certain New York landmark the Statue of Marly. At least temporarily. My head cheerleaders, Jane Franklin and her husband, former *New York Times* reporter and current *Washington Spectator* editor Ben A. Franklin, helped give focus when both I and the words tended to yaw. Award-winning biographer Max Holland read various drafts and gave penetrating comments and support. Investigative author Dan E. Moldea, the gutsiest writer I know, provided top-notch strategy and advice—his Web site, Moldea.com is well worth visiting for any investigation. And a standing ovation for my dogged lead research assistant, Laird Barron, a fine writer himself, who, having completed a thousand-mile Anchorage-to-Nome Iditarod dog-sled race, knows how cold yet rewarding the long haul can be.

A special thanks to author William Least Heat Moon, who, one night over drinks at the Blue Moon in Seattle, broke a psychic logjam at a critical time.

Other authors who helped include biographers Edmond Morris and Sylvia Jukes Morris, Bill Bryson, John Heilemann, David Kaplan, Tom DeMarco, Ken Auletta, Robert X. Cringely, Michael Drummond, Wendy Goldman Rohm, Edward Roeder, Nicholas Lemann, David Bank, Bob Metcalfe, Stephen Silbiger, Frank Sulloway, Larry Jay Martin, Adam Clayton Powell III, Scott Armstrong, Stephen Manes, Clarence Page, and Walter Cronkite.

Journalists who contributed include *San Jose Mercury News* columnist Dan Gillmor, and reporter Kristen Heim, *Seattle Post-Intelligencer* reporters Dan Richmond and James Wallace, Jean Gooden and Brier Dudley at the *Seattle Times,* the *Detroit Free Press*'s David Zeman, and former *Slate* editor Michael Kinsley.

Editors and writers have disagreed ever since Moses brought down the fifteen commandments, and readers generally benefit from the robust exchange. My talented editor, Henry Ferris, wielded a skillful, hidden hand while often leaving whole sentences intact, sometimes even full paragraphs. Sarah Beam, Kristin Green, Lorie Young, Greg Villepique, Jayna Maleri, and Kyran Cassidy at HarperCollins helped as well.

When beginning a book I throw out a large net, with small webbing, and trawl various data banks—hauling in the catch, dumping it on the deck called a desk, separating the entrails from the entrée, the flotsam from the fillet. Every now and then you find a pearl. String the pearls together and you have a story line. I started by tossing out a wide net at the core of our intellectual infrastructure, our national Library of Congress, the fountainhead of the free flow of facts in a free and thinking world. There is no greater single information resource on earth, nor a more helpful professional reference staff, than this mother of all libraries, even though some library officials seem intent on turning it into a book museum. Special thanks to an *über*-LC reference librarian, Dr. Thomas Mann, a friend whose faith in the project never waned.

Other libraries that helped include the Suzzallo-Allen, Oleguarde, and Foster libraries at the University of Washington, and the Missoula Public Library in Missoula, Montana. Michigan libraries include the Stockwell-Mudd libraries at Albion College in Albion, the Baldwin Public Library in Birmingham, the Farmington Public Library in Farmington, and the Bloomfield Township Public Library (one of the best regional libraries in the country), plus the Bentley Archives and the Hatcher graduate library at the University of Michigan. On the East Coast the New York Public Library, Philadelphia Free Library, Boston Public Library, Bangor Public Library, and Camden Public Library in Maine were good resources, as were the Pucey and Houghton Libraries at Harvard and the Harvard Archives. In Florida, the Jacksonville Public Library, the main and Sunset branches of the Ft. Lauderdale Public Library, Delray Beach Library (unique in that it's a private library but free and open to the public), and the Key Largo, Big Pine Key, and Key West Public Libraries were all helpful.

At the high school level Dr. Terry Piper, Roxanne Roberts, John Campbell, Gerald Hansen, and Beverly Hannett-Price were most helpful. Post-secondary academics who weighed in include Drs. Judith Lockyer, Wesley Dick, and Larry Steinhauer at Albion College, Professors Christopher Peterson and Thomas Kauper at the University of Michigan, Kevin McDonald at the University of California, and Rodney Brooks, Mike Hawley, and Patty Maes at MIT. Thanks to the public relations staffs at Harvard College, the Harvard News Service, Harvard Business School, and the Stanford Graduate School of Business Administration.

Public relations folk tend to light on writers like black flies in northern Minnesota on a hot summer day when you're sweating a waterfall. Microsoft's flacks were exceptional. In fifteen years of professional writing I have never come upon a less helpful group of public affairs people than Microsoft's propagandists. That was probably their intention. Contrasting that are the world-class PR people at the 2000 Camden Technology Conference in Camden, Maine. Led by Sue-Ellen Roper McClain, of the Portland, Maine–based Hauptman & Partners Communications, Kate Rathmell and Jennifer Boogs went out of their way to get me every interview I requested and all the background data I needed. Kudos to the press flacks at Procter & Gamble, the Ford Motor Company, the National Archives, the Smithsonian, and the Securities and Exchange Commission.

Writing an unauthorized biography of a man heading a wealthy, non-lawsuit-averse multinational (with a head lawyer named Neukom) required some legal advice. First among those offering such counsel is a master of the legal universe, N. Frank Wiggins, a partner in the venerable Washington, D.C., law firm Venable, etc., etc. Staff attorneys helped at the both the Seattle and national chapters of the ACLU, the Reporters Committee for Freedom of the Press in Arlington, Virginia, and Mike Filopovich at the Federal Defenders Service in Seattle.

Special thanks to Stuart Moore, Katalin Sallai, Janet Lee Michaud, Ugly Dave Coyne, Laura Coyne, Janet Fishman, Bruce Harris, Kip Schisler, Petra Hellthaler, David Duerden, Greg McBrady, the three Js at Mona's—Jason, Justin, and Jennifer, Greg and the staff of Zorba's in Washington, D.C., Judy Roberts and her crew at 220 & Edison's in Birmingham, the Dinosaur Cafe in Missoula, Deep Geek, Mary Burns, Eric Lemnitzer, Jack Oram, whomever invented the spell check, the History Channel, the Biography Channel, Whitney Lee, Byrd Stewart Leavell, Christy Fletcher, Ron Marquard, Christine Price, and April Goldberg.

Finally, I know of no flawless book ever written or published, and make no claim that *Bad Boy Ballmer* is the first. Any mistakes in the text are mine.

NOTES AND SOURCES

This biography is the product of a survey of numerous public documents, books, and articles, augmented by over 150 interviews of people who generously, sometimes begrudgingly, gave of their time and knowledge. Many dozens of people interviewed for the book asked not to be identified. Of course, their wishes are honored. One source, working at Microsoft, decided to go by the name Deep Geek and is listed as such. The primary sources for *Bad Boy Ballmer* were correspondence and interviews that I conducted between 1999 and 2002 with the following individuals:

James Adams	Douglas Coupland
Peter Alder	Robert X. Cringely
Gordon Alter	Walter Cronkite
Ken Auletta	Tom DeMarco
John Perry Barlow	Bill Dewey
Hank Borgman	Whitfield Diffie
Rob Borgman	Michael Drummond
Rodney Brooks	Irving Dworkin
Philip Caldwell	Olga Dworkin
John Campbell	Esther Dyson
Jamie Coldre	G. C. Follrich
Casey Corr	Alain Frene
Kelly Corr	Ira Glasser

Jean Gooden	Bob Metcalfe
Don Gregario	Cameron Mhyrvold
Beverly Hannett-Price	Carol Munger
Gerald Hansen	J. W. Munger
John Hansen	Phil Nuygen
John Heilemann	Dr. Christopher Peterson
K. C. Jensen	Beth Portier
Dan Jiggitts	Adam Clayton Powell III
Bill Joy, Jr.	Michael Radner
Bill Joy, Sr.	Todd Rich
Kevin Kallaugher	Dan Richmond
David Kaplan	Ed Rider
Jerry Kaplan	Wendy Goldman Rohm
Dr. Judith Kaplan	Mary Jo Salter
Mitch Kapor	Mark Schmall
Ted Kartes	Steve Silbiger
Thomas Kauper	Drexel Sprecher
Kurt Keljo	James B. Stewart
Aviva Kempner	Linda Stone
Michael Kinsley	Cheryl Tsang
Nicholas Lemann	James Wallace
Elmore Leonard	Ken Wasch
James Love	Brandon Watson
Li Lu	Jeff Weedman
James Mason	Walter Whitman
Rob Mason	

Three months after I interviewed one person he asked that his comments be taken off the record, a strange request but one that I honored. A Microsoft vice president, Doug Burgum, initially agreed to sit for an interview, then backed out when Ballmer's office informed him that the biography was unauthorized.

Another Microsoft vice president, Robert L. McDowell, who authored a book for HarperCollins in 2001, with a preface by Steve Ballmer, failed to return phone calls. Steve Ballmer, Bill Gates, Paul Allen, Scott McNealy, Ray Noorda, Judge Thomas Penfield Jackson, Jim Clark, and Rachelle (Shelly) Ballmer all declined to be interviewed.

Bad Boy Ballmer builds upon the body of Microsoft literature, of which eight books were indispensable: Stephen Manes and Paul Andrews's *Gates: How Microsoft's Mogul Reinvented an Industry—and Made Himself the Richest Man in America;* James Wallace and Jim Erickson's *Hard Drive: Bill Gates and the Making of the Microsoft Empire;* Paul Andrews's *How the Web Was Won;* James Wallace's *Overdrive: Bill Gates and the Race to Control Cyberspace; World War 3.0,* by Ken Auletta; *Pride Before the Fall,* by John Heilemann; *The Microsoft File,* by Wendy Goldman Rohm; and *Breaking Windows,* by David Bank.

In researching the biography I frequently used the *New York Times,* the *Washington Post,* the *Wall Street Journal,* the *San Jose Mercury News,* the *Seattle Times,* the *Seattle Post-Intelligencer, Seattle Weekly, Time, Newsweek, The Atlantic Monthly, The New Yorker, Wired, Fast Company, Business Week, Forbes, Fortune,* and the *Washington Spectator.* Freedom of Information Act (FOIA) requests were made of the Central Intelligence Agency, Federal Bureau of Investigation, Social Security Administration, Internal Revenue Service, Immigration and Naturalization Service, and the National Personnel Records Center's Military Records Center in St. Louis. All provided quick responses to my requests. Eighteen months after receiving a FOIA request for Fritz Ballmer's passport file—public information upon death—the State Department had failed to provide any requested information. A FOIA request to the U.S. Secret Service is, as of this writing, pending. On-line sources include The Register, CNET Investor, and Company Sleuth, along with

Moldea.com. When relevant, I have cited the sources directly in the text. Further sourcing can be found on the Web site www.badboyballmer.com, along with copies of public documents, including parts of Fred Ballmer's Nuremberg personnel file.

The principal sources for the introduction and chapter 1: *Current Biography: World War 3.0; Skid Row*, by Murray Morgan; *Sons of Profits*, by William C. Speidel; and *Papa Hemingway*, by A. E. Hotchner.

For chapters 2 and 3: The Nuremberg personnel file and the INS file of Fritz Hans Ballmer; *The Reckoning*, by David Halberstam; the Ford Motor Company 1972 Annual Report; historylink.org; *World Book Encyclopedia Yearbook, 1972; The Anatomy of the Nuremberg Trials*, by Telford Taylor; *The Jewish Phenomenon*, by Steve Silbiger; *A History of the Jews in America*, by Howard M. Sachar; *It's Always Something*, by Gilda Radner; *"But What If The Dream Comes True?"* CBS Reports; and *Inside The Nuremberg Trial, vol. 1 and 2* by Drexel Sprecher.

For chapters 4 and 5: Various Harvard yearbooks, *Gates; Hard Drive; The New Imperialists*, by Mark Leibovich; Robert X. Cringely; records of Detroit Country Day School; *Unheard Witness*, by Ernst "Putzi" Hanfstaengl; *The New Rules*, by John Kotter; Procter & Gamble's 1978 Annual Report; *The AOL Story*, by Kara Swisher; the *Detroit Jewish News*; and *Co-leaders: The Power of Great Partnerships* by David Heenan and Warren G. Bennis; and *How the Web Was Won*, by Paul Andrews.

For chapter 6: *The Silicon Boys and Their Valley of Dreams*, by David A. Kaplan; *Microsoft First Generation*, by Cheryl Tsang; and *Accidental Empires*, by Robert X. Cringely.

For chapters 7 and 8: Harvard and Radcliffe Class of 1977 Five Year Anniversary Report; *Renegades of the Empire*, by Michael Drummond; *Hard Drive; High Noon*, by Karen Southwick; *The Microsoft File*, and *Breaking Windows*.

For chapters 9 and 10: *Startup*, by Jerry Kaplan; *How the Web Was Won*, by Paul Andrews; *Netscape Time*, by Jim Clark; and *The Microsoft File*.

For the remainder of the book, *Breaking Windows*, *How the Web Was Won*, and *The New Imperialists* were used.

SELECTED BIBLIOGRAPHY

Allen, Tim. *Don't Stand Too Close to a Naked Man.* New York: Hyperion, 1994.

Andrews, Paul. *How the Web Was Won: How Bill Gates and His Internet Idealists Transformed the Microsoft Empire.* New York: Broadway Books, 1999.

Auletta, Ken. *World War 3.0: Microsoft and Its Enemies.* New York: Random House, 2001.

Bank, David. *Breaking Windows: How Bill Gates Fumbled the Future of Microsoft.* New York: Free Press, 2001.

Berg, A. Scott. *Lindbergh.* New York: Putnam Publishing Group, 1998.

Brinkley, Joel, and Steve Lohr. *U.S. v. Microsoft.* New York: McGraw-Hill, 2001.

Calkins, Richard M. *Antitrust: Guidelines for the Business Executive.* New York: Dow Jones-Irwin, 1981.

Chernow, Ron. *Titan: The Life of John D. Rockefeller, Sr.* New York: Random House, 1998.

Clark, Jim, with Owen Edwards. *Netscape Time.* New York: St. Martin's, 1999.

Coupland, Douglas. *Microserfs.* New York: ReganBooks/HarperCollins, 1995.

Cringely, Robert X. *Accidental Empires: How the Boys of Silicon Valley Make Their Millions, Battle Foreign Competition, and Still Can't Get a Date.* New York: HarperBusiness, 1996.

Deutschman, Alan. *The Second Coming of Steve Jobs.* New York: Broadway Books, 2001.

Drummond, Michael. *Renegades of the Empire*. New York: Crown, 1999.

Eisenach, Jeffrey A., and Thomas M. Lenard, editors. *Competition, Innovation and the Microsoft Monopoly: Antitrust in the Digital Marketplace*. Boston: Kluwer Academic Publishers, 1999.

Ferguson, Charles H. *High St@kes, No Prisoners*. New York: Times Business, 1999.

Formisano, Ron. *The Great Lobster War*. Amherst: University of Massachusetts Press, 1997.

Freud, Sigmund. *Civilization and its Discontents*. New York: Norton, 1961.

Gardner, John. *On Becoming a Novelist*. New York: Harper & Row, 1983.

Gladwell, Malcolm. *The Tipping Point: How Little Things Can Make a Big Difference*. New York: Little, Brown & Company, 2000.

Gookin, Dan. *Word 2000 for Windows for Dummies*. New York: IDG Books Worldwide, 1999.

Grove, Andrew. *High Output Management*. New York: Vintage, 1983, 1995.

———. *Only the Paranoid Survive*. New York: Doubleday, 1996.

Hailey, Arthur. *Wheels*. New York: Doubleday, 1971.

Halberstam, David. *The Reckoning*. New York: William Morrow and Company, 1986.

Hamilton, Edith. *The Greek Way*. New York: W. W. Norton, Reissued 1993.

Hanfstaengl, Ernst "Putzi." *Unheard Witness*. New York: J. B. Lippicott, 1957.

Heilemann, John. *Pride Before the Fall*. New York: HarperCollins, 2001.

Heenan, David, and Warren G. Bennis. *Co-Leaders: The Power of Great Partnerships*. New York: John Wiley & Sons, Inc., 2000.

Hesse, Hermann. *Beneath the Wheel*. New York: Farrar, Straus & Giroux, 1968.

Hotchner, A. E. *Papa Hemingway*. New York: Carroll & Graf Publishers, Inc., 1999.

Huxley, Aldous. *Brave New World*. New York: Harper & Row, 1946.

Kaplan, David. *The Silicon Boys and Their Valley of Dreams*. New York: William Morrow and Company, 1999.

Kaplan, Jerry. *Startup: A Silicon Valley Adventure*. New York: Houghton-Mifflin, 1995.

Kidder, Tracy. *The Soul of a New Machine*. New York: Atlantic Monthly Press, 1981.

Leibovich, Mark. *The New Imperialists.* New York: Prentice-Hall, 2001.

Lewis, Ted G. *Microsoft Rising . . . and Other Tales of Silicon Valley.* Los Alamitos, Calif.: IEEE Computer Society, 1999.

Manes, Stephen, and Paul Andrews. *Gates: How Microsoft's Mogul Reinvented an Industry—and Made Himself the Richest Man in America.* New York: Touchstone, 1993, 1994.

Mansfield, Ron, and J.W. Olsen. *Mastering Word 2000.* San Francisco: Sybex, 1999.

McClelland, David. *The Achieving Society.* New York: Free Press, 1967.

McDowell, Robert L., and William L. Simon. *Driving Digital.* New York: HarperBusiness, 2001.

Metcalfe, Bob. *Internet Collapses and Other InfoWorld Punditry.* Foster City, Calif.: IDG Books Worldwide, 2000.

Moody, Glyn. *Rebel Code: The Inside Story of Linux and the Open Source Revolution.* New York: Perseus Publishing, 2001.

Morgan, Murray. *Skid Road: An Informal Portrait of Seattle.* Seattle: University of Washington Press, 1982.

Oates, Joyce Carol. *Expensive People.* New York: Vanguard Press, 1968.

Page, Clarence. *Showing My Color: Impolite Essays on Race and Identity.* New York: HarperCollins, 1996.

Radner, Gilda. *It's Always Something.* New York: Avon Books, 1989.

Rohm, Wendy Goldman. *The Microsoft File: The Secret Case Against Bill Gates.* New York: Times Business/Random House, 1998.

Sachar, Howard M. *A History of the Jews in America.* New York: Alfred A. Knopf, 1992.

Silbiger, Steve. *The Jewish Phenomenon: Seven Keys to the Enduring Wealth of a People.* Atlanta: Longstreet Press, 2002.

Siwek, Stephen, and Howard W. Furchtgott-Roth. *International Trade in Computer Software.* Lanham, Md.: Quorum Books, 1993.

Southwick, Karen. *High Noon: The Inside Story of Scott McNealy and the Rise of Sun Microsystems.* New York: John Wiley & Sons, Inc., 1999.

Speidel, William C. *Sons of the Profits or There's No Business Like Grow Business: The Seattle Story 1851–1901.* Seattle: Nestle Creek Publishing Company, 1967.

Sprecher, Drexel. *Inside the Nuremberg Trial,* volumes 1 and 2. Lanham, Md.: University Press of America, 1998.

Swisher, Kara. *AOL.com.* New York: Times Books, 1999.

Taylor, Telford. *The Anatomy of the Nuremberg Trials.* New York: Alfred A. Knopf, 1992.

Tsang, Cheryl. *Microsoft First Generation: The Success Secrets of the Visionaries Who Launched a Technology Empire.* New York: John Wiley & Sons, Inc., 2000.

Wallace, James. *Overdrive: Bill Gates and the Race to Control Cyberspace.* New York: John Wiley & Sons, Inc., 1997.

Wallace, James, and Jim Erickson. *Hard Drive: Bill Gates and the Making of the Microsoft Empire.* New York: John Wiley & Sons, Inc., 1992.

Webster's New World Dictionary of Computer Terms, third edition. New York: Prentice-Hall, 1988.

Wiener, Lauren Ruth. *Digital Woes: Why We Should Not Depend on Software.* Boston: Addison-Wesley, 1993.

Wilson, Mike. *The Difference Between God and Larry Ellison (God Doesn't Think He's Larry Ellison).* New York: William Morrow & Company, 1998.

Additional sources available on the web at *www.badboyballmer.com*

For any questions contact: *badboyballmer@hotmail.com*
Re: Source Question

INDEX